ABANDONED MINE

ABANDONED WINE

CHINESE WRITING
TODAY · II

selected *&* edited by
HENRY Y H ZHAO
& JOHN CAYLEY

with a foreword by
GARY SNYDER

wellsweep

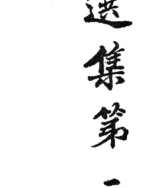

SPECIAL THANKS to Desmond Skeel and Katie Hill for their help in the preparation of this volume.

NOTE
This publication is the second biennial selection of works in English translation from the best of the Chinese literary magazine *Jintian (Today)*. *Abandoned Wine* covers the eight 1992–93 issue of *Today*. Please note that the actual selection of pieces was undertaken by Henry Y H Zhao in close co-operation with the other editors and regular contributors to *Today*. This book is a selection made by contemporary Chinese writers and critics themselves.

ISSN 0968-4670 (*Chinese Writing* Today, Number 2)

ACKNOWLEDGEMENTS
Brian Holton's translation of Yang Lian's 'The Garden on a Winter's Day' is included in Wellsweep's collection of Yang Lian's later, shorter poems, *Non-Person Singular* (1994); numbers 1 & 3 of the sequence were also published in *Conjunctions* 23 (Annandale-on-Hudson, 1994). Gregory B Lee's translations of 'There is no' and 'Watching the sea' by Duo Duo were printed in an appendix to *Chinese writing and exile*, edited by Lee (Chicago, 1993). Part of Hu Dong's story 'The Mask Outside the Library' was published in *Another Province: new Chinese writing from London* (London, 1994).

This selection copyright © *Wellsweep* & The Today Literary Foundation.
First published in 1996 by
The Wellsweep Press, 1 Grove End House, 150 Highgate Road, London NW5 1PD
in association with the Today Literary Foundation.

ISBN 0 948454 24 5 paperback

BRITISH LIBRARY CATALOGUING-IN-PUBLICATION DATA
A catalogue record for this book is available from the British Library.

Designed and typeset by *Wellsweep*

FOREWORD

GARY SNYDER

From a semi-fantastic tale out of Younghusband's expedition to Lhasa to a surreal delve in the language of scholarship; fantasy academies and subtle sexualities; exile *anomie* and bumptious confidence; from apartments in Berkeley to memoirs of harmless aesthetes trapped by the Cultural Revolution, this anthology is a window into the minds and lives of some of the world's finest young writers. It's to be celebrated that such a cosmopolitan and high-quality journal, speaking (in a way) for international Chinese literary culture, manages to keep itself going without official support from any nation or major institution.

Today is always 'today'. But there is some flex in how big 'today' might be, and just what is it that we consider to be the 'present moment'. Some would say that this post-ice-age span of the last 10,000 years that scientists call the Holocene, with its current climate and biota, is our human 'present moment'; is our human 'day'.

This anthology of writings from recent issues of *Today* is a bit like that, for it is fully and immediately contemporary, but some of these pieces make a radically imaginative stretch back into cultural memory — the sense of a vast cultural landscape is always present here. These writers are now in many different places, they are members of a Chinese culture that has several nations and many enclaves. Some of the writers are presently in exile, some are fully at home living far from the old river basins of the Han people, and many are living in China. Yet, with subtlety and reflection, with magical turns, with surreal power, virtually all these pieces of poetry and prose manifest a sense of loss, a soul-home-sickness, that runs parallel with their emerging confident internationalism, and a deep knowledge, a love-hate, of the past. It can be said that right now, today is a very long day, a day of seeking new birth.

That's what I thought as I read these pages: it is an account of being in the Bardo realm, the time/space between births, and the soul's search for the loving couple that it will be born through to get back into the world. Liu Zaifu, now living in Boulder, writes 'reincarnation is difficult'. Truly. But not impossible. And to be unsure, to be between stances, between certainties, is always the freshest, the most creative place to be! This displaced place might be denigrated; we were recently talking about how the socialist critics of the past took inwardness, personal vision or quandary, as signs of 'decadence' — (to be decadent in the occident requires much wickeder stuff) — but in any case, the nature-literate critic replies that decadent/decayed materials are nutritious, the rotten is sweet to the right critters (crows, vultures, or bears), and that for all of us writers, this century demands not only a strong stomach but a good appetite. We need to be able to eat the past, even if it is a bit rotten, to be, then, both intimate with our souls and with history. And to go on.

We find poems and stories strongly in the moment, mixing with antiquity as in Nan Fang's 'Beautiful Landscape'. The image I get from this and several other pieces (Hu Dong, 'The Mask Outside the Library', Zhong Ming's 'Trying Swords with the Daoist "Great Man" Ruan Ji') is as though the past, present, (and future?) are all contemporary, all locked in cells in some great samsaric prison, the past and the present trying to communicate with each other by rapping through the walls. I sense here a harking-back to earlier popular narrative, the magical tales from Ming and Qing. To do justice to the diversity of this anthology it must be said that no single characterization is adequate to it all, though.

Huang Ziping, in his essay 'Dances with the Other — Writing at a Critical Moment' brilliantly explores the difficulties perceived in being 'in the shadow' of the non-Chinese literary world; anxieties of influence; but suggests that simultaneously the non-occidental literatures cast shadows too — and we are all dancing in and out of each other's dark and light. I suggest that we (late twentieth century cultural types of all backgrounds) join this performance without fear, and jettison worn categories and judgements, 'modern' and 'postmodern' or whutebba, and get on with today, the big today of the Holocene and this very moment, here and now in the book in your hand. We are all of us about to be born again.

CONTENTS

CRITICISM AND BELLES LETTRES

FICTION — II

棄 酒 《 今 天 》 雙 年 選 集 第 二 集 目 錄

ABANDONED WINE

O

FICTION — I

MEETINGS

GE FEI

translated by Deborah Mills

In the dim and distant past, a Chief Magician in the Potala Palace made this prediction: in 1904, which would be the Tibetan year of the wooden dragon, there would be a great catastrophe in Tibet. On different occasions the priest described in detail the nature of this catastrophe, but never explained clearly where it would come from.

At the beginning of the summer of 1903, an expeditionary army for the invasion of Tibet, made up of a hotchpotch of British soldiers and Indian Sikhs and Gurkhas, stealthily sneaked along the Disita River Valley into Khamba Dzong. The origins of the catastrophe were finally becoming clear.

1

On their way to Khamba Dzong, the expeditionary army, under the leadership of Colonel Francis Younghusband, had come across no other obstacle than the heavy rain swirling over the plateau. The vast and lonely plateau seemed to be in a deep sleep and the legendary shepherd army of Tibet was still nowhere to be seen.

Whichever way you look at him, Colonel Younghusband was an adventurer in the true sense of the word. After graduating from Sandhurst, his military career began in the Meerut and Kashmir regions of India. In the autumn of 1886, he stole alone into the Chinese interior, leaving a trail all over the plains of the north-east, Mongolia, Xinjiang and the Kunlun Mountains. In Colonel Younghusband's view, his most recent appointment as commanding officer of the British expeditionary force was entirely a result of his own remarkable military talent and rich mountain experience. This view was totally different from the initial feelings of the Governor-General of India, Lord Curzon. When the governor first saw Younghusband he was deeply impressed by the headstrong, rash and impetuous nature of this young officer. Younghusband was undoubtedly the most suitable choice to take command of a war in a mysterious country like Tibet.

The army set up camp at Khamba Dzong on a plain by the side of a little darkly shining stream. From here they overlooked the whole of the Targan river valley; the peak of Mount Everest towering in the distance seemed close at hand, and the silver-grey peaks and ridges piled high with snow, each one rising higher than the other, glittered with a dazzling radiance.

The beginning of summer in June was the season of good weather in this region, when flowers and grasses blossomed in abundance. Colonel Younghusband was sitting on a tree stump in his tent, and with a depressed look on his face was playing a game of Erlut chess with Major Bretherton, a game they had just learnt how to play. Bretherton's mind seemed to be elsewhere; he kept turning to glance in the direction of the silent valley. His glances appeared highly significant and seemed to stir up the anxiety which Colonel Younghusband had been bottling up for some time.

After the troops had entered Khamba Dzong, they had fallen into a period of endless waiting. In his last letter, Curzon had hinted that the British parliament felt quite undecided as to whether or not the expeditionary army should occupy Chumbi in the near future, then seize Gyantse and advance on Lhasa. This indecisiveness and procrastination was a mixture of feebleness and artificial posturing. Colonel Younghusband was worried that it would put the British troops at a strategic disadvantage and give the Tibetans time to gather a large army. At the end of his letter, Curzon warned him that there was no reason to act rashly before the negotiators from China and Tibet had arrived at Khamba Dzong.

The River Targan trickled quietly through the valley, passing through an area of low scrub thicket and patches of land where highland barley was struggling to grow. Colonel Younghusband could see the blurred silhouettes of British soldiers scattered about in twos and threes in the valley. Day after day they had been hanging around there, collecting specimens of fossils, plants, butterflies and insects. The valley was covered in plants of the buttercup family and cluster on cluster of azaleas; the flowers grew so thickly that, looked at from a distance, they glittered red like burning coal. The wind of the plateau blew diagonally across the plain; apart from the trickle of water from the stream, all around was shrouded in a listless silence.

At midday, a man dressed as a missionary, riding one of the small horses that are native to Tibet, was coming slowly towards the camp along the narrow track that ran around the edge of the valley. The arrival of this man gave Colonel Younghusband and the Major an excuse to put an end at last to their dull and insipid game of chess. The Colonel impatiently tossed a piece onto the board and stood up.

"Look, some one's coming."

"It looks like a priest," said Major Bretherton.

"It's that Scot we met a few days ago."

Major Bretherton was silent. His eyes were full of worry, and he anxiously regarded the silhouette of the missionary out on the plain, as if the announcement of his visit brought with it some sort of mysterious danger.

Bretherton had been a close friend of Colonel Younghusband when they were young; on the eve of Younghusband's being given the order to enter Tibet, he had Bretherton transferred from far-off Kathmandu to his own command, putting him in charge of transport and supplies. Bretherton was by nature an honest, frank man, faithful in the discharge of his duties, and a capable military supplies officer, but, as Colonel Younghusband later realized, not everyone could manage to live in a place like Tibet. On the first day Bretherton entered Tibet he was overcome by fear, and the continuous scourge of dysentery had reduced him to a shadow of his former self. The sound of chanting from the Lamaist temples always made him feel uneasy, and over and over again, in a fearful tone of voice, he said to his friend and protector, "Perhaps we will never reach Lhasa."

Between ten o'clock in the morning and one in the afternoon, a total of three people came one after another to visit Colonel Younghusband's camp command post. They were the Scottish missionary John Newman, the Head Lama of Tashilhunpo monastery and the resident Chinese official in Tibet, He Wenqin.

It was impossible to see three people when it was just coming up to lunch time. Colonel Younghusband, from intuition and interest, without hesitation selected one of them (namely the Head Lama of Tashilhunpo monastery) for an interview, and sent the other two away to wait in suspense in the corn fields outside the camp.

The Head Lama made an unforgettable impression on Colonel Younghusband as soon as he appeared in the camp, with his skinny body, his wrinkled face and his long scarlet robes swaying emptily. He had obviously appeared not as an official negotiator, but to persuade him as an individual. His refined, courteous manner and generous

17

appearance complemented his high monastic position. What startled Colonel Younghusband was that this lama from the labyrinths of a monastery in the back of beyond was proficient in both Chinese and English.

At first their conversation involved the skilful use of a string of sensitive terms such as invasion and occupation. From this it was evident that the Head Lama was by no means ignorant of the current trends in foreign strategy. From religious practices and medicine they moved on to magic and miracles, but finally there arose a serious difference of opinion in the field of philosophy.

In his youth, Colonel Younghusband had made a sketchy study of the works of Spinoza and Leibniz, and therefore had enough general knowledge of philosophy to start a debate with the lama. Within two hours, they had already wasted a lot of breath quarrelling over whether or not the earth was round. Whatever one may say about it, the interview was quite encouraging, in particular because the many peculiar and incredible views of the Head Lama took root in Colonel Younghusband's memory without his being aware of it.

In the area where corn was growing outside the camp, the meeting between the Chinese official and the Scottish missionary, on the other hand, seemed quite relaxed.

He Wenqin had come thousands of miles, with the weight of his mission from the great Qing empire on his shoulders, in order to see Younghusband, and the latter had inexplicably rejected him, had shown him the door, and forced him to hang about waiting with a missionary.

It appeared from the way He Wenqin and John Newman met each other that the two men had not only met before, but also that they were quite well-acquainted. Still, they seemed able to celebrate the rituals of people meeting afresh.

The missionary, his face wreathed in smiles, walked towards He Wenqin with both arms outstretched, as if to embrace him. He Wenqin, however, backed away through the corn.

Several British officers outside the camp saw everything without understanding the whys and wherefores. No one knew what the two men in the wide expanse of corn were actually talking about. The missionary seemed to be rather interested in the long silk gown He Wenqin was wearing, for as soon as he had finally managed to get close to He Wenqin, he threw up a corner of the long robe and twisted it with his fingers. This overly intimate action would have been indiscreet in the traditional etiquette of either China or England.

2

It was afternoon when the Head Lama emerged from Younghusband's tent, and the sun was shining on everything. He did not go straight back to Tashilhunpo near Shigatse, but instead took a different road. After many years of being lashed by the cold wind of the plateau and burnt by the strong sun, his face was as dried up as a sheepskin.

As his horse danced unhurriedly down the Targan river valley, the Head Lama saw the lone silhouette of the Scottish missionary riding along the riverbed. The Chinese official who had been waiting with him earlier was nowhere to be seen.

Newman had not come to Khamba Dzong to see Younghusband; his real intention had been to wait for He Wenqin. Colonel Younghusband's refusal to see any negotiator from China had both hurt and depressed the Qing dynasty official. In his gloom he had left Khamba Dzong and returned all alone to his Chinese village of Cangnan. The missionary's horse was walking slowly and the Head Lama soon caught up with him. A gap remained between the two men and they rode separately along the reddy-brown river valley under the blazing sun.

The summer wind blew over the mountain ridges in their direction, concealing a cold hint of ice and snow. Black and white ducks and snow doves warbled among the trees and grasses, and a torrent of water from a waterfall in a nearby ravine made a distant and monotonous din.

Perhaps in order to distract himself from the weary loneliness before his eyes, the Head Lama began to chat to the missionary. Throughout this irrelevant conversation, the Head Lama frowned constantly, his heart heavy with worry.

Colonel Younghusband was a difficult man to tackle. Although he was not actually opposed to Tibetan Buddhism (in fact he even harboured a cautious curiosity towards it) nevertheless, his arrogance and cold indifference made it difficult for someone to get close to him. The Head Lama not only had not managed to prise out of him any useful information, but had not even had an opportunity to raise with the Colonel what he had originally planned to, which was to try to dissuade the British army from the idea of pressing on to Lhasa. And there were some things he had been able to say, even though he had not wanted to. In addition, there was a great discrepancy between the evaluations made by Lhasa and the true facts, as the British had apparently already made all the necessary preparations for going deep into the interior of Tibet, and their occupation of the sacred city of Lhasa was just a matter of time.

At dusk, an enormous red and white castle appeared before them and the Head Lama reined his horse to a halt. Since he was about to take his leave, the Head Lama invited the Scottish missionary to spend the night with him at the castle (purely out of politeness). Newman was thinking of refusing gracefully, but instead heard himself immediately accept the invitation — which just shows how difficult he found it to restrain himself in either word or deed.

This event had at least two consequences: looking back on it with hindsight. It was the start of a series of later misfortunes, but just then the idea that the Christian missionary and the great Tibetan lama were about to spend the night under the same roof made both men very nervous.

This eastern-style castle was built on a hill in the middle of the plain. It was a rambling, untidy building, six storeys high. There were courtyards to the front and rear, and outside the courtyards were tethered seven or eight Tibetan horses. Ravens were perching in rows under the eaves and on the walls, cawing and squawking. In a hollow in the hills not far to the left of the castle was a Buddhist nunnery. Several nuns were queuing up to go down to the river to draw water.

In the last few years, Newman had never been allowed to enter a genuine Tibetan-style castle, so he decided to make the most of today's opportunity. As darkness was beginning to fall, after they had eaten a hurried meal of roasted barley and highland barley wine in the dining room, the missionary asked if he could have a look round the castle. The Head Lama deliberated for a moment, and then nodded his head in agreement. A young servant boy quickly brought them an oil lamp.

As they went up along flights of stone steps, the dark, sinister labyrinth of a building gradually revealed itself before the eyes of the missionary. On the second floor of the castle Newman saw an enormous storehouse of old-fashioned armaments. The room and the passage were full of hay, black gunpowder, rusting helmets, shields, breastplates and matchlock rifles. These objects were relics of days gone by, discarded and unused for a long time, their surfaces covered with a thick layer of dust, but the rows of prayer wheels set in niches in the walls, after years of being touched by people's hands, appeared bright and shiny.

The moonlight shone in through the arrow slits in the walls, turning the Head Lama's face a dark bluish colour. The light sent an icy cold shiver over Newman's whole body.

Newman apparently felt that in these circumstances it would be highly unprofitable to argue about the merits and demerits of the two religions (in the past he had seen such disputes with the lamas as part of his sacred duty). However, since the Head Lama had already started a conversation, out of politeness he managed grudgingly to put in the appropriate replies, disputes and corrections.

"In fact, we have never thought that the Christian religion contained any defects," said the Head Lama, after leading the missionary to a room where sutras were stored, on the fourth floor, "and indeed, we have never sent anyone to Scotland, or to London, to do missionary work. All religions possess similar characteristics, though they give rise to completely different customs. For instance, you generally describe Tibetan people as 'dirty'. It's true that we don't wash very often, but the difference between us and you Westerners who splash around in a bath tub is that the Tibetan custom is to bathe in the pure, clean wind. It is similar to curing someone of an illness; the Chinese method is to palpate the wrist of the sick person; yours is to slide a round piece of metal backwards and forwards across the sick person's chest, but in Tibet, whether a person is ill or not is decided by the noise he makes when he urinates into a wooden bucket..."

"Quite so," the missionary chimed in, "but there is one thing I have never understood, which is that you believe in Buddha, but how do you know that Buddha really exists, or where he exists, and in what way do you understand the hardships of this mortal life?"

"In the Christian religion, on what do you base your knowledge of Jesus' existence?" countered the Head Lama.

"On miracles," replied Newman.

"What miracles?"

"For example, according to biblical records, the prophet turned a creeping reptile into a rigid walking stick..."

"But that's just a type of sorcery," interrupted the Head Lama, laughing gently, "In Kashmir, India, and in Tibet, there are many roving artists who are masters of this art..."

Newman's face turned red with shame and rage, and he was just thinking of making a stern rebuke, when the Head Lama of Tashilhunpo monastery patted him on the shoulder, and in a mysterious voice said softly, "Come with me, I've got something to show you."

Guided by the uncertain light from the flickering lamp, Newman followed the Head Lama downstairs. They passed through one long, narrow corridor after another, all blackened by smoke and soot, and through several secret rooms, and finally came to a small, secluded courtyard at the back of the castle.

"What do you think that is?" The Head Lama gestured towards a tree in a corner of the courtyard.

"A tree."

"Go closer and look at it more carefully." The Head Lama passed him the oil lamp he was holding.

Whichever way you looked at it, the tree was at first sight no different from other trees. The crown of the tree was bushy and disordered with tangled, higgledy-piggledy branches, and these heavy branches stretched out beyond the boundary wall. The missionary did not know what sort of tree it was, but the strange sound as the wind rustled the leaves made him realize that it actually was different from most other trees.

Newman raised the lantern and went slowly closer, but was quickly brought to a halt by fear of what he saw: on each leaf of the tree there was, clearly outlined, the lifelike image of a Buddha. The leaves were a dark, blackish green, some a little deeper, some a little paler.

"You can stroke the leaves with your hand," the Head Lama said in the darkness.

Newman carefully examined the leaves, which were all wet with drops of dew, and then stretched out his hand to peel off a piece of bark; on the new bark the image of a laughing Buddha reappeared.

"Is this one of the sacred trees which were mentioned by the Abbé Huc?"

The Head Lama nodded.

Newman had once read in a book that in 1884 the French Abbé Huc had seen a similar phenomenon at the foot of the hill on which stood the Tar monastery in Qinghai.

"How many trees like this are there in Tibet?" asked the missionary.

"At least two thousand," the Head Lama told him. "Apart from a very few, most of them are unknown to man."

"Could I pick a leaf to take with me?"

The Head Lama smiled, without saying yes or no.

The Head Lama and the missionary spent the second half of that night on an open-air terrace right at the top of the castle. A Union Jack on the battlements made a flapping sound. The flag was a sign that the British had once occupied the castle, and made them unconsciously turn their conversation to the business of the British army's invasion of Tibet.

"There's only one way to stop the British troops entering Lhasa," Newman warned the Head Lama.

"Which way is that?"

"Kidnap Younghusband."

This conversation actually took place at dawn on the following day; caressed by the cold wind, the missionary saw some women from the nunnery kneeling among the groves on the river bank washing Tibetan rugs and discussing something loudly in Tibetan. The sound of their laughing carried unhindered over a great distance....

3

Due to weather conditions, the British army's original plan to launch an offensive along the Guru-Tuna line on Christmas Eve had to be postponed until the following spring.

On the 16th of January, 1904, Colonel Younghusband's 23rd Engineers pushed forward to a position beyond the Guru canyon. At the same time, a large Tibetan force had in anticipation already occupied all the elevated positions above the gorge. The Guru gorge was the gateway to Gyantse, and seizing the fortress of Gyantse was the most important objective of the British in their plan to enter Lhasa.

Over the last few days, Colonel Younghusband had been faced with his biggest problems since entering Tibet. On the one hand, the atrocious weather conditions had exacerbated the soldiers' problems with the lack of oxygen, and pneumonia and dry coughs were wreaking havoc in the camp. Younghusband was worried that if the situation lasted another two or three weeks, then the already weak transport line would be unable to supply the troops with enough food. On the other hand, the British government was still urging Colonel Younghusband to do his utmost to find a way of negotiating with the Tibetans. This could not fail to seem contradictory: the arduous journey into Tibet, the hardships and dangers, the endless trudging over mountains which the army had endured in the two-year preparation for this expedition, were not after all for the purpose of a military victory, but merely for one tiny diplomatic initiative. The Colonel found this very hard to bear.

On January 17th, Colonel Younghusband decided to negotiate directly with the leader of the Tibetan army. If the Tibetan troops had not withdrawn from the Guru gorge within five hours, then despite opposition from England, he would teach these complacent Tibetans, their heads buried in Lamaism and their own recklessness, a necessary lesson.

Colonel Younghusband's talks with the Lhasa Depon commanding the Tibetan army took place on the sandy ground of the Guru gorge. They lay full length on a Tibetan rug and carried out their talks with extreme difficulty through a poor interpreter. The Lhasa Depon's stubbornness and self-confidence infuriated Colonel Younghusband. He kept harping on the fact that if the British did not withdraw immediately to the mountains south of Yatung then "the great earth would suddenly split asunder" and "the world would be totally annihilated". And then the deeply patriotic Depon launched into a long description of these imminent disasters.

Younghusband obviously felt that his self-esteem had been somehow wounded. He drew the interpreter to one side: "Tell that Tibetan that the world belongs to Allah; the earth belongs to the Pasha and heaven belongs to the lamas, but that all this must be ruled over by the British."

The negotiations were concluded in this manner.

At twenty to three in the afternoon, Colonel Younghusband and Major Bretherton were huddled up in a tent in the temporary command post gazing after a strike force of one hundred British and three hundred Indians as they entered the deep and silent gorge.

The Colonel's way of thinking was this: as soon as the British cavalry had penetrated deep into the gorge, the Tibetan force, armed with matchlocks and primitive bows and arrows, would be unable to ignore them. Once they started loosing their arrows, the Tibetan army's flank would be met by a powerful attack from the Maxim machine gun squad. On the eve of the first opening of hostilities, Colonel Younghusband looked solemn and depressed. Major Bretherton, standing by his side, trembled constantly from excessive agitation; they could not have predicted all that happened next.

The most regrettable thing was that the Tibetans showed enormous patience over the affair: they watched in silence as the British troops marched into the gorge, and from start to finish did not fire a single shot.

The troops who had been given the task of armed provocation carried on walking slowly round the gorge, and returned the same way without having achieved anything. Younghusband was on the verge of losing his temper and impulsively issued a second command: the strike force should climb up the gorge and "chase the Tibetans away like London policemen dispersing a crowd of demonstrators in Trafalgar Square."

Finally, at dusk, disaster struck.

The Tibetans began noisily pushing and shoving each other in a sea of confusion. They had neither received an order to retreat, nor heard a signal to resist. When the British soldiers charged up the gorge, demanding that they give up their weapons, the Tibetan troops, although complaining under their breath, were very unwillingly relieved of them.

The Lhasa Depon was deeply enraged by the humiliation which was suddenly taking place before his eyes. At the same time, he felt that the battle had already left him out in the cold. Beside himself with anger, he let out a great roar, grabbed his revolver and ferociously blew off the lower jaw of one of the British soldiers.

The honesty, restraint and conciliatory approach shown by the Lhasa Depon and the government troops during this incident of provocation made a deep impression on the British journalist on the battlefield, but the Tibetans had already lost any chance of preventing the heavily armed British troops from carrying out a cruel massacre of "those simple innocent shepherds."

As the Tibetan soldiers milled down the gorge like a flock of sheep, they were fired upon by two Maxim machine guns and nearly three hundred rifles.

Amidst the violent noise of gunfire, the Tibetans dispersed incomprehensibly slowly in the direction of the woods. Major Bretherton several times in a row warned Younghusband that shooting blindly at unarmed Tibetan soldiers was obviously going against the basic aim of advancing into Tibet. Colonel Younghusband smiled coldly and lit a cigar.

"War has always been like this," said the Colonel casually. "War is war, after all, and not playing around with some sort of Chinese massage. A few corpses and some fresh blood might give the soldiers some stimulation and at the same time ease the pressure on our nerves, which have been strained and depressed since we arrived in Tibet."

After a moment Colonel Younghusband, with some regret, said, "Actually the present situation is a mess: the Tibetans are totally incapable of returning fire. If some reason could be found for it, I would like to see the Tibetans furnished with modern, British-made weapons, so that the two armies could come and have a proper fight to the death on the wide plain beyond the gorge."

At midday on the 20th of January, Colonel Younghusband led his British command through the gorge, and set out, vast and mighty, towards Gyantse

The Colonel, riding a big Indian horse, dozed off under the shining profusion of sunbeams. The glaciers and river valleys, forests and swamps along the march seemed unreal, like a painting in oils. The landscape and scenery of the area were quite similar to that of the Swiss Alps — peaceful and pure, luxuriantly beautiful, absolutely silent and still.

Even the criticism from England could not spoil Colonel Younghusband's delight in the scenery or his good mood. Parliament's comments on the recent battle of Guru were predictable. They attacked the British troops for carrying out a massacre of simple Tibetan people. And a snide article in *Punch* read: "We are very sorry to learn that the sudden attack by the Tibetans on our troops at Guru spoilt the scenic photographs that the officers were taking."

As far as Francis Younghusband was concerned, there was now only one thing left which could move him. Day and night he hungered to see the sacred city of Lhasa, now only a few hundred miles away. Apart from Thomas Manning more than a hundred years earlier, he would be the first Englishman to enter Lhasa. The previous evening, while lying in his tent on the banks of the river Guru, he had had a profoundly significant dream. In the dream he saw an amazingly tall Tibetan woman standing on the banks of Lake Namu-tso; her scarlet head-dress and many heavy robes were being blown aside by a light gust of wind, revealing her beautiful body.

On the endless march, the air was everywhere full of the cool fragrance of trees; flowering saffron, crocuses and snow lotus covered the valley; below the snowy mountains lush green forests of scrub and needle-pine stretched unbroken like brocade, and heaps of agate and Buddhist pagodas could be seen all over the place.

But just then, dangers, the nature of which Colonel Younghusband could not have anticipated, were quietly fermenting; at the very moment that he was marching towards Gyantse, a Tibetan strike force made up of 1,600 Khamba tribesmen was hastily converging on Shigatse in southern Tibet. This strike force was to steal quietly into

Gyantse on the secret orders of the Head Lama of Tashilhunpo monastery (the origin of these orders being the impromptu suggestion of the Scottish missionary) and, at some point in the near future, launch a surprise attack on the British expeditionary force's centre of command — Colonel Younghusband's command post.

4

On leaving Phari castle, after a long and arduous three-day trudge, John Newman came to the damp mountain region of Gongbala.

From the ridge of the Gongbala hills, Newman could see a miserable scattered village at their foot. The crude wooden houses built higgledy-piggledy among groves of trees looked from a distance like so many ruined birds' nests. On the bank of a little river at the south-east end of the village stood a stone compound, an old-fashioned, apparently Ming dynasty-style building. It was in fact the abode of He Wenqin.

The village where He Wenqin lived was situated in a wooded area about seventy *li* east of Gyantse. The village, called Cangnan, rarely saw the sun all year, but the high rainfall meant that plants such as berries, cherries, tea and sugar cane grew in abundance.

Eleven years earlier, this grain collector of the great Qing empire had set out on the interminable journey — half work, half exile — along the course of the old canal. After stopping briefly in Chagang in Gansu and Yushu in Qinghai, he finally reached Tibet in the autumn of 1893.

With the passage of time and the change in his geographical concepts, the beaded screens on the gaily-painted pleasure boats in the ancient city of Yangzhou receded daily in his memory. He was like a beetle anxious to return to a deep place inside a flower's stamen, as day after day he waited for an edict from the Emperor and yearned to return once more to the illusory moonlight of the four and twenty bridges.

He Wenqin's house was quite near the hot springs at Cangnan. Every day at noon he would see a few Tibetans and merchants and pilgrims from foreign parts come to wash at the spring. And if the happy-natured women, their faces smeared all over with oil and the dried blood of animals, had never been washed clean by the spring water, he might never have discovered their natural beauty. The Tibetans of the Cangnan area knew how to enjoy themselves and they were well aware that the iron and sulphur in the spring water were good for the health. If the water was not hot enough, they would set light to some dried horse manure and heat up rocks in boiling water, then roll them into the spring. As a result, the air around He Wenqin's house smelled faintly of horse manure all day.

One morning, He Wenqin was awoken with a start from a deep sleep by a hubbub outside his room. Outside the west window of his bedroom he saw a foreigner performing magic for the Tibetans near to the spring. His housemaid told him that this foreigner had already been staying in Cangnan several months and that he could do as many magic tricks as a pomegranate has seeds.

He Wenqin told the maidservant that she could invite this foreign fellow in any time she liked and get him to give a performance of all these magic tricks of his.

That evening, the foreigner, wearing a long black robe and a straw hat followed the maidservant into He Wenqin's courtyard. This was the first meeting between He Wenqin and John Newman.

Since He Wenqin knew nothing about Christianity, he imagined Newman to be an Indian pilgrim wandering in a strange land, who relied on performing magic to make a living. On this occasion, Newman had brought with him several black metal instruments. His modest, patient performance, in which great attention was lavished on every detail, quickly won over and delighted the maidservant, but He Wenqin showed little interest in these bizarre phenomena. In the end, Newman introduced He Wenqin to two valuable commodities: a camera and a high magnification microscope.

Newman explained that, with the former, one could fix a person's image on to paper without in any way harming the body of that person, and that with the latter one could make the lines on a map instantly thicker. He Wenqin shook his head to show that there was no way he was going to believe such bizarre theories. So Newman gave an on-the-spot demonstration: stretching out his hand he grabbed a louse from the floor and put it under the glass of the microscope. When He Wenqin saw that, under the microscope, the louse had suddenly turned into a mouse, he was so amazed he could not speak.

Later, He Wenqin admitted openly to the missionary what his real feelings had been at that moment: "For a minute I thought that time was playing tricks on me."

Newman was an experienced old China hand. More than ten years ago he had begun his career as a missionary following a group of Jesuit missionaries through the Yangtze basin, and had spent a long time in the area around the ancient cities of Jiangning and Yangzhou. This experience provided him and He Wenqin with inexhaustible topics of conversation.

Although the missionary and He Wenqin quickly became close friends, their relationship was not always a happy one. In He Wenqin's opinion, Newman's overly warm and intimate behaviour towards him (such as embracing him) always caused him alarm and agitation. When the missionary kept urging him to become a Christian, then He Wenqin felt even more unhappy. But because it was their first meeting, he had to be polite, and he did not utter a word of protest.

In 1903, when the British army suddenly invaded China's southwestern highlands, the prospect of a serious national disaster posed a grave threat to the friendship between He Wenqin and the Scot.

Newman rode his purple-red Tibetan pony unhurriedly up to the front of He Wenqin's house. It was very quiet in the courtyard. A group of lush green tangerine trees laden with fruit was swaying in the wind. Creeping vines climbed all over the low wall of the yard and an ornamental streamer with sutras on it slanted diagonally through the courtyard.

The maidservant told him that He Wenqin was in the middle of his midday nap, and that if he did not have any pressing business he could wait in the study. The maid's tone of voice was icy and uncomfortable to listen to. It reminded Newman of the time he and He Wenqin had met at Khamba Dzong, when they had parted on bad terms, and a kind of dull depression took hold of him.

As the missionary walked towards the courtyard gate, He Wenqin was in the back room but he was not asleep. Through a shuttered window and the waving tassels across the two open doors he could see Newman's fading shadow. But he did not feel like getting up and seeing him straight away.

A few days before, he had set out for Khamba Dzong on the instructions of China's chief minister in Tibet, with the aim of holding talks with Colonel Younghusband of the British expeditionary force. If he could halt or delay the British in their bold march on Lhasa, the chief minister in Lhasa would guarantee his return to a post in China within the year. But the outcome of his mission to Khamba Dzong had been very disheartening. That arrogant, conceited Colonel had had the effrontery to say that he was of "too low a rank" to meet him.

Since the British troops had appeared in the Chumbi river valley, he had written several times to the chief minister, suggesting that the imperial government urgently send troops from Qinghai. They could then launch a decisive attack on the British on the plains of Gyantse before the British reached Lhasa. His suggestion instantly met with a stern rebuff from the chief minister. This led He Wenqin to draw several pessimistic conclusions: apparently even the ancient empire itself was experiencing unprecedented disorder and misfortune and the fact that the Sichuan troops who had originally been garrisoned in Qinghai were being re-assigned one after another to posts in China was proof of this. It appeared that the imperial government's control over its south-western border had in fact already ceased to exist except in name.

In a sense, the declining state of the nation was at one with the misfortunes of the individual. Whenever a merchant convoy of yaks passed through Cangnan, heading west for India and Sikkim, an uncontrollable feeling of homesickness welled up in him. He often dreamt of the mastheads of ships outside the city of Weiyang, of its deep and quiet streets and alleys, and of the sweet smell of osmanthus wafting in after a night of wind and rain. When he awoke in the morning, to his surprise his face would be covered in tears.

That evening, the missionary came into the sitting room wreathed in smiles, as he had done so often in the past. He saw He Wenqin standing miserably in front of a map, on which he was marking circles and dots with a pencil.

"Your people have occupied Gyantse," He Wenqin told him.

"Our people?" said the missionary evasively. He could feel the coldness and indifference in He Wenqin's voice, and sensed that he had a lot weighing on his mind.

"They have killed over a thousand Tibetans at Guru gorge," He Wenqin still had his back to him.

"Mr He, do try not to worry," Newman walked over towards him, "the British will never succeed in reaching Lhasa."

"Why not?"

Newman was on the point of saying something when a Nepalese pilgrim dressed in Muslim attire came in. He had a blue cloth bundle clasped to his chest.

The Nepalese pilgrim handed the cloth bundle to He Wenqin, and then, without so much as a grunt, bowed and withdrew.

"What's in the cloth bundle?" asked the missionary.

He Wenqin did not reply. He put the bundle on the table and opened it very carefully. It was a brand new German pistol.

He Wenqin skilfully loaded a bullet into the chamber, revolved the chamber once, and pointed the muzzle at Newman.

"Mr He, is this some sort of joke?" The missionary's face turned red, then white, and his smile suddenly appeared rather forced.

He Wenqin's expression was calm, but he had a frenetic gleam in his eye: "If your Jesus really is in Heaven, he can protect you in the underworld."

Then he pulled the trigger.

Newman covered his face with both hands, as if trying to block out a blinding light.

"Mr He…" he cried.

He Wenqin casually fired the second round, but as before the chamber was empty. He looked in disappointment at the pistol, sighed, and without more ado put the gun on the table to one side.

The missionary had been pouring with sweat, the muscles on his face were twitching uncontrollably, and tears spilled from his eyes. He stood in the middle of the room, still in a state of shock, at a loss what to do next. After a long while, he appeared to have recovered from his fear and come back to his senses. In a strange tone of voice the missionary shouted at He Wenqin: "Mr He, I did not enjoy your evil theatricals one little bit, not one little bit!"

He Wenqin smiled and reached over to pick up a teacup from the table.

5

News of the attack by the British expeditionary force on the Tibetan army at Guru spread quickly to the Tashilhunpo monastery in the south of Tibet. A young lama returning from saying prayers, told the Head Lama that according to reports from shepherds in Gyantse, the British troops must have killed several dozen Tibetans in the Guru gorge.

Two days later, a pilgrim brought more detailed news to Shigatse. After the cruel attack, shepherds from the Gyantse region had discovered a total of 321 corpses of Tibetan soldiers in the dense stony grasslands. (Dealing with these corpses presented unprecedented problems to the only two priests in Gyantse who could conduct celestial burials.) The whereabouts of even more Tibetan soldiers who had been taken prisoner was unknown.

The news was deeply shocking to the Head Lama of Tashilhunpo monastery. He had already had a premonition of it, but once the incident had actually occurred, the great lama, hitherto so adept at controlling his emotions, could not prevent tears from pouring down his cheeks.

News that, after crossing the Guru gorge, the British had pressed on into Gyantse, followed soon after. The Head Lama decided to bring forward his plan for curbing the activities of Colonel Younghusband.

Over a thousand Khamba tribesmen converged on Shigatse in the space of a single night. These men had been enlisted especially for the occasion from among the shepherds of the south-east mountain region. They were tall, with ruddy complexions, and coiled round their heads they wore head-dresses of red cloth.

The Head Lama met them on a main road outside Tashilhunpo monastery, and then, according to an ancient religious rite of those parts, patted them on the crown of their heads.

On the Head Lama's orders, this strike force of Khamba tribesmen was to hasten to Gyantse — arriving before the third of May — and launch an attack on the British army's position at midnight on the fourth. If the attack was successful, they should seize Colonel Younghusband, hold him in the forest on the shores of the Yamdok-tso and await further instructions. The Khamba commander in charge of the attack and the Head Lama sat on the sand by the roadside, discussing in great detail the various difficulties and their possible solutions.

Finally, the young Khamba leader asked the Head Lama: "But how will we recognize the man we are after?"

"Oh, I almost forgot," laughed the Head Lama, clapping himself on the forehead. Then he drew a piece of card from his bosom and handed it to him.

It was a photograph of Colonel Younghusband, sent to the Head Lama several months ago by John Newman.

The commander took the photograph and his eyes widened in surprise. The man in the photograph had a thin face, with a thick growth of beard round the corners of his mouth. His epaulets and the insignia on his chest were clearly visible — he looked as lifelike as a real person. The Khamba leader stared at the photograph and then immediately threw it on to the ground as if it had burnt him like a hot coal.

"You don't need to be afraid," the Head Lama said gently, "it's not a paper mirror, nor is it a demon; it's a daguerreotype: the technique was invented not long ago by a Frenchman."

The strike force set out from Shigatse before dawn on the 25th of April. The Head Lama accompanied them through two mountain passes. By then the sun was already rising and a mountain road, as fine as a sheep's entrails, appeared before them. The Head Lama led the Khamba commander to the bank of a mountain torrent by the roadside.

"This mountain road leads straight through to Gyantse," the Head Lama told him with a dark and solemn expression on his face. "Once your attack has been successful, put a log into the Gyantse river here, and tie your red head-dress onto it, and the current will bring your portent of good tidings back here to me."

The Khamba leader nodded.

As they were taking their leave, the anxious leader thought of something else and asked, somewhat hesitantly: "In the unlikely event that we fail, what should we do?"

"Fail?"

"I mean, in the unlikely event that our plan fails, what sort of signal should we send you?"

The Head Lama stopped in panic. The question had come out of the blue. He thought for a moment and then patted him on the shoulder saying: "You cannot fail."

When the Khamba troops had vanished in the warm gentle rays of the sun, the Head Lama did not return to Tashilhunpo monastery, but sat down on a wooden bridge over the river. He sat silently with crossed legs like a yogi, and never moved from this position.

Over the past few short months, the chaotic business of the war had given the Head Lama the most unusual experiences of his life. He had decided on the plan to attack Gyantse all by himself, and without even reporting it to Lhasa, since he was concerned that his report would provoke unnecessary disputes there, which might in turn cause his already fundamentally weak plan to miscarry. Even if Lhasa had approved the plan, news of it might still have leaked out and made the British take greater precautions. The forthcoming attack had swept the Head Lama even more deeply into the military affairs and politics which he had always detested, and he had no way of knowing if the gods of the underworld would protect his strike force. Since the Buddhist elders had not uttered a peep about the British massacre at the Guru gorge, the May 4th midnight attack could hardly avoid being seen as contrary to their wishes. The inner peace and harmony he had attained by his single-minded practice of Buddhism seemed to have been thrown into chaos in one fell swoop, while the complexity of many problems had long ago far exceeded the scope of his imagination. But if the surprise attack on Gyantse could prevent the British from entering the sacred city of Lhasa then whatever happened, it was worth the risk.

The river trickled and flowed on its tranquil way, lapping the floating grasses on either side of the channel and making little eddies around each of the bridge pillars. Milky-white buttercups and mountain flowers were blooming all over the mountainside.

On the opposite bank of the river was a small Tibetan village. The low black roofs of the houses were covered in stacks of dry grass, and piles of pure white cloud hung low, pressing down on the houses. Many-coloured streamers with sutras on were strung like netting between the houses, linking them all together. Some streamers and strips of cloth reached as far as the trees, stretching unbroken to the end of the bridge by the river. A crowd of large fat ravens were perched on the walls, and innumerable twittering tits chirped incessantly in the depths of the forest.

At noon, the Head Lama saw several women sidle past him over the bridge. They carried cane baskets on their backs, loaded with dried horse dung and blocks of ice recently chipped from the mountains. The enormous blocks of ice in the baskets glittered like diamonds. As they walked towards the village, the women kept looking round to stare at him, all the while discussing something in whispers.

That evening, the village women appeared by the river again, bringing the Head Lama beef, sweets, some wine, and a Tibetan blanket to ward off the cold. So as not to disturb his meditation they deposited these provisions at the end of the bridge and left without a sound.

The Head Lama sat at the end of the bridge as silently as a rock, the icy cold wind brushing against his face, the night frost forming softly on his body, but he paid no attention to the food and blanket. The next morning food arrived in a steady stream; they took away the food from the previous evening and replaced it with fresh. The living Buddha and the lamas from the nearby monastery and some monks who were passing through came one after another to sit next to the Head Lama. They did not know why the eminent Head Lama had chosen such a place to sit and meditate, but they quietly sat around him anyway, beating drums and chanting. And when evening came, the lamas and monks softly drew nearer to him so that their bodies would protect him from the chilly winds of May.

6

On the fourth day of Newman's stay in Cangnan, a British soldier disguised as a Tibetan arrived secretly from Gyantse. When he saw Newman at He Wenqin' house, he gave him a letter written personally by Colonel Younghusband. In the letter, Younghusband ordered the missionary to come immediately to Gyantse, without giving any particular reason.

Mr He Wenqin had gone out as soon as it got light; the servant girl had seen him walking in the direction of Moon Wood, carrying a double-barrelled shotgun: it looked as if he were going hunting.

Newman waited by the stream outside the house until the sun had set behind the mountains, to say goodbye to He Wenqin, but there was no sign of him. By dusk he was being constantly pressurized by the British soldier. So, feeling frustrated and forlorn, he set out on the road to Gyantse.

The missionary arrived at Gyantse the next morning. The supply officer, Major Bretherton, was outside the camp to meet him. The young officer looked even thinner and more sunburnt than at Khamba Dzong. The unfamiliar climate and insomnia had left dark lines on his face.

Bretherton told him that as the British force penetrated ever deeper into the Tibetan interior, battles would become more and more savage, and the number of woundings and fatalities among the soldiers would therefore increase. Colonel Younghusband hoped that he would stay with the camp for the next two months as army chaplain.

Newman found the idea inconceivable. He told Major Bretherton that he was a clergyman, a free missionary, and that apart from his instructions from the Church at home, he had no interest in and no reason for taking on other duties. "Even less so," Newman explained, "seeing as I can't stand the sight of blood."

Major Bretherton smiled patiently at him: "Mr Newman, you are now in Colonel Younghusband's battlefield command, not a Scottish diocese. I can sympathize with the fact that you cannot stand the sight of blood, but if Colonel Younghusband ordered you to drink a dish of sheep's blood right this minute, I'm sure you wouldn't refuse, would you?"

When Major Bretherton put it like this, it did not leave the missionary much room for manoeuvre.

As early as 1785, the Jesuit mission in Tibet had for various reasons been disbanded. The parishes they had established were later taken over by the French Lazarists. However, the Lazarists made no more progress in China and Tibet than had the Jesuit mission. Their unfortunate experiences in Tibet had a significant effect on the missionaries: they were often pessimistic to the point of despair about their mission and these feelings eventually led to their concluding that "Tibet's native religion is perfect and without flaw."

After working for more than ten years in China's Yangtze river basin as a missionary, Newman had returned to Scotland for a time. The failure of the Church in Tibet had inspired in him an intense fascination for this region. In Newman's opinion, the rich experience he had gained working as a missionary in China's interior was sure to be useful in Tibet. It was obviously unrealistic to expect the whole Tibetan population to become Christians overnight, but at least he could make an opening there for the Christian faith.

In the summer of 1894, he crossed the Kashmir Basin and the mountains of north-western India in the company of a group of border traders and arrived alone in Tibet. He had brought with him a few of the latest achievements of Western civilization in the hope that he could use them to rouse the Tibetans from their Himalayan hibernations. Among these achievements were a camera, a telescope, several microscopes, some tinderboxes and a dozen or so printed pictures. In several years of missionary work Newman had narrowly missed being successful: if smallpox had not carried off a certain three Tibetans, he sincerely believed that they would eventually have become Christians. Later, when Newman happened to meet He Wenqin at the Cangnan springs, the humorous Chinese had said, apparently in jest: "If you could bring the smallpox vaccine to Tibet, you'd have as many Christians here as there are sheep in Lhasa."

Like many Chinese, He Wenqin was not opposed to Christianity. The young official was tall and fair-skinned with his hair combed back into a long glossy black pigtail. With his elegant deportment and gorgeous brocaded silk robes he looked more like a woman. The moment Newman set eyes on him in Cangnan he was strongly attracted by his appearance. For a time they were spending whole days together, hardly ever out of each other's sight. They took tea together and discussed ancient Chinese poetry. They rode out together on horseback and hunted in Moon Wood. They went to Naqu in northern Tibet and attended the big horse trials... As time passed,

Newman's secret plan to convert He Wenqin to Christianity became nothing more than a simple religious duty.

The days in Gyantse were dull and uninteresting. It happened to be the rainiest season in the Gyantse area. A fine drizzle began every day at noon and continued to fall until dusk. Newman's living quarters were on a slope near the Baiju temple, where a few Turkish-style tents formed a circle on the barren ground. All around it was completely bare, without a tree or a plant in sight.

The British expeditionary army was in a state of anxious anticipation. Since the attack at the Guru gorge, opposition from parliament had become more intense than ever. Newman noticed that for the last few days, Colonel Younghusband had been constantly down-hearted, and that a frown had never left his face. It seemed as if the whole camp had run out of patience with the damp and gloomy weather.

While out for a stroll one time, Colonel Younghusband rather dejectedly told Newman that even if parliament suddenly agreed to his plan to march on Lhasa, for strategic reasons the advance would have to wait at least until the end of the rainy season, because if they advanced in the rain, the British army ran the risk of having its extremely long and fragile supply lines cut by the Tibetans.

Bretherton seemed rather more approachable than Colonel Younghusband. He often came to Newman's tent for a chat after meals. In his youth, Bretherton had studied the history of religion for several years at theological college, but his interest in religion was limited to knowledge and textual research and had never involved belief or faith. In the same way as certain mystics in the Church at home, Bretherton's guess was that Jesus really existed. He told Newman that some years ago when he was stationed in Kathmandu, he had done some on-the-spot investigations in India and Kashmir, and in these areas where Buddhism flourished he could almost feel "that the spirit of Jesus was hovering in the air." In southern India, someone had taken him to see a dark and secret chamber. Judging from the veiled suggestions of the local Buddhists, after Jesus had been nailed to the cross, he had not died immediately. By means of his own consummate yoga skills and by great good fortune, he had survived, and had spent his declining years in this secret chamber in India, devoutly practising Buddhism, and indeed attaining the great age of eighty-one.

"There is also the strange case of Kashmir," Bretherton said to Newman with a reverential expression on his face. "The peaceful and beautiful landscape of mountains and river valleys described in the Old Testament can be seen all over the region, and I have a feeling that Kashmir is the land "flowing with milk and honey" of the biblical stories."

Newman had a very contradictory reaction to Bretherton's talk. It was similar to the attitudes men are said to have towards women: contemptuous, disgusted, and at the same time lusting for them.

Bretherton was a man with a vivid imagination and also, in certain respects, a good man. It was obvious that since this young man, brought up on the banks of the River Thames, had arrived in Tibet, he had lived in fear of the strange, secret worship of the spiritual, and had been plagued by fantastic conjectures and premonitions. During their stay in Gyantse, he more than once said to Newman, "A great catastrophe is creeping up on us."

On the morning of the second of May, the sky, which had been covered in thick dark cloud, finally showed signs of clearing. Although the grassland was still sodden with rainwater, a group of British officers started a game of football on the extremely muddy slope. Another group of soldiers went down to the Gyantse river and started chatting to some Tibetan women who were doing their washing. The women had not seemed to mind the mild jesting of the soldiers, but dalliance seemed to be overstepping the mark, and they hurriedly turned and left the river bank.

That afternoon some Tuoben monks passed through Gyantse fort on their way west and had to endure the interrogations and close scrutiny of the British soldiers. These Tuoben monks brought Newman some surprising news: on their way here they had noticed the greatest amount of Buddhist activity they had seen since arriving in Tibet. Several thousand lamas and a living Buddha were sitting in a circle on both banks of the river. The sound of their chanting could be heard several miles away.

That night, Newman secretly slipped out of Gyantse, and hastened to the place where they were gathered. He did not then realize that the Head Lama of Tashilhunpo monastery had already been sitting quietly on that river bank for the last seven days, nor that starvation and exposure had brought him to the brink of death.

7

The British army had spent the period of heavy rain in Gyantse in a state of endless waiting and had collapsed into utter despair. Colonel Younghusband received one report after another: some soldiers had gradually lost all self-control and had raided the Baiju temple and Gyantse's antiques market, looting treasures and molesting women. And the Tibetan population of Gyantse were no longer as tractable or agreeable as they had been: their highly secretive reprisals actually led to two low-ranking British army officers disappearing without trace from the banks of the Gyantse river.

Bad news came as usual from England. Curzon was suddenly relieved from his post as Governor-General of India, and his replacement was the extremely senile Lord Ampthill. This seemed to indicate that Colonel Younghusband had lost the last bastion of support for his march on Lhasa. Finally, in mid-April, Younghusband received a telegram from London in which a high-ranking government official tactfully urged him to resign.

On the other hand, the Tibetan officials in Lhasa had abandoned all hope of negotiating with the British. Troops drafted from the Kham area were continuously arriving in the mountains north of Gyantse and building military fortifications and defensive walls at the southern foot of the Karo mountains. These recently drafted troops were equipped with fairly modern weapons, among which were rifles with a range of over two thousand yards. Colonel Younghusband had ordered an advance party to launch a trial attack against the Tibetan army's position, but they met staunch resistance from the Tibetans.

Before dawn on May third, Colonel Younghusband, after a sleepless night, finally made a bold decision. He ordered most of the troops stationed at Gyantse to go directly to attack emplacements in the Karo mountains, under the command of Major Brander. Colonel Younghusband seemed to have foreseen that if they did not deal the Tibetans a fatal blow before they had completed the construction of their fortifications, then this defensive wall, stretching on for miles, would sooner or later become an insurmountable obstacle to the British advance on Lhasa.

Major Bretherton was stubbornly opposed to this plan, because if the main force of the British army went off to the Karo mountains, then the command post at Gyantse could be left in great danger. Once the Tibetan army found out about the British army's manoeuvres and attacked Gyantse, then the centre of British command would be finished off in one fell swoop.

Although Major Bretherton's concern was not unreasonable, it enraged Colonel Younghusband. His face grave, he sternly reminded the Major, "Remember that our enemy is not the French army under Napoleon's, but a crowd of shepherds from primitive tribes."

That evening, seven hours after the main British force had withdrawn from Gyantse, unlucky omens appeared.

Several dozen Tibetan POWs who had been recovering from their wounds in the British army hospital suddenly and mysteriously went missing. At the same time, several Tibetan maids and porters employed by the expeditionary army left without a word. In addition, according to reports from army scouts, on the plain, twenty miles outside the command post there had appeared a team of draught oxen — nobody knew where they had come from. Under cover of darkness they had quietly entered a dense forest on the opposite bank of the Gyantse river.

Colonel Younghusband took no notice of these suspicious occurrences, but carried on as before, going to Major Bretherton's quarters after supper to play Erlut chess. Perhaps he was worried that the public dressing-down he had given Bretherton that day might have damaged their long-standing friendship, and thought that a calm, good-tempered game of chess would help to disperse the cloud that lay over them.

By midnight a heavy rain had again begun to fall. Claps of thunder boomed continuously and the fierce wind made the tents flap and rattle noisily. Over the last few days, Colonel Younghusband had actually begun to feel rather tired, and half-way through the game he dozed off in a cane chair.

At two o'clock in the morning, in a howling gale, an attack force of sixteen hundred Khamba tribesmen came stealthily and silently to the edge of the camp. The British were totally unprepared for this attack. The camp fires had long ago gone out and it was pitch dark. A few black and white ducks and cuckoos cried restlessly in the bushes around the camp.

A newly-conscripted Indian soldier was discovering that the greasy Tibetan food totally disagreed with him, and was kept awake all night by thirst and stomach-ache. On the third occasion that he went out of the tent to relieve himself, he noticed the silhouettes of a number of people swaying about near the perimeter of the encampment. Then, in a flash of lightning, he saw several muskets protruding over the battlements of the wall. The new soldier was obviously scared to death, for he remained rooted to the spot for four or five minutes-in the dense curtain of rain before coming to his senses and sounding the alarm.

The sound of gunfire startled Major Bretherton into action. He shouted to the sleeping Younghusband and then rushed into the compound outside the camp behind several security guards.

For a moment Colonel Younghusband could not work out what had happened outside. Bewildered, he came out of the tent in his pyjamas to the patter of concentrated gunfire from the Tibetans. He saw several dozen Gurkhas scurrying hither and thither around the courtyard while an old regimental army doctor wearing white shorts trembled in their midst.

After a moment of confusion, Major Murray, who was in charge of camp security, led the soldiers of the guard to Colonel Younghusband's side and clustering around him they withdrew to a patch of scrub land outside the camp.

Despite their advantage of secrecy, the Tibetan troops responsible for the attack knew practically nothing about assault tactics. If, at the start of the attack, they had crossed the defence wall and struck the heart of the British army position, then the expeditionary army and its command would have been completely overwhelmed. But as it was, the fact that they remained lying flat on top of the wall, shooting blindly, gave the British army time to organize an effective resistance.

As the fine light of dawn rose from the darkness, the assault force on the wall was exposed to fire from the British Maxim guns. The attack lasted until five in the morning, when the situation began to show real signs of deterioration.

When a hundred or more Tibetan soldiers had been left dead beside the wall of the camp, the Tibetan army began to retreat along the Gyantse river towards the south-west. On the right side of the camp, three hundred or so Khamba tribesmen had withdrawn into a stable. Major Murray reckoned that he could capture them all at once, but Colonel Younghusband, still extremely ruffled, ordered the machine guns to be positioned in front of the stable.

With a few furious bursts of fire, the plan that the Head Lama of Tashilhunpo monastery had spent so many months mulling over had finally failed.

The losses sustained by the British army from this attack were extremely limited. Five soldiers died in the battle, including one captain of cavalry.

The first thing Francis Younghusband did after the attack was summon the war correspondent, Henry Naylor, to his command post. On Colonel Younghusband's orders, he would dictate a communiqué which Naylor was to send, post haste, back to England. This communiqué made a massive overstatement of the losses sustained by the British during the Gyantse attack — these losses suddenly rose to sixty-three.

"The Tibetans can never have dreamt that their foolish attack would assist my grand design," Colonel Younghusband said to Major Bretherton.

"Do you think parliament will approve your plan now?"

"We are in fact already on the road to Lhasa." Colonel Younghusband lit a cigar. "This attack is the key which opens the door on the antechamber, and it will not be long before we'll be able to use it to unlock the great gates of the Potala."

Major Bretherton seemed to be about to say something, but then quickly changed his mind. Their good fortune in averting disaster had done nothing to raise his low spirits.

"When do you count on starting the general offensive?" Bretherton asked after a moment.

"Tomorrow," Colonel Younghusband quickened his step, "as long as nothing unexpected happens, we will capture Zhebang monastery next week."

Inside the reed shack that served as a field hospital, wounded soldiers were lying all over the grass floor, and doctors and nurses were bustling about anxiously. Bretherton noticed a Tibetan soldier fearlessly having his leg amputated without anaesthetic. The calm composure of his face was incredible, and formed a striking contrast to the moans of pain from the wounded British soldiers.

Bretherton went over to him, and through an interpreter, had his first conversation with a Tibetan.

"It's not such a bad thing, having my leg sawn off," the Tibetan soldier said to him.

"Why not?"

"Because next time we fight, I won't be able to run away."

When he heard this reply, Colonel Younghusband, who was standing to one side, couldn't help bursting into laughter.

8

He Wenqin did not return from Moon Wood until after dark. The servant girl, watering the irises in the yard, told him that Mr Newman had left Cangnan at dusk. The missionary had waited on the sandy river bank outside the house until the sun fell below the mountains, hoping to say goodbye to him. "He looked as if he had something he wanted to tell you." He Wenqin said nothing. He threw the Big-eyed antelope and several snow cocks that he had been carrying on his horse onto the floor, then strode vigorously towards the back yard. Although he had come to dislike the missionary more and more, Newman's abrupt departure left him with a feeling of emptiness and desolation.

As the British expeditionary army pressed on towards the Karo mountain fortifications, one after another, Tibetans and merchants fled the area around Cangnan. For even if the village, only a few dozen miles from Gyantse, was not going to be the field of battle itself, it would still be right on the edge of it. Every day, large groups of Tibetan soldiers riding in ox-carts passed through, setting out along the Masuo river valley towards the Karo mountains. What with malnutrition and the arduous journey, they seemed completely exhausted. They travelled very slowly through the gorge, flanked on either side with chestnut trees. You would not have thought , to look at them, that they were bound for the fields of war; they looked more as if they were off to the prairies of northern Tibet for the annual horse trials.

On May twenty-first, 1904, a Chinese courier crossed the Gongbala mountain range and arrived at He Wenqin's front door. He handed Mr He a letter written by the chief Chinese minister in Lhasa himself.

In his harshly-worded letter, the chief minister criticized He Wenqin for having "lost an opportunity through hesitation" and for being "ineffective in negotiation." He also hinted at his having had too close an association with the British missionary, or even, by these failings, encouraging the British to make a big push towards Lhasa.

"And what's all this about your being too low in rank?" At the end of his letter the chief minister had written: "You are the formidable envoy of the great Qing empire; this Younghusband is a mere colonel..."

In view of He Wenqin's serious dereliction of duty and thus his obvious unworthiness of the Emperor's kindness and favour, the chief minister ordered him to lock himself away and think on his mistakes while awaiting his punishment.

That evening, a heavy rain once again came gushing from the heavens. The dense raindrops pattered against the paper windows, and threads of damp night air invaded his study from between the door leaves, bringing in the luxuriant scent of cool resin. He Wenqin sat under the oil lamp staring at the curtain of water coming down from the eaves like tassels, and passed a sleepless night.

In the ancient city of Yangzhou, periods of heavy rain usually occurred during the season when the plums were turning yellow and ripe. The continuous downpour made the flowers of the scholar tree and the gardenia produce a seductive fragrance, and drenched the branches so that the trees were dark green all over. In the evenings when night fell and people were asleep, He Wenqin would often remain alone in the little hut and listen attentively by the dim candlelight to the wind and rain in the night....

Now it was all so far away. The masses of pretty women and beaded curtains that filled his memory now seemed hollow, unmoving and lifeless, Although the chief minister's letter had not elaborated on how the Emperor, assailed by disaster at home and abroad, would punish him. He Wenqin had read his fate between the lines. Now that the road home, in his hopes and dreams, had been cut off, these times of chaos had already cast him far aside.

The next day at dusk He Wenqin mounted a yellow-maned Naqu horse and rode alone out of his house into a thicket overgrown with oak and chestnut trees by the river. In his drunken stupor he saw the maidservant come running out of the courtyard, so he pulled on the horse's reins. Tears were streaming down the maid's face and the sound of her clamouring vibrated in his ears, but he could not make out what she was saying.

Scattered gunfire sounded across the ridge of the Gongbala hills. By the time the sound reached this side of the hills it was very faint and indistinct. He Wenqin gave the reins a shake and the pony bolted along the stony ground through the wood. He saw the silhouette of the maidservant by the river growing smaller and smaller; turning his head, He Wenqin gave a careless laugh and waved at her.

The warm sunlight rested lazily on the curving lines of the course of the river. Flocks of birds hopped about on the rocks by the river. He Wenqin whipped his horse on to a fast gallop. The rushing river water and a large expanse of fringed iris swept swiftly past his eyes. At that moment, He Wenqin did not even know where he was going, but the beautiful warm sunshine and the cool breeze caressing his face offered him a contentment and peace of mind he had never felt before. He could not stop himself letting out a great roar as he headed for the distant snow-covered mountain peaks, each one rising higher than the other. Distant and illusory echoes rose swiftly one after another in the stillness and peace of the valley.

The sky gradually began to darken. The Masuo river suddenly changed its course as it approached Lalong. Following the dark, gloomy band of trees and coarse grass that meandered towards the north-east, He Wenqin at last caught sight of the silver-grey snow line on the tops of the Karo mountains.

The Tibetan army was encamped on a broad patch of mustard-growing land to the north of the Karo pass. The camp fires had been lit much earlier and the air was full of the floating smells of horse dung and incense. Groups of Tibetan soldiers clasping muskets were sitting huddled around the fires. Their faces were dark and expressionless. In front of a blue-coloured ancestral fortress in the Karo pass, a few soldiers clasping stringed instruments were playing and singing. In He Wenqin's memory, the soldiers' folk-songs were very like the lullabies of the boatmen from the region of rivers and lakes: low and deep, coarse, grating, lacking in rhythm, and yet full of sadness.

He Wenqin rode slowly through the middle of the soldiers. When he came to a wall surrounding the outside of the camp, an aide-de-camp of the Lhasa Depon stopped him in his tracks.

"You can't go any further," the aide told him in halting Chinese, "the British 32nd Pioneers are positioned not three hundred yards south of the wall."

He Wenqin seemed not to have heard him. He whipped his horse, who leapt down the gentle slope of the pass and the thick blackness quickly swallowed him up.

"The British machine guns will make mincemeat of you!" the aide yelled after him.

He Wenqin did not know why he wanted to go to the British encampment. Nor did he know where his scrawny Naqu horse would finally take him.

In the end, He Wenqin never actually reached the British encampment. Once in the great miry wasteland, spanning an area of glimmering, low-lying marshland on the left side of the Karo mountains, the pony recognized the road, cautiously skirted round this area and turned into a dense forest on the shores of the Yamdok-tso, not a hundred yards from where the British army was encamped. By this time, He Wenqin had already fallen into a drunken sleep on his horse's back and was oblivious of everything.

The next morning, woken by the cool morning breeze, He Wenqin found himself lying on the bank of a little stream, his body covered in a thick layer of frost. His horse was drinking from the stream, snorting and whickering.

On the opposite bank of the river, He Wenqin caught sight of the coil of a scarlet head-dress which kept appearing and disappearing in the undergrowth. A large Khamba tribesman was cutting wood on the bank of the river. The sound of chopping echoed hollowly through the forest. He Wenqin led his horse across the river and went up to the man.

The young man was apparently a soldier who had just retreated from the battlefield. He had a bullet wound in his thigh and hobbled as he walked. He Wenqin helped him finish felling the birch tree and then the two men sat down on the sandy riverbank.

"Have you just fled from the fortifications at the Karo pass," asked He Wenqin.

The Khamba man shook his head. "I've come from Gyantse."

"Gyantse?"

"At dawn on May fourth, we attacked the British headquarters at Gyantse. But we lost, and the British forced us into a stable, set up their machine guns and fired into it. But I wasn't killed, so I hung on until dark and then made my escape."

"What are you doing here cutting wood?"

"It's like this," said the Khamba man, "I must send a signal to the Head Lama of Tashilhunpo monastery, because he told me that if we were successful, I had to put a log into the Gyantse river and bind my headband onto it. But our plan failed…"

"So you should send a signal of failure," said He Wenqin casually.

"The problem is that it never occurred to us that we might fail."

He Wenqin frowned, as if realising the Khamba man's dilemma.

"What do you intend to do then?" he asked.

"I thought of getting you to kill me, the young man said with a dismal expression. "You could bind my dead body to the log, then the Head Lama will understand everything."

"I see what you mean," He Wenqin regarded him sympathetically, "but I can't kill you. Take your time and think of something else."

When he had finished speaking, He Wenqin stood up and prepared to leave. By now the sun had risen. In the brilliant sunlight, a myriad white butterflies were fluttering about in the thickets by the river. As

He Wenqin led his horse up, getting ready to think about which direction to take, the Khamba man had already stolen up behind him with a sharp knife in his hand. All of a sudden, He Wenqin felt an icy blast in the small of his back, which spread quickly through his whole body....

He was still alive as the Khamba man dragged his body towards the river bank. A confusion of bright light stabbed at his eyes so that he could not open them properly, but he could still smell the fresh scent of plants and feel the warmth of the sunlight.

A moment later he could feel his body floating downstream, and then the icy water covered his face....

9

The Head Lama of Tashilhunpo monastery had kept watch on the banks of the Gyantse river for ten days, but he had still seen no sign of the birch log signalling good tidings floating downstream, which seemed to a certain extent to confirm the prediction made many years before by the Chief Magician of the Potala Palace.

John Newman arrived in haste to find the Head Lama already at his last gasp. Just before the end, the great lama, who had lived all his life in seclusion in the monastery at Shigatse, left two testaments. One of them concerned the trials and tribulations he had endured in his life, his enlightenment into and understanding of the Buddhist classics, the funeral arrangements after his death, and so forth. This was hastily written down by two learned living Buddhas. But the other testament had to do with the greatest secret in the history of Tibetan Buddhism. Being the only person there to hear it, Newman got the impression that the Head Lama hesitated to relate this story to him.

Once upon a time, a young Israelite called Isa, after enduring many hardships and dangers, arrived alone in the foothills of the Himalayas. He studied Buddhism with great devotion in a monastery and became familiar with the Buddhist classics. He was naturally intelligent, with extraordinary powers of understanding, and after a few years he had cultivated himself for the attainment of future bliss. A number of teachers of the sutras in India, Tibet and Kashmir recognized his great worth, and it appears that they foresaw the extraordinary future achievements of this young man, for they did everything they could to persuade him to stay and spread the Way in the Himalayan region. But one bright moonlit night, the young Israelite set out in secret on the long journey back to Jerusalem.

"The young man Isa was Jesus Christ," the Head Lama told Newman. "Although it is unknown by most people in Tibet, there are two rolls of sutras recording this piece of history which are still kept today in a secret room in the Dazhao temple in Lhasa."

The Head Lama of Tashilhunpo monastery passed away quietly at midnight that night. The people built a Buddhist pagoda in the place where he had passed on in order to commemorate his achievements and his virtuous character.

One morning, just before the completion of the pagoda, He Wenqin's corpse finally floated by. The various species of fish in the Gyantse river, and the birds and wild animals from the woods had picked all the rotten flesh from his body. In accordance with the customs of the Han Chinese, after dragging his remains from the river, Newman and the local Tibetans did not give him a celestial burial, but instead buried him under a patch of poppies by the pagoda, and planted a tangerine tree on top of the grave.

Shortly after dealing with He Wenqin's burial, Newman left Tibet. He hired a horse and cart and returned to Scotland by way of Yatung in southern Tibet. With him he took a prayer wheel and a shiny black pigtail. The pigtail had been given to him as a present a year ago by He Wenqin. On his cold and lonely journey, Newman often examined it, and could not prevent tears from running down his face, for even after it had left the nourishment of the human body, the pigtail continued to grow surreptitiously ...

As Newman's cart was passing through a stage near Yatung, a British reporter told him that the expeditionary force led by Colonel Younghusband had occupied Lhasa a few days earlier.

That night the Scottish missionary lay in the inn under the dim lamplight, and for a long time was unable to go to sleep. As he casually turned the pages of the Bible at the head of his bed, a wind-dried leaf fell out of the book onto the floor. Newman picked it up with a pair of tweezers and examined it repeatedly under a microscope: the leaf plucked from the sacred tree actually looked no different from a leaf from any ordinary tree: the lifelike images of the Buddha which had once been on it had long since ceased to exist...

On the 30th of July, 1904, the British troops under Colonel Younghusband reached the banks of the Tsangpo river, twenty English miles outside Lhasa.

Major Bretherton never saw the shining golden flame-like roofs of the Potala. The forebodings of doom he had been experiencing since arriving in Tibet finally became reality: while the British troops were fording the surging torrent of the Tsangpo river, Major Bretherton and two Gurkhas fell into the water and were lost.

Three days later, Colonel Younghusband led the army into Lhasa. Although the lamas sent out negotiators of varying status in an attempt to prevent the British troops from entering the Potala Palace, Colonel Younghusband still forcibly carried out the storming of this majestic, mysterious, magnificent and splendid sacred temple.

Bretherton's fatal accident and various other problems which arose after entering Lhasa made Colonel Younghusband feel more downhearted that he had ever felt before. On September 7th, not having received any instructions from the British government, he rashly agreed to sign an internationally binding, but quite farcical, treaty with the Tibetans.

Not long afterwards, a letter sent by the head of the India Office, Broderick, arrived in the hands of the former Governor-General of India, Lord Curzon. In the letter, Broderick criticized Younghusband for being a vulgar man with no breeding. "Everything he has done in Tibet shows that he lacks an adequate understanding of the political situation between Europe and Asia in the twentieth century. For the sake of our country's honour, Colonel Younghusband's removal would seem to be more or less inevitable..."

On the final evening of his interminable Tibetan expedition, Colonel Younghusband rode alone to the edge of Lake Namu-tso. Under the snowy peaks of the Nyainqentanglha mountains, for a moment, Colonel Younghusband forgot where he was. He felt as if the deeply-established opinions he had held, including even his awareness of time itself, had all changed unimaginably since he had arrived in Tibet. In his ears resounded once again the frail old voice of the Head Lama of Tashilhunpo monastery. They had been at Khamba Dzong at the time, in the command post, and he and the Head Lama had had a blazing row about some matters of geography. The Head Lama, with an unbelievable obstinacy, had told him,

"The earth is not round at all; it's triangular, like the shoulder-blade of a sheep."

DISTANCE

BAI GUANG

translated by Duncan Hewitt

I suppose I did wonder whether I had fallen in love with her. At the time I couldn't give myself a coherent answer. The time I spent with her passed very quickly, and touched me deeply, but I was never able to get close to her. She said, when I'm with you I feel really happy. Her words, her calm gaze, left me suspended in a welcome ambiguity. She did it very well, I thought. I found it all very appealing.

Then Feng Jian came into my life, and eventually into her territory, into those lovely times we spent together, those evenings of alcohol and affection — later the grim, cold and heart-rending memories.

I met Feng Jian at a party early one summer. We got talking about the old town where I live. Its name is complicated — San Francisco — apparently something to do with a saint from a long time ago. But its Chinese name is very straightforward: Jiujinshan — Old Gold Mountain. Feng Jian said he didn't live here, he was on the other side of the Bay Bridge, at Berkeley. The party was a constant hubbub of people coming and going, but our common language drew us together, and we spent a long time talking. We got into a detailed discussion about the bridge which connects San Francisco and East Bay, and the bay below, which is named after the city. Half way across, the bridge disappears into a tunnel, through a small island which rises out of the sea. The bridge is so long that even at top speed it takes as long it takes to smoke a cigarette to drive across. The sight of this great bridge bestriding the bay had instilled a great self-confidence, and buildings of all kinds had sprung up along the shoreline around the bay, and so the bay area of San Francisco had become a splendid place. You ought to have a good life in America, Feng Jian remarked. These philosophical discussions aside, he said he'd help me look for a car to buy, and we arranged to meet at the weekend.

Summer over here is not so different from the other seasons. The nights are still very cool. I left the lively party behind and went back to my little apartment, wondering what to do next. Sleep is the most natural thing in the world, but it's also the most boring. So as usual I started drinking beer. I leafed through some of the financial magazines I always felt I ought to read, did my best to memorize some of the commentaries and figures, until the alcohol began to make me feel drowsy and I succumbed to sleep.

In the daytime my time wasn't my own. In the office I drew up tables, made phone calls, held earnest discussions about problems, felt smug about how capable I was, or made excuses for the things I couldn't do. After work I dived into the subway and came home, and set about making phone calls chasing up people and places with cars for sale. After a while I gradually realized that my dream of finding the ideal, most beautiful car at the lowest price was costing me too much time and effort, and that I ought to call it a day. Towards the end of the week I settled on a car, and stopped making any more phone calls. That evening, as usual, I casually heated up some noodles to fill the hole in my stomach, allowed my thoughts to wander for a moment to how I'd like to have a wife, got nowhere, and so started reading magazines. I needed to find things to talk about to impress my colleagues, so I'd get promotion. A few years earlier, on the other side of the ocean, I'd laughed scornfully at this kind of artifice. Now I observed my devotion to it, even in what was meant to be my spare time.

At the weekend, I went to the garage with Feng Jian, and confirmed that the car really was all that I'd hoped for. On the way there he asked me how long I'd been tormenting myself over this car. More than two months, I told him. He said, that's cool. I asked if he thought I'd been wasting my time — and my life. He said, if you weren't so busy how would you realize that there wasn't enough time. In fact there's never enough time. In America being busy is as commonplace as lawns.

After we'd driven the new car home, I asked if he had any plans for the evening. I hesitated over whether to ask him to eat with us, or whether to invite him the next day instead. I was trying to imagine the scene when he met her. But he said he had to hurry home; he'd call me the next day. After all he was in Berkeley, just twenty minutes drive away.

She was at Berkeley too. So you've bought the car at last? she asked. I said I didn't have the patience to carry on looking. I said I urgently needed something to convince myself that my life was moving forward.

That's not like you, she said. She looked at me, her eyes were very pretty. Have some more vegetables, she said.

This restaurant on the fringes of Berkeley was a place we had specially selected. Perhaps it was because of its name, 'Wei yuan', The Flavour Garden. Or perhaps because of the beautiful view from the window. The landlord had quite a struggle to keep the place going, and the restaurant was always very quiet. I knew him quite well now, and I often suggested all kinds of half-baked ideas to him, but he never took any notice. I decided he must have a better idea than me of how to make a living. The one thing that annoyed me slightly about him was the fact that he'd jumped to the conclusion that we were lovers. This gave her all the more opportunities to apply some kind of unspoken pressure and add to my sense of unease. It was an issue I always avoided.

I'd known her for almost a year now,

I'd been in America a long time and my experience of life here was that contact with women had become an imaginary game to me. But she was different. I had concluded that she was very attractive. She spoke very calmly and she had a gorgeous smile. It was easy to fall for her.

Yet she said she didn't have a man in her life. She also said she didn't intend to stay single.

Early on Sunday evening Feng Jian phoned. I was very excited. In this place, when people say they'll phone you, you don't take it too seriously. Everyone knows that unspoken sense of being too busy. Feng Jian said, has the new car been put to use? Is there anything you can't use a second-hand car for, I asked him.

"Old cars are too noisy, they drive you crazy," he said.

"Because you can't listen to music in peace, you mean?"

"And because you can't have a nice quiet chat."

I knew what he was talking about. But it wasn't easy to start joking about your love life with someone you didn't know very well. So I changed the subject and invited him for a meal. He said there was no need. When I persisted he asked me if I liked drinking. You can get all kinds of fancy spirits in San Francisco's Chinatown, but we decided to stick to beer this time, since I had to work the next day. I made a solemn promise that we'd find an opportunity to drink spirits one day. So he came over in his car; within a quarter of an hour he was ringing on my doorbell.

Feng Jian's regular beer was different from my usual, but we each liked the other's favourite too. So we decided to abandon the American custom of each choosing our own drink, and stick to just one kind of beer instead. We agreed to toss a coin to decide which it was to be. We came up with my choice, a Dutch beer, which comes in bottles with green labels. His was a German beer, with red labels — though he said that when it came to people he preferred the French. After supper we went to buy some dried beef; he said it wasn't really convenient to go to his place, so we went back to my little apartment,

I learnt that he'd been in America for seven years. He liked America a lot, it was free and easy, you could do whatever you wanted. But he'd been in college the whole time. He'd delayed for a long time and then transferred to Berkeley, to be sure of getting a good job. Like many people, he thought you wouldn't find a good job unless you had a degree from a good university. When I attempted to dispute this, he just said it was easy for me to talk, but with a degree from Berkeley he'd get a good job.

I also learnt that things weren't going well between him and his wife, and that they were more or less leading separate lives. "When we first got married I wanted to change, but in fact things just got worse," he said, and then intoned solemnly, "Marriage is the highest price a man can pay."

I said he was too narrow-minded. He said he was using up all his energy trying to stop his marriage from grinding him down. I found it hard to imagine, since I'd never been married. I could only conjure up a vague picture of married life: a sense of emotional stability, making progress at work, making love twice a week, that kind of thing. He told me it was unusual for him to share even a single moment's intimacy with his wife in two months. He said he didn't know why.

"Wouldn't you like to have a baby?" I asked.

"Sometimes I think I would," he said.

His wife was very keen to have a child. And it would be born an American, after all. But Feng Jian said he thought he was still too young. On the other hand, he said, I struck him as someone who'd start to think about children once I'd been married for a while. I couldn't argue with him. If I understood correctly, he meant that I was more or less worn down already. Feng Jian went on to expound on how short life was, how he didn't want to rush towards the next stage. He said America was a good place, one shouldn't feel too sorry for oneself. At this point I looked up instinctively, to see the expression on his face. The scars of life had left me with an extreme sensitivity to anything fake, but what I saw at this moment was utter sincerity, and a trace of heroism.

I told him that I had had a real struggle to find work. I'd really suffered, physically as well as mentally. In the end I'd come to my senses and stopped holding out for the perfect job, and so this demeaning and exhausting process had come to an end. At this Feng Jian suddenly sat up straight, and said loudly that I had become a degenerate. Above all, he said, one must follow one's instincts. "This is America," he said. He said that the fact I was so prepared to repress myself showed I was still constrained by old habits. Everyone has their limits, I said. I said when people have been worn down to a certain point, they simply have to bow their heads. "And what would happen if you didn't lower your head?" he asked.

I told him I didn't have the strength to be so self-indulgent.

We finished the beer, and I took out a bottle of wine which I'd had in the fridge for a long time. It was left over from when I'd visited a vineyard in a valley in the hills nearby, while I was still a student. I was feeling so happy today that I decided it was time to drink it. Feng Jian read the label, told me I had good taste. I said buying this bottle of wine had had nothing to do with good judgement. There weren't any wine glasses, but Feng Jian said it didn't matter, and went to wash some cups. As we started the wine, Feng Jian told me that when people talked about "wine, women and song," this was the kind of fine vintage they had in mind. Then he asked why I wasn't married.

I said I still couldn't get used to being so close to one woman.

He asked what I meant. I said that when I was confronted with a woman I had this strange inexpressible sense of distance, which I could never overcome. He decided I was talking rubbish, he said reproachfully that women were very important to men, women brought love, and love gave you hope.

"You're too romantic," I said.

When he started talking about the importance of the romantic spirit, I said I didn't want to divorce myself from life. Immediately I realized this kind of talk was a bit heavy to say to someone I'd only just met. But Feng Jian said, "You ought to have better luck than me."

I got to sleep very late that evening. It was middle of the night before Feng Jian left. I felt that we'd both said too much. I'd had a similar experience before, in that land across the ocean. It was a dingy, dust-blown, crowded place, but what had happened there had left a deep impression on me.

Though I had spent the whole evening disputing Feng Jian's fluent arguments, he had made an impact on me, and I now felt uneasy. I had a nagging sense that he was implying that I had been a participant in my own annihilation. As I slipped gradually into an uneasy sleep, I was troubled by fleeting snatches of another mystifying tale. It seemed to be saying: if you come too close, you might trigger a tragedy.

The next morning the alarm shook me, still half asleep, out of bed. On my way to the office I did my best to pull myself together and assume the correct expression. Today I was supposed to be going with my boss to assess a wholesaler, so I had to look sober and sensible.

The first guy I saw when I came through the door greeted me with a "Hi, what's going on?" He just meant it as a friendly greeting.

"Not much," I said. This was my standard reply.

"Great," he said, looking absolutely delighted.

"How are you?" I enquired.

"Pretty good," he said.

"Super," I said, looking absolutely delighted.

The boss was busy. I loafed around, idly mulling over a few trivial matters. Fragmented images came back to me, of Feng Jian the night before. After half an hour the boss came out of his office, and told me urgently to hurry up and get ready, we were late. I said everything was ready. He said that was great. Then he started chatting to someone else. They chatted for a long time, I think it was about something that had been on TV the night before. Although I felt rather anxious, I was very patient — I felt there was nothing I could do about it. In the end we were in such a hurry that we barely had time for lunch.

On our next enchanted evening at the Flavour Garden, I told her about Feng Jian, told her how he liked drinking too. I also said he was very straightforward, that he was a good man. "So it's that easy to be a good man in your opinion, is it, you just have to be straightforward?" she said.

"What I meant was that he was good-hearted." I told her how Feng Jian had wished me good luck for when I got married.

"You've only just met him," she said. Then she said, "Feng Jian.... it's an interesting name."

"I easily take a liking to people," I said, "not like you."

She glanced at me, then said have some more vegetables. After a while she said, you seem very cheerful today, has something nice happened?

"Well, at least I'm starting to hope for something nice to happen," I said.

"Starting to hope?"

"That's right."

"So what did you do before?"

"I suppose I was a bit crazy."

She still looked rather uncertain. "Isn't it true," I said, picking up a piece of spinach and gulping it down, "that somebody, or perhaps two people, had a pretty hard time trying to make you like them?"

"Are you serious?"

"Don't take it like that, it was a genuine question."

She believed me, and said, "I guess it is. I suppose there are people who've tried to extract affection from me."

"And you wouldn't give it?" I asked.

She smiled. She smiled and looked at me. All I could do was ask: "What are you thinking?"

"I suppose I wasn't exactly overwhelmed by their interest, OK."

I murmured an apology, felt very awkward, lowered my head down and started drinking. After a while she asked me why I was interested in such things. I hesitated, then said I couldn't understand why such a lovely woman had no one to care for her emotionally, no one devoted to her, that it seemed an injustice. She asked me what I meant by lovely. Her eyes were twinkling, her tone of voice was plain and to the point.

What I was trying to say to her, in fact, was very simple. I asked her why she didn't want their affection.

"I can't talk about other people's good and bad points like that," she said.

"Well you can talk about it in the abstract then," I said. "It's you I want to know about, not other people."

She betrayed a hint of embarrassment. I hadn't really expected that, and thought maybe it wasn't embarrassment. She had simply averted her gaze, out of step with the rhythm of her speech. Perhaps she was thinking about other things, other people, that had nothing to do with me. She couldn't accept excess, she said, and she couldn't accept dilution.

"Dilution?" I repeated.

"Well, for example, if you could only talk about green cards, cars, and houses, then I wouldn't bother coming here."

She admitted that these were things she constantly found herself thinking about. She'd changed her job, and was just trying to get a new green card.

Things like this were a nuisance, and time consuming, but the value was self-evident. She agreed. It was still worth making the effort for it. But what about afterwards? she asked me next.

For her part, as her pursuit of the good life increasingly went according to plan, she felt ever less interested in it. As days and nights passed her by, she felt no emotional involvement, even began to forget what it meant to be moved. Boredom dominated her days, she said.

"Talking to you is the only thing that holds any interest for me," she added.

"You're embarrassing me."

"Why?" A hint of a smile shone in her eyes again, her voice was even more blunt than before.

I began to feel vaguely uncomfortable. As soon as I sensed the desire to get closer to her, I immediately felt exhausted. I said, "I must already be going grey."

She didn't respond. But she didn't just glance at me as she usually did. She was staring at me. The sunlight streaming through the window caressed her gently, emphasizing her stirring figure. I felt my heart skip a beat. Hastily I told myself, it doesn't have to be like this, this distance suits you very well.

I regained my composure, and she stopped staring at me like that. Narrowing my eyes I looked out through the window, the lawn outside seemed very soft and peaceful in the gentle sunlight. I blamed Feng Jian for my abnormal state today. It was his bluster which had set me thinking about these senseless things.

"Are you going to turn completely pallid?" she asked.

"It doesn't matter if I do — I'm used to it," I said.

We reverted to our original easy chatter. It was all abstract, far removed from reality. Nothing else happened, except the landlord misunderstood a few more times. Afterwards I took her home. The sky was just growing dark, and the unchanging ritual of night began once again with the lighting up of the street lamps. Before she got out of the car, she asked whether I wanted to come in and sit for a while.

I knew I wasn't in the right frame of mind. I also knew that this was a one-off invitation. I feared I might let her down, make her feel unhappy. And I could also feel the desire in my heart growing more and more real. "Why are you staring like that?" she smiled. "I said do you want to come in and sit down for a while?"

I felt I was already behaving badly. But what I said was, "OK, but I've got things to do later."

"Then go and do your things straight away."

As she spoke she opened the car door. I felt a bit uneasy, a bit angry with myself, a bit awkward. I got out of the car too. Leaning on the door I said wait for me to park the car. She said, "Seriously: you go and do your things. We can talk next time." She really meant it — her expression showed she was serious. I watched her go up the steps, and suddenly felt clearly that I — and I alone — was very unfortunate.

After I left her, I showed up at a party. It was in a musty old building. Big solid chairs arranged in a circle took up half the room, the other half seemed full of big cupboards. I blindly invited the girl who happened to be sitting next to me to dance, and got quite a fright when she got to her feet: she was a head taller than me. Bracing myself I took her by her vast waist, and began to dance, my legs floating rather uncertainly across the carpet. I did my best to assume a carefree manner, but the girl looked more and more expectantly for me to say something. I had no choice but to start mumbling aimlessly about some harmless topic, and then gasp in admiration as she told me how she had dreamed of becoming an astronaut. As she realized my total empathy with her, her awkwardness turned first to profound thoughts, and then to exuberance, and when the music finished she led me over to the cupboards and told me to watch, then launched into a handstand, her huge body thrusting upwards and swaying precariously. As I hastily stretched out a hand to support her, the sight of her vast thighs made me very embarrassed. When her body had righted itself I said that was great, then glancing all around me said I had to go outside for a moment.

I got away from the woman with the massive body, and went out into the corridor. I needed a cigarette. The corridor was in a teaching block; there was a couple in the doorway of the next classroom peeping inside. I realized I'd just seen the girl at the party, her pink make-up was very attractive. I decided that the large woman had been blocking my view completely, and that there were must be plenty of pretty young women in there. With this in mind I went back inside, but the classroom was completely empty. The chairs were arranged in a square, with a row of cupboards on the other side. My bag and overcoat had ended up on the chair nearest the door, the coat neatly folded and placed next to the bag. My mind suddenly felt completely empty. I went out into the empty corridor, then into the empty school yard. A gust of chill wind brought me to my senses. My bedding had all fallen off.

I tried to come to a Freudian interpretation of this dream, but I got nowhere and so went back to sleep. The next day, Sunday, I got up very late. My whole body was so heavy with sleep that I felt exhausted by the slightest movement; there was nothing for it but to do nothing at all, with a clear conscience. This I did until dusk, when I felt a bit hungry, and phoned Feng Jian. He wasn't in. His wife wasn't exactly friendly so I couldn't leave a message. I had to go and boil myself some noodles.

I threw myself into the next week's daily routine. But something seemed to have changed. I began to feel a kind of revulsion at my work. I did a lot of different things, but my basic job was to let the others — my boss and my colleagues — know what the buyers in the market expected from our company, and how we should respond. I used all kinds of charts and statistics plus plenty of random speculation to show how well I was doing, and my overall boss thought I was contributing a lot. I guess I'd never really liked doing this kind of standard American work, but now my dislike for it was becoming really disturbing.

The other thing that was worrying me was a pervasive sense of her. Even our first meeting came back to me clearly. I was looking for work then, networking wherever I could, and one of my many working lunches happened to be with her. I soon realized she wouldn't be able to help me, but I went through with the lunch, in fact I prolonged it: she brought a hint of romance to the little restaurant. But I was in a pathetic state at the time, my head full of talk about my CV, and my imagination went no further than how wonderful it would be to go to bed with her. And so I tried to take a short cut, saying some crude and inappropriate things; she gently stopped me short. She said, be a bit more clear, she didn't understand what I meant. During the brief moment of silence that ensued, I suddenly realized that her charms were not simply of one particular kind.

I was supposed to call her straight away but the strain and rushing around involved in finding a job got in the way. When I did see her again I felt awkward at how neglectful I'd been, and put a stop to those sweet fantasies. I remained at a point not far away from her, yet not close to her either. I often wanted to see her, to talk to her. That's all it was. She made it clear that she greatly enjoyed spending this time with me. I thought she seemed quite ambivalent, and I began to wonder whether I didn't also feel quite ambivalent about being together with her like this. I don't like to seem uncertain in front of a woman, and so I convinced myself that she hadn't made an impact on me. And in fact, apart from the time I spent with her, I very rarely thought about her. But now something had changed, she was starting to move into my life, to infiltrate my memory and my imagination.

Feng Jian phoned to arrange to meet for a drink at the weekend. I hesitated. I said why don't we call each other nearer the time. He asked me how I'd been recently. I said fine. I asked him why his wife was angry with him again. He asked how did I know. He said that was the bread and butter of family life, I'd understand when I got married.

I'd arranged to meet her at the weekend. It was very rare for us to go to the Flavour Garden two weekends in a row, but she didn't seem to mind at all. She showed no sign that there was anything out of the ordinary. I suppose I didn't feel that it was anything out of the ordinary either, I simply felt very happy when I looked at her. When I hooted on the horn and watched her come down the steps, walk over to the car and open the door I felt a great sense of joy. Once she was inside she looked at me, stretched out her hand, tapped the gear lever, and said, "Let's go."

At this point I still had no idea at all what this woman symbolized. Because of the way she had taken hold of me in the last few days, I had started to survey her territory, but all I could see were some insubstantial possibilities. I still couldn't be sure who she was: The distance yawning between us was hard to gauge. The only sequence I could imagine was: throwing oneself into pleasure; anxiety and foolishness; sinking into warmth; feeling pain; warmth again; pain again; and finally heartbreak. I simply didn't know that, in her territory, this was all far stronger than I imagined.

The difference between today and our previous meetings became apparent early on: at supper time we talked about my past love affairs. She said she had doubts about whether I had had a love life. "So I'm that useless, am I?" I said.

"That's how you seem"

I said this was most unjust. I went on to say that I could tell her an imaginary love story.

"Tell me how you chase girls," she said.

"OK, are you ready?"

"I'm ready."

I told her that a bright, vivacious girl from China had started dropping a few hints, and so I had pursued her, putting into practice all the tricks I'd heard of. I imagined that my description of those petty clevernesses was accurate, and so the calm woman sitting opposite me would see that I knew how to win a woman's affection. Would she start to look at me in a different light? As I spoke I was wondering all the while what I would do if she didn't want to listen. "And then?" she said.

I carried on, right up to my final seaside walk with that vivacious girl. "Along the way we had a nice chat," I said, "and I found plenty of opportunities to make it clear that my feelings for her had already reached a certain point, but each time her reaction was non-committal, half-embarrassed. When we reached the seaside, we went to a very elegant restaurant, which I knew she would like, and she didn't object when I paid the bill. After our meal we went down to the shore; just when I was doing my best to use the waves as a metaphor for my emotions, she sighed that there weren't enough real men in this world, so I hurriedly started trying to act more like a real man."

She smiled. She had a beautiful smile.

She said she couldn't imagine how I could play the part. But she said it didn't matter, it was great, I should carry on talking.

"She pushed me away. I asked what it was, she said it was nothing, so I tried again. Again she wouldn't have it. I ignored her. Then she said what's the matter with you. I said you don't like me, do you? She said that wasn't true. She didn't know what the problem was either. She drew close to me and touched my hand, said gently, "You're not angry are you?" Then I plucked up my courage again, and again she skilfully deflated it."

She said I was making up the story as I went along.

"This really happened," I said. "I warned you."

She said it was very original.

"I was original or she was original," I asked?

I said that the girl had probably wanted to test me out: she needed time to make an thorough investigation. I said I didn't blame her.

"And afterwards?"

"Afterwards, because I was too busy, I gave up," I said.

"And she didn't come to look for you again either?"

"She did."

We had just about finished eating. In that brief moment of silence I saw her hand stroking the napkin. Her hands could make all kinds of movements.

"I still don't think you could chase a girl like that," she said.

"Are you saying I'm not that passionate?"

"That's not what I mean."

I was going to tell her that that girl was typical of the young Chinese women who come to America — you have to chase them like that. But I thought this seemed a bit brutal, and so I didn't say it. I observed that my story was pretty boring, and asked whether she had any better ones to tell. She said she didn't.

But, she said, she could have.

She said it just needed my participation. I asked what she meant. She said she wasn't such a good talker as I was, she was afraid she couldn't tell stories properly. Then she pointed out that we'd finished the 'green' Dutch beer, and asked whether I wanted another bottle.

As I was taking her home I asked her whether she had any beer in the house. She said she hadn't, but she had some very good tea, and asked me if that would be OK. We'd already arrived. I said wait for me to park the car. As we were going upstairs she told me it was Longjing tea. I told her Longjing was my favourite kind.

Her house was very neatly decorated, the colours plain and cool — in keeping with her style. The pictures on the wall prompted a few moments of idle chat. Then the water boiled and she got up and went out. As she went, I watched her from behind, watched the way she walked; my heart skipped a beat and I found it hard to keep my composure.

"So you used to be a pretty modest person then?" she said as she came back. She made the tea, then sat down softly and leant back in her chair. She raised her head slightly, gathered a few hairs into their correct position. All the time I watched her.

She caught my eye, looked back at me. She was very calm. I averted my gaze. I felt terribly clumsy. But I could still cope, I managed to keep the conversation going.

She put on some soft piano music. Her speech was still very quiet; gradually it melted into a caress. I was starting to find it very hard to talk to her, discovered how utterly useless I was. During the moments of silence while she was out boiling the kettle, I wondered why I still hadn't drawn closer to her. But then the lessons of American life made me carry on as if nothing had happened. Night fell.

Her expectation, which gradually became obvious, had the same calm force as she herself. Perhaps to avoid an awkward moment, I said, I've always been modest. She pursed her lips. "I think you're incredibly arrogant just now," she said.

"Perhaps you shouldn't be so perceptive."

"But you're fine like that." She blew on her tea leaves, her elbow was as high as her hand holding the cup. "It would be a waste if you weren't like that."

"Don't mock me."

"You're always joking. Don't do it any more, please."

I didn't know what to say; anxiety gripped me. But just when I was about to succumb to a fit of trembling, I realized that I still didn't want this. I couldn't see myself occupying her territory. I suppressed the urge, felt an immediate sense of sadness. I'd been cut off from this kind of feeling for so long, I just wasn't used to it any more.

Confronted with such an emotional moment I felt uneasy. In the silence I noticed her eyes take on a gloomy aspect; all I could do was start talking again. I said to her, "To people in the wilderness, it doesn't matter whether something is wasted or not."

I'd talked about the wilderness to another friend before. That friend told me there were three kinds of love. She was an academic, who had always had a fascination for studying American culture. The definition of the three kinds of love had come from an American: sexual attraction, compassion, and the love of one individual for another. I asked whether the last kind could be divided up further. She said that the American thought it was the most difficult kind of love. "So the States has a very high divorce rate," she said. Then she said that my theory about the wilderness blurred the line between what was difficult and what was easy: "It's actually very difficult." She agreed with the American. I wanted to tell her that I wasn't looking for the third kind of love, I was used to maintaining a distance. I even maintained a certain distance from the English language; if I spoke it for long I felt exhausted. I thought that this was something which life in America had given me.

I averted my eyes, moved away from her and turned towards the room. A fleeting sense of opportunity, a faint taste of sweetness, had snatched at me. I stopped at the door to the bedroom, and felt somehow unfamiliar, far away.

"A wilderness?" she said. It was as though she had only just heard. Her eyes were downcast, her voice weak.

I saw her put her teacup down on the table. I saw her lean back in her chair, cradling her hair in her hands. Now she was watching me.

She said, "I admire how casual you are."

"People are changed by their surroundings," I said.

"You're OK."

I had to go. I got up and said goodbye; with an effort she got up from her chair to see me out. I said she didn't need to; she didn't insist.

The nights at this time of year were cold and silent. I filled up with petrol, gave the car a quick wash, went back to the supermarket to buy a few necessities and a large quantity of beer. When I got home I set about tidying the place up. Afterwards I settled into a comfortable chair. I put one of the green labelled bottles of Dutch beer down in front of me. I opened it. The first mouthful always gave the best sensation. Following my regular routine, after the first mouthful I lit a cigarette.

I thought of Feng Jian. It was already half past one in the morning. I thought about it for a long time, then finally called him. I pinned my hopes on the fact that students are night owls. He was. And he came over straight away, with a box of his German beer.

"Doesn't your wife mind you coming out so late?" I asked him.

"If she does I don't know about it. Anyway, it's the weekend."

He tossed a coin, and this time it was the German beer which won. He was in high spirits, like someone who'd just had some good news. He started talking about the women he'd been involved with before, talked a lot about how to get along peacefully with girls, how to avoid quarrels or embarrassing moments, heartbreak and angry scenes. I asked him whether he had felt emotionally involved. He said when you're in love you don't worry about things like that. So I said what about your romanticism? He said there were many aspects to life. He said you can always find something about a woman that moves you. He said otherwise how could you bear such desolation. I told him I was jealous of his ability to retain his affection. He said in fact he was envious of me, that my love was real.

"What do you mean by that?" I was taken aback. It was only now that it dawned on me why he had started talking about women the moment he saw me.

He explained that he had only wanted to exchange a few ideas with me; if I didn't like talking about things like this, then he begged my pardon.

"Are you saying that I'm up late drinking because of a woman?" I asked.

"Well, I thought you'd must have just been with a woman."

I was surprised at his sensitivity. "I had supper with a girl," I said, "but that's a long way away from love."

"Is she a nice girl?"

"One in a million."

"Hey, that's great." Feng Jian clinked his glass against mine, drank a mouthful.

With an effort I tried to explain that real love was still far away. I told him she was a nice girl but I couldn't find the emotion within me. At this Feng Jiang launched into an all-out attack on me. Then he again produced his theory that there was something moving about every woman, and said that any man worth his salt should spare no effort in seeking out and appreciating that sense of vitality. Otherwise you're dead. You really are. He said this was one of the main things he had reaped from his years in America. "You should learn how to live," he said.

I wasn't in a good mood, and told him that I'd gotten something from America too. "Yes," I said, "before you get to the touching moments you have to endure a lot of suffering; I'm not as patient as you are."

"Hasn't the Bay of San Francisco taught you about breadth of spirit?"

"It's taught me about being generous to myself."

"That's enough, that's enough. Tie them to the bed, let them scream. That's what you ought to do."

"Just don't shrivel up after you've tied up the wrong person, eh mate?"

After that we cut out the crude talk; drinking's still the best thing, I said. Drinking was safe. I said people had limits, they couldn't endure any kind of pressure.

"That's an excuse. It could just be weakness, the fear of being hurt. You can't just give up like that," he said.

I said I'd already given up.

Feng Jian fell silent. The sounds of the night gradually grew clearer, the lawn outside my window was shrouded in the darkness of the moonless night. When I came back from the window, Feng Jian was sitting quietly on the bed, leaning back against the wall. Rotating his glass slowly in his hand, he started to talk about his wife. He had a very good wife, in fact. Way back, when she had strayed innocently into his sights, trusting him and liking him even if she didn't understand him, his heart had filled with gratitude.

But Feng Jian didn't say why things weren't going well at the moment. He simply said: If only we'd met later.

Again he asked what the girl was like. He asked whether he could meet her.

I told him, in terms of innocence, she was like his wife. She wasn't calculating about money or about green cards. I said, you ought to meet her.

We'd finished the German beer. I asked Feng Jian if he wanted to toss a coin again, said I had more beer left over. He hesitated. I said perhaps we shouldn't, we didn't want to get into a situation where we'd have to break the rules. The law said you weren't allowed to buy alcohol at this time. So what could we do, since we'd run out of the German stuff.

"Is she very special to you?" Feng Jian asked. He stopped for a moment, then explained that he wanted to know whether I was getting closer to her. I said I wasn't. I said, "She's called Xiao Di." Then I read out her phone number. "Give her a ring first."

He said he remembered. He'd heard of such a person before.

Feng Jian told me that she had strung a lot of people along, then had married a wealthy old American. He made it sound very convincing, said she'd made a fool of me.

"Who told you she'd married a rich man?" I was very surprised.

"Everyone says so."

"We're not talking about the same person."

"Her name's Xiao Di, right?"

"Then it is her. I've just had supper with her, even went to her place for a while. She lives alone. She says America's a let-down."

Feng Jian's expression seemed very remote. He picked up two of the green labelled bottles, shook them, opened one using the other. Then he stood the bottle up straight, letting the drops of foam spill over the back of his hand. He looked at me. I drained my glass and held it out. He filled it very carefully, so that there was a thin layer of foam on top. He wiped his hand and said slowly, "From what I've heard, she's not beautiful."

I said, "Have you ever seen her?"

"But she's very captivating."

I felt I should wait to see what he said next. I suppose I nodded my head. He went on.

"When she says America's a let-down, don't you think she might be talking about you?"

"In what way?"

"Meaning you're stupid because you're the only one who doesn't chase after her."

"Really?"

"She's very calm, very cool, and you're left unable to open your mouth, right?"

"No, she can be a very warm woman."

Feng Jian was adamant that I ought to be in love with her. He attacked me from all sides, reproached me, encouraged me, sighing frequently about what a shame it was, and we got through quite a few bottles in this way. I presented all my reasons, all my views, but I knew that his mind was made up. In the end I said, when you see her you'll understand. You'd find it very hard to fall in love with her just like that.

The sky had grown light. The morning was very fresh, but I felt very weary. The sour taste in my mouth proved to me again that I was no longer young. I slept for a long time. It was already afternoon by the time I woke up. I sloped around until the sun began to fade, then started thinking seriously about what I should do now. Feng Jian had left before I woke up. He left a note, asking me to call him. He hoped to ask me again who Xiao Di was when I was sober.

I didn't know what I would say, so I decided to go for a walk by the sea. I knew I really ought to be making use of the time to sort out the papers I needed for my green card, and there was the proposal I was supposed to present at work the next day, and I needed to call the landlord to fix the hot water in the bathroom, and I'd already got a fine for not paying my phone bill, and there was the registration document for my new car, and clothes to wash.

It takes between thirty-seven and thirty-nine minutes from my place to the beach, if the traffic is favourable. I had discovered this particular stretch of beach when I had just arrived and was exploring the area. I thought then that I would come down here often to see the sea. But in fact I very rarely came. On the other side of the ocean, a few years back, to get to the seaside used to take me five hours by train, plus two bus journeys of one and a half hours and a half an hour. Now, when it was so easy, I had gradually forgotten all about it. The car slipped and slithered quietly along the winding road, like a fish, the fading sunlight shining straight through the windscreen.

I felt very calm. I'd put on a lot of clothes, so I could follow my inclination to sit on the sand near the breakers. The sun was moving towards the horizon, the water turned leisurely into spray. I thought about how these waves were coming in from the Pacific. They were very pure, as they rose they showed me their azure underbelly.

I paid a price for this. On Monday, in a meeting at work, I couldn't answer some of the questions put to me. They weren't very happy, and that included my overall boss, who had always liked me a lot. I still had to rely on them for my Green Card, but actually I was focusing more of my attention on my own state of mind. I just couldn't concentrate on the table of market analysis coordinates in front of me. I looked at myself in a new light, as though watching a frozen river thaw in the warm season. Now and again I got up and wandered around: it was as though nothing would be right unless I messed a few more things up first.

Soon it was the weekend again. I only ever saw her at the weekend. We usually arranged our meetings by phone well in advance;

occasionally we just phoned at the last minute on Saturday. I felt very hesitant about whether I should phone her. I felt that the way our last meeting had ended seemed no longer to permit a last minute call. Then I decided I should call Feng Jian. On Wednesday he'd left a message on my answerphone telling me about a party at the weekend, but I still hadn't returned his call. Last Sunday when I got back from the seaside I'd phoned him and asked why he didn't just go and see her himself, instead of asking me about her; he said he just wanted to be sure whether I had got emotionally involved with her. I said I hadn't.

Feng Jian answered the phone, said his friend was having a party this evening, in Berkeley, asked me whether I was interested. I said OK I'll come. He said be careful. I asked what he meant. He said it was nothing. I sensed that his wife was in the room, so I said: "Xiao Di's coming, right?" He said yes. I said even if you can't bear to explain yourself, you'd better stay polite. Feng Jian said I shouldn't worry, he'd treat her well.

Because I had so many things to do which I'd been putting off I didn't go until very late. I hadn't got everything done, but I decided to leave the rest until the next day. The party was very well organized, the music was just right and the sound system was excellent. The host had used soft lighting to illuminate the people dancing in the living room. Around the sides people with glasses in their hands were chatting animatedly. I warmly shook hands with the host, who was a giant of a man, and told him my name; he said he'd heard Feng Jian talk about me, please come in. I said what about Feng Jian. He said he'd gone out. He leaned towards me a little and whispered "he went out with a beautiful girl." I asked if they'd gone to get some cigarettes, he said he wasn't sure, then said any friend of Feng Jian's was a friend of his and told me to make myself at home.

I joined in with a few conversations. Xiao Di had actually been a bit unfair. People weren't just talking about houses and cars and green cards, they were also talking about stocks and gold and starting companies, there was even one group who were discussing politics. Something to do with the Fourteenth Party Congress. I went from one to the other, got tired of talking, decided to dance. A quick look round showed that all the women there had a man with them. I didn't want to offend anyone, so I gave up on the idea. I knew that if Feng Jian were here he'd be sure to say I was useless. I went back and joined a group of people who were discussing the gold market, as I had some money invested in it myself. As the conversation went on I decided I'd be better off withdrawing the money and spending it.

Of course Xiao Di wasn't there either. It had been remarked upon, and I was expecting Feng Jian to be criticized. He had a wife, after all. But all I heard was envy, or rather jealousy. No one pointed out that he was a married man. Everyone was convinced there was a rich old American, but nobody could give precise details. The general sentiment seemed to be: you ought to go for it with women like that. Some people even said the Americans didn't play fair and that all the good women had all been taken, that kind of thing. I had the impression that all these confident-sounding bachelors were all talk and no action. This was a product unique to the States, I thought. And I was such a product myself, only a different kind — no talk and no action.

They mentioned something else which had happened in America. I knew the person they were talking about, he was called Bai, like me. It was all about guns. Mr Bai had had two guns, they'd both been fired, people had been killed.

I recalled him, pale and sober, wearing a neat pair of glasses. Every five minutes the person telling the story sighed: "How could such a cultured young man actually shoot someone dead?" I looked around me, everyone was listening, but they didn't show any signs that this was anything out of the ordinary. In fact it must be very easy, I thought, life can be a very fragile thing. "And then?" I asked.

"Afterwards he was arrested," he said.

This was in America, he said again. I could imagine how Mr Bai had bought guns and bullets in America, how when he was feeling depressed he'd taken aim at someone, how he'd got high on the idea of snuffing out their life.

I'd met Mr Bai in China. It was in a tastefully decorated house. I'd read a story he'd written, got talking to him about his choice of words. Naturally, we strayed off the subject of the story itself, and had a very pleasant conversation. The story was set during the Cultural Revolution. It was about a tough fearless Red Guard who had the Counter-Revolutionaries on the run. But somehow the other side found out that he was in love with a woman, and used her as a bait to lure him into their trap. The next night they tied him to a pillar, forced him to watch while a big thug raped her before his eyes. Afterwards he almost lost his wits. At the end of the story he became a monk. The details in the story were brilliantly observed, meticulously establishing the image of a hard man, then watching him being destroyed by a woman.

I had a lot of contact with Mr Bai after that, but it was all restricted to our writing. It never occurred to me that his stories revealed that he knew all about heroism and ruthlessness. Like everyone else I subscribed to the view that he was just a bookworm; hearing of his fate now I was quite amazed.

It seemed like Feng Jian wasn't going to come back. The host had the same feeling. He obviously felt very awkward. I guessed he was a good friend of Feng Jian, perhaps he'd even arranged the party at Feng Jian's request. Was her name Xiao Di? I asked. He said yes. I said I knew it. He asked whether she was going out with anyone — I said no. "Then it's a disaster," he said.

"What's the problem?" I asked.

"Feng Jian and his wife aren't exactly getting on well at the moment — did you know?"

"So?"

"That Xiao Di really knows a few tricks — if Feng Jian isn't careful he might give in under the pressure."

"Surely not." I said.

He didn't go on. I gave him a light, told him in cases like this there was no point anyone else worrying. He said Feng Jian's wife was a really good person too. I said most people in the world were. He said Feng Jian was too impetuous. He said he was too romantic. He said it was bad to draw so much attention to yourself. Eventually he said he didn't blame him, that girl really wasn't bad.

I said a few more vaguely coherent things, and gradually discovered he wasn't listening to a word I said. He seemed wracked with anxiety. So I started asking him about the specification and price of his sound system. I had a cassette recorder, which I listened to a lot. Now I thought I really ought to have a sound system like his.

Afterwards it started to rain. The fine drizzle continued until the next morning, giving me an excuse for an extremely low level of efficiency when I got up. As I sorted out a few things, my mind kept wandering to the image of Mr Bai. Yes, there was another way of existing in America, not just the kind of feeble inactivity which we practised. But that kind of violence and pain were too much to bear.

Feng Jian phoned, said it was raining, asked if I fancied a drink. I said I was very busy, another day. He said we'd still hadn't got round to drinking spirits. I said we definitely would some time.

I didn't ask him where he'd been the night before. I just didn't seem to be able to say the words. I could tell from his suppressed excitement that he wanted to broadcast his happiness, but I could find no common ground with the woman in his thoughts. Now that another man, swept up by the romance of love at first sight, had encroached on her territory, the rhythm of my heart was broken. I no longer had any understanding of her.

It occurred to me that I had quite a few friends scattered around America who I hadn't been in touch with for a long time, so I made a few phone calls, talked a lot of incoherent nonsense, felt even worse. I decided to call it a day, wound up my alarm clock, and fell into a fitful sleep.

I went to the seaside again this week. I discovered that the road to the coast was favoured with some lovely scenery. It occurred to me that in fact I knew this already, that I had painstakingly explored them soon after I first arrived here. Now I let them slide past the car windows, an accompaniment to the music. I even sang along with the music a little.

The company gave me a warning of dismissal. But I was busy analysing and assessing my present state, and the ways in which I had changed. I decided that since coming to America I had learned how to protect myself. I had maintained my equilibrium ever since, protected by distance, not influencing, not being influenced, as though hibernating. But now desires were springing up everywhere. This was very dangerous, I concluded. And I realized that I couldn't afford to pay such a high price. I continued to go about my business through force of habit, even though my heart wasn't in it; at the same time I gradually began to perceive the temptation which was luring me towards disaster. It was the source of all my desires. It was something I had sensed long ago, in another land. At the time my conclusion was that it was impossible, and unnecessary, to discover what lay behind it. I had simply allowed that constant temptation to cling to me. In those days I could afford to pay any price.

The fines from the telephone company grew larger, I felt cursed. I felt I was too busy and didn't have the time to deal with the problem. I phoned them again to enquire, again they told me to wait, a machine said all lines were busy at the moment, as usual I didn't wait.

I saw Feng Jian again — I hadn't had a drink with him for a while and I suppose I was missing him a bit; and I thought that by now I wasn't under Xiao Di's influence. We went out for dinner together, I saw that he was in a state of confusion. He said I'd misled him. With a smug expression I said that as far as I knew she wasn't very beautiful. He said don't joke about it. "She might kill me," he said.

"I've heard someone say that eagerness to catch fire conceals a desire to end up as ashes." I went on, "He suggested sailing quietly in a boat with a red sail."

I could tell Feng Jian wasn't really listening. His eyes were shining, his whole body cloaked in weariness. After we'd eaten I abandoned the idea of going for a drink, said I had to be home early. Just before we parted, Feng Jian told me he was now living at Xiao Di's.

That night, in the warm glow of the lamplight, I slipped into a state of torpor. There was no longer any need to flick through magazines and documents — they were of little significance to me now. My new sound system had taken their place, and with a sense of shame I turned up the music until it filled every corner of the room. At dinner Feng Jian, full of love, had criticized me again: "Why do you always stay so aloof." Feng Jian said she was water. Her gentleness was a stream, her strength was a waterfall.

Now though, amidst the music and the lamplight, I felt profoundly affected. The image of Feng Jian and Xiao Di before my eyes was so vivid that my attempts to avoid it were no use any more. In my imagination I walked towards Feng Jian, saw how water can twist a man's obsession, dissolving it into a few timeless moments. I saw Feng Jian slipping into the boundless waters, in front of him the image of Xiao Di could not be blotted out, and yet was somehow indistinct, he wanted to shout at the top of his voice, he wanted to do all kinds of absurd things for her sake. But I remained in a state of calm. I said to him: "This is just a fantasy created by your own desires." He said it wasn't. I said your fantasy is growing, turning. Now it's covered over your sky. He said you're wrong.

He said all this is real. She is inexpressibly wonderful.

So I had to accept that Feng Jian was right, it was all very real. From this moment on, each day when he went out he would see a different sun. The sun's enhanced rays would flicker through the green leaves to fall embellished on his body, then spread out, giving colour to everything around him.

Autumn crept up languidly on San Francisco bay. Its onset was not easy to detect because there was no change of colours but the change in me was continuing. Things had got even worse at work; on several occasions I had really wanted to see Xiao Di. I could imagine how radiant she must look in the flush of love, and I knew that once the tide of passion had receded, I would have missed the chance to experience that splendour. But I didn't want to disturb Feng Jian. I resorted to my old technique of unconcern.

One weekend afternoon, I came to Berkeley for an event which everyone had been talking about: it had been organized in honour of an inspection team from China. A confident skinny type wearing glasses was making a speech, I guess it was something about what good prospects lay in store for those of us who'd studied in America. It didn't take long for most of the audience to congregate in the corridor outside, leaving only the people in suits in the front row sitting there neatly. I wasn't sure why I had come; maybe it was because I was having a hard time and yearned for the atmosphere of the old days. And indeed the inspection team did bring with it a familiar odour of mainland China, but this just made me feel even more ill at ease. It was like turning the faded pages of a book. I realized that with time and distance, all those stories etched on my mind had become washed out and purified; they were no longer part of my reality. I was incapable of experiencing the same kind of feelings again. They were so remote that even regret was superfluous. There was no point in regret. I forced myself to laugh at myself, got up and went out into the corridor. There was a lively discussion going on. I thought I'd probably feel a bit better for having a chat.

I saw the guy who'd told the story about Mr Bai again at another party. Again it was at the house of the big man who'd been so anxious about Feng Jian. I made sure I joined in the conversation, but nobody mentioned Mr Bai again. Feng Jian was mentioned a few times, but only very vaguely, there wasn't much in the way of fact. As the conversation ran through a whole string of unconnected subjects, my hopes came to nothing, and I turned my attention to the music. The soft music formed a very pleasant background; watching all those happy people I realized that life always went on.

I wondered again whether I could get closer to them.

My friend who studied America noticed the state I was in. "You're depressed, Bai," she said. I told her things weren't going well at work. "Are you in love?" She was very perceptive, she rushed over to me, but my customary quick-wittedness had deserted me, and I suddenly found myself lost for words. I suppose she interpreted my silence as confirmation, because she said, "I'm really happy for you."

The cycle of Feng Jian's love had already entered the doldrums, and we sat together drinking again. I'd reverted to my state of solitary drinking some time ago. I understood Feng Jian, and he knew I understood him. Autumn had left as unobtrusively as it had arrived. I said to him, it's because you're too close to her.

He looked as though he was having a hard time. I told him that all love had its ups and downs, he said he knew this but it didn't make his suffering any less real. He asked me how I was doing, I said I was working very hard. I said I was under a lot of pressure.

"Did you know Xiao Di's been sacked?" he asked.

He said he hadn't been able to persuade her, she just didn't take her Green Card seriously, she was too naïve.

"You still haven't got a divorce?" I asked.

Feng Jian smiled. "I know you can't understand that I can still get on with my wife."

"What trick have you pulled?"

"I've gone away to a conference."

"And what if you bump into her on the street?"

"Have you ever bumped into anyone you know on the street?"

"As a matter of fact, I have. That's one big advantage of America."

Feng Jian said unhappily that he wanted the conference to end, wanted to go home for some peace and quiet. Each day, when he looked at Xiao Di, he felt powerless, could do nothing but force himself to feel love for her. As he looked into her eyes, or at her face, he felt weak and lacking in passion; what's more he was constantly discovering some or other new shortcoming. He said he knew this was perfectly normal, but there was something about this woman which made him balk at putting up with it. "She isn't like other women," he said, "her love makes you feel dissatisfied with yourself."

"Maybe things would be better if you were apart for a while." I resorted to conventional wisdom.

Feng Jian didn't mention his techniques for getting along with women, nor did he mention what kind of mood Xiao Di was in at the moment. I really wanted to know, but I didn't ask, and concealed how much this woman meant to me. At the moment it was Feng Jian's state of mind which mattered.

When we finished the beer, we went out to buy some more. Once we were out on the broad streets, with their regular street lamps, Feng Jian grew gradually calmer. It was late at night now, and the streets were very quiet. On the way back I turned off the radio, and the soft hum of the engine could be heard. "I envy you," Feng Jian said. I said it was easy for him to talk. He said you really hurt me.

When we started drinking again, Feng Jian started talking about her unpredictable shifts of mood. He said she was often depressed, and at these times she deployed all her charms towards him, which he found very tiring. And yet he had to conceal his weariness.

"You shouldn't do it in front of her," I said.
"You really shouldn't," I said.

As the night grew more silent, so Feng Jian's frame of mind grew more stable, and his speech gradually regained its normal pace. He asked me if I had really been to her house. I said what do you mean. He said he got the impression Xiao Di didn't really know me very well. When he mentioned my name, she acted exactly as she did when he mentioned anyone else. "Well, she knows how to act," I said.

"I say to her, it's Bai Guang, the one you used to go to the Flavour Garden with," Feng Jian said.

"What do you say things like that to her for?" I felt slightly put out.

"Because, at the time, I was really jealous of the time you spent together."

Xiao Di had told Feng Jian that she often met people for dinner at the weekend, just for something to do. Her impression of Bai Guang was that he was a good talker, and drove a new car. "You're so demanding; do you want me to swear I've never had a relationship with him?" she said to Feng Jian petulantly. Feng Jian asked why Bai Guang hadn't attained such happiness. Xiao Di said, "I've got you and that's enough."

"That was a long time ago," Feng Jian told me, "I've been looking for an opportunity to ask you ever since."

I understood Feng Jian, but the sense of unease welling up inside me was very persistent. Most painful of all was the icy chill which had descended on my heart. There was a moment of silence between us. Once I felt calmer, I asked Feng Jian:

"Did she tell you I'd mentioned you to her a long time ago?"

"No. Did you?"

"Yes."

Feng Jian was perplexed. When he first met her, the phrase "My name's Feng Jian" had been completely new to her. She had even said, "Your parents were pretty stupid to give you a name like that, didn't they realize it would sound like the word 'fengjian', meaning feudalism?"

"Well she'd probably forgotten, it was a long time ago, when I'd only just met you," I said.

I carried on making excuses for her to myself; I came up with a whole string of reasons, and eventually decided that at the time I'd simply been indulging in wishful thinking. I admitted to Feng Jian that I'd misinformed him, that I'd never been close to Xiao Di after all. He eyed me suspiciously.

"So you don't trust me."

I got up to get some more drink from the fridge. The chill was deepening, I felt a stab of pain in my mind. By the time I reached the fridge, the sense of grief had already passed.

I filled Feng Jian's glass, put the bottle, which was still half full, down on the table, then opened another and filled my own glass. I drank a mouthful, lit up a cigarette. Feng Jian was concentrating on blowing smoke rings. I said:

"Why are you so stupidly belligerent?"

Feng Jian looked serious, saying he was a bad person, he shouldn't have asked Xiao Di these things in such detail. He seemed to have lost his customary cool and confidence. Abandoning my habitual circumspection, I told him I was annoyed with him for ruining my designs on Xiao Di, even though I understood him. And I also told him that I was even more upset at how Xiao Di had talked about me. I acknowledged that my feelings towards her had gone beyond friendship.

"Are you furious with me?" he asked.

I told him not to be stupid.

"Are you jealous of me?" he asked.

I said I was.

Afterwards I told him I didn't have it in me to go round and wipe her out, and I didn't want to. He laughed, and clinked glasses with me.

We went on to discuss the psychology of jealousy, I told him about the theory of the three kinds of love. We even painstakingly divided the third kind of love up into new categories.

While I wasn't paying much attention, the company postponed getting me my green card. Where once I would have hit the roof, now I could just grin and bear it. I felt I was reaping what I'd sown. Now all I asked was that the company didn't sack me, I could worry about the green card later.

I got less and less sleep as exhaustion took hold of me and wouldn't let go. I didn't do anything with those extra hours, just frittered them away trying to restrain myself from phoning Xiao Di. However hard I tried I found it hard to believe that I could have been so wrong, that at my age I could have been so foolish as to delude myself with wishful thinking. This feeling was so persistent that it overwhelmed any other explanations my brain could produce, and was dragging me bodily towards an emotional abyss. I felt that all I wanted was to walk towards her, not say anything. And then we would walk slowly beneath the setting sun. Under the silvery moon I would stroke her shoulder, inhaling her scent, until our bodies were in perfect harmony.

"I've been meaning to phone you for ages," Feng Jian said. We talked on the phone for a long time. He told me his supervisor was annoyed with him, and he had to make himself concentrate. On top of this his wife was taking steps to divorce him. He angrily accused Xiao Di of destroying his life. "It's only love, she takes it so seriously." He said he didn't want to see her again, one marriage was enough. He even asked me if I wanted to go after her, said she was very attractive, he really hoped another man would come on the scene, and so on. I thought this was too much. He'd completely lost control, was totally out of it. I arranged to have a drink with him at the weekend. I said I'd just lost my job.

He was shocked, wanted to come over straight away. I said I had too much to do, let's leave it until the weekend. In fact I didn't have anything to do apart from selling my car, I just wanted a few quiet days on my own. Go to the seaside or something. I mentioned drinking spirits, he said OK.

In the past I'd always seen Xiao Di at the weekend. I waited until the time I should have been parking my car outside her house, then phoned her. I don't know why I called her just before I was going to meet Feng Jian. Xiao Di answered the phone in English, I said who I was in Chinese. "Bai Guang? Oh, is something the matter?" she said.

I said it was nothing. I said I was just ringing to say hello. Then I hung up.

Feng Jian and I got blind drunk, really punishing ourselves. I didn't utter a single consoling word all evening, just listened as he told me fervently one minute that she was good, the next that she was bad. In the end it all came down to one thing, which, in his confused state, he had decided: she had destroyed his life. I never got the chance to tell him how come I'd been sacked; in fact I wasn't in the mood anyway. I was more preoccupied with the remarkable strength of the five grain spirit.

In my dream, the one thing I couldn't rid myself of was the way Feng Jian, loosened up by the alcohol, described her eyes. "There's something about the way she looks at you that knocks you right off balance."

The next day I had a splitting headache. Feng Jian hadn't left. He was fit, even at a time like this he still felt like making something to eat. I always had noodles with an egg and a few bits of cabbage, but he said we can do better than that today. The two of us went out to buy food, he asked me what I was going to do about a car, it was no good having no money and no car. I said I was thinking of buying a cheap second-hand car. He said my stereo was worth a lot of money, I said I didn't want to sell it. I said if things don't work out I can go and get a job in a restaurant. He said he could lend me some money. I said I still had a few savings, I'd get by for the moment.

I told him I simply hadn't been up to the job. Another reason was that I'd been so affected by observing how much in love he was that my mind was in turmoil, and I spent most of the time day-dreaming about women. He said he'd rather not have such an all-consuming love. I said don't be ridiculous, another two days and you'll be off to another of your conferences. He said not this time. He said he really wanted to leave that woman. He said he couldn't cope with her emotions. He went on and on, and his talk again grew more and more wild, he started saying how wonderful, how intoxicating she was, then said she was so haughty and aloof, the best woman in the world, she was unbearable.

The food Feng Jian cooked was really very good; I was as surprised by this as I had been the first time I saw his sensitive side. My headache diminished. He asked me what I was planning to do later, I said I didn't know. I asked him when the next Berkeley disco would be; I said I was intending to find myself some romance. He asked me whether I was still going to look for a job, I said love wouldn't stop me doing that. He mentioned that Xiao Di had recently got a clerical job, she was very pleased with it. I said I hadn't decided what kind of job I wanted yet. Actually I hadn't even started to think about it.

Feng Jian told me that the single women at the university discos had more suitors than they could cope with, and I'd have to join the queue. And he went on to describe, in depressing fashion, the prospect of queuing up at the back of the ranks of admirers. I couldn't really understand this, since two of his own romances had begun in this very way. "But I'm a bad boy," he said. However, he said, when it came to destroying other people's happiness, there was no need to queue up. I told him I had no interest in starting feuds with husbands or boyfriends. He said I didn't need to worry about it, everyone was used to this kind of thing. "Force of circumstance, you know," he said. I still insisted I didn't want to mess around with wives or girlfriends. I said at the very least it would be a lot of hassle. He said queuing up was a hassle too. I said I could just take it easy and wait until all the others were exhausted. "You've always got to set yourself apart from the mainstream," he said.

I told him, actually I phoned Xiao Di yesterday.

He looked at me in silence. I could tell he wanted to say something but was doing his best to hold it back. We'd more or less finished our meal; in the silence he carried on eating the last few grains of rice, started clearing up his side of the table.

"Do you understand why I did it?" I asked.

He went out to the kitchen. He came back and sat down, carrying a cup of Longjing tea. "She could hardly remember my name," I said.

"So haven't you forgotten her?" At last Feng Jian spoke.

"No."

I'd finished eating too. The table had been wiped completely clean, Feng Jian was about to go. "But now I can start forgetting her," I said. Feng Jian sat down again, lit a cigarette. He asked me why. I said because she doesn't want to know who I am any more.

Again I asked him, "Do you understand?"

Feng Jian said he understood. Again he stopped himself from going on. "What is it?" I said. He said it was nothing. "You ought to tell me," I said.

Winter had begun to strengthen its grip on the calendar, I discovered by chance. This revelation reinforced my dismal frame of mind, and for the time being I gave up looking for work. I wouldn't see Feng Jian for a while, because he felt that if he wasn't able to breathe a word about Xiao Di it would all be very artificial. When he was about to leave he patted me on the arm, said I'm your friend for ever, but for the moment it has to be like this. So once again I went back to drinking alone. I became a regular at the deep blue sea, and in a park in the heart of the city I discovered a secluded hillside overlooking the green waters of a little lake. Feng Jian had told me, you shouldn't think about her anymore. And so Xiao Di's cold words were invested with a concrete significance. The sky above the bay of San Francisco gave no hint of the season; as I gazed up at it I felt terribly, terribly depressed.

"Bai, I don't think this is shameful at all," my friend who studied American life told me. This time she had been explaining another theory, from another American; the gist of it was that the romantic spirit had gradually withered away over the course of the twentieth century. "The romantic spirit is a precious thing," she said. "But I still don't quite understand why you don't hurry up and find another job. Can you explain again, please?" Her speech gradually became slower, she was looking at me in a kindly but inquiring manner. I said I'd start looking again. Then I explained that in fact I hadn't really got involved in a romance. "Well you did lose your job," she said. I pursued this train of thought, explained how Feng Jian and I had divided the third kind of love into new categories. I told her people often thought they were in love, when in fact it was all based on illusion and misunderstanding. "But as far as they're concerned it's a real emotion," she said.

This friend gave me the final push, and I began to visit some other friends I'd made recently. The final topic of conversation at dinner that night had been the fact that, early on, she had discovered that I was rather anti-social. So I sprang into action. The one I saw the most was the big party host, and his lovely, warm-hearted wife. They had some great music at home. I quickly discovered that although everyone was so busy they could hardly cope, they really longed for social contact. Contact diluted the sense of meaninglessness which filled everyone's lives. People extended a helping hand to me too, and let me know about all kinds of job opportunities. And so I began the painful struggle of searching for work.

All thoughts of looking for romance were frightened out of me when the big guy's wife started to show an interest in introducing potential girlfriends to me. "The main thing is to look for work," I said. Sitting in front of my computer I thought long and hard about how best to add my work experience since graduation to my CV. I bought lots of envelopes and stamps, waited for a lot of calls and made a lot of calls, raced all over the place in my noisy old wreck of a car. Feng Jian was constantly drifting back into my consciousness, having passed through the added embellishment of other people; the sensation grew increasingly pronounced; finally I interrupted my efforts to ingratiate myself with every personnel manager in town, and made my way to Feng Jian's door.

The reason the situation seemed so serious was because of a conversation at the big guy's house, where he said he could no longer consider Feng Jian a friend. "He just can't handle women, it's intolerable," he said. I'd come to listen to his music. I'd heard people discussing Feng Jian's love life, saying he was acting out of character, had lost his style, but I'd always assumed these were groundless rumours, people letting their curiosity run riot. I hadn't paid them any attention. I set the CD player to replay, got a bottle of beer out of the fridge, and asked the big guy what he was talking about. "You don't know?" he said.

The first charge against Feng Jian was that he'd got divorced. The second was that he kept swearing that he was going to leave that woman, yet to this day he was still with her. The third was passing his friends' warnings on to her. The third charge rather annoyed me, but I refrained from joining the big guy in his cursing. Afterwards the big guy casually told me a story about Xiao Di. His description smacked of reasonable prejudice; I could see the scene before my eyes. Feng Jian and Xiao Di walk elegantly into the dance hall at Berkeley. Feng Jian ditches Xiao Di, grabs another girl to dance with. Feng Jian dances passionately, Xiao Di sits in the front row, all her attention focused on the way he's dancing, enjoying it. No one can get her to move. Feng Jian is joking and laughing with everyone; she doesn't utter a sound. Now and again she says a few words, just to tell people who try to get her a drink or ask her to dance that she's waiting for her boyfriend to come and do these things. When the dance finishes Feng Jian walks elegantly out of the dance hall, with a beaming girl. She gets up too, politely turns down the well intentioned people who offer to help, doesn't even telephone the college security office, simply sets off on her own and goes home. "Can that be right?" the big guy asked. "And within a few days the fucking jerk goes back to Xiao Di again."

I discovered from other people that Feng Jian had quarrelled with the smug girl from the dance. In a moment of viciousness he'd told her she had no taste and lacked breeding, he'd even hit her. This woman, who only moments before had experienced the joys of passion in Feng Jian's wife's bed, had, with a sense of terrible injustice, denounced him in English to the police; in Chinese she'd let the other wives and girlfriends know just how dreadful men were, and they had swiftly and efficiently broadcast news of this outrageous scandal. One version of the scandal was: it was at Xiao Di's instigation that Feng Jian was hurting other people, in order to satisfy her jealous nature. The big guy got Feng Jian out on bail, but then dropped him.

Feng Jian never returned my phone calls. I found it very hard to accept that he'd passed on his friends' warnings to Xiao Di, but allegations of this kind were becoming increasingly frequent and increasingly specific. One of the accusations was that he'd even hit someone. Afterwards I realized that it probably wasn't because of Xiao Di that Feng Jian was avoiding me. I had the impression that, because his friends no longer acknowledged him, he'd shut himself off, so I went round and pinned a note on his door. I said I wanted to have a drink with him. His phone call came. In a hesitant voice he asked me repeatedly whether I really wanted to see him. I said what the fuck's wrong with you. He said OK then.

I drove my old car onto the bridge, across the bay of San Francisco, and arrived in front of the house which Feng Jian's wife had once forbidden me to visit. Winter, already well advanced, had brought a chill to the air, but there was a fire burning in my heart. First I wanted to find out whether or not he really had done these things. Then I wanted to ask him why.

It was a disdainful expression which Feng Jian presented to me when he opened the door. I noticed he looked haggard, but I simply put the drink down on the dining table, walked over to the other side of the living room, and crouched down to look at the sound system at the foot of the wall. "It's not as good as yours," Feng Jian said from behind me. I sensed a certain caution, which wasn't his style. He didn't make any further sound until I had finished adjusting the volume and had come back to the table. The languid sound of "Brothers in Arms" echoed through the room. The tape had been out already, so I guessed Feng Jian probably listened to it a lot. I'd never heard it, but I thought the cover and the names of the songs looked quite good.

"This is the first time we've had a drink here," I said. I opened a bottle and started to pour.

Although Feng Jian was sitting down, he was still on edge. As he opened a bottle he said "You've got something to say to me?" I came straight to the point. I asked him how much of what other people, including me, had said, had he passed on to Xiao Di? "That's enough. You can get out." With startling speed Feng Jian was on his feet again.

His eyes were bulging in an ugly way; the skin of his face was crimson and greasy and looked as though he hadn't washed it for a long time. With a sense of revulsion I slowly got to my feet, with a feeling that things between us were growing frosty. This disconcerting vision in front of me ought to be destroyed, I thought coldly.

I walked as far as the doorway, then turned round. He was still standing rigidly beside the table, staring at me viciously. In this frosty atmosphere my voice grew quiet.

I said: "What's the matter with you?"

Feng Jian said, "You're no different from all the rest of them. You're a hypocrite too."

I said: "You haven't got the guts to admit you've done something dreadful."

Feng Jian said: "If you don't get out now, I'll help you with this bottle."

The expression on his face gave me the same message in an even more ugly manner; his hand shook with fury as he poured the beer violently into the glass. The froth spilled over the top and soaked the whole table. As this was happening I took off my watch, stuffed it into my back pocket. As revulsion welled up inside me my heart grew even harder and more resolute.

When he came towards me, I said to him, "Come outside."

In the parking lot in front of the house the two of us stood facing each other, very close together. Feng Jian hadn't brought the bottle with him. I was wondering whether there was more to say, but he'd already made his move. With a thud his lunging fist rocked my face, and through the pinpricks of light which filled my vision I caught sight of the cruel expression on his coarse face.

Then I hit him.

In a fit of fury I didn't notice that Feng Jian very soon stopped fighting back. I finally stopped my hand when I saw blood spurting from his mouth; his body began to sag, he sat down on the ground.

Panting for breath, I was unsure for a moment what to do. I saw him wipe his mouth with one hand, while the other supported him on the ground. The awkward silence continued until he got to his feet, and I began to realize that people had seen us at it. I also realized that he hadn't retaliated at all. Eventually he spoke, "You fought pretty well."

He said, "Let's go into the house and sit down, the police'll be here soon."

During those days when Feng Jian was nursing his wounds, I heard another version of the rumour. It was true that he'd got divorced. It was true that he couldn't leave Xiao Di. But the story was false. Whether or not he'd hurt another girl didn't matter. In the end though, it was true that he'd had a fight, the police had come, and he'd soon have to go to court. The charge of fighting had nothing to do with me. By the time the police had arrived, Feng Jian had already tidied himself up, and, with a quite startling presence of mind, had grinned broadly and told the police that he'd been practising Chinese-style boxing, that's why the neighbour hadn't seen any boxing gloves.

I believed Feng Jian's version of the story. While Xiao Di had been with him she'd got to know some of his friends. One guy, a perpetual student, seemed to think he was more attractive than Feng Jian, and was always looking for an opportunity to have a heart to heart talk with Xiao Di, to explain some profound thoughts to her. He told her that most people were too crude to be able to grasp the full goodness of a woman as exquisite as she was. He said he was the only person who realized just how exquisite every part of her body was, that she was a true masterpiece of nature. He explained that he had formally fallen in love with her, and that people who, like him, could distil the spiritual treasure stored up by mankind over thousands of years into a living passion were as rare as the phoenix or the unicorn; he asked her to think it over seriously. Xiao Di, who was experiencing the pain of love at the time, lost her customary warmth, and told this devotee of the soul that she wasn't able to satisfy his desire to sleep with a woman. Rather annoyed, Xiao Di had told Feng Jian about this friend; Feng jian didn't seem to care, even said you should be a bit more generous, it's not easy chasing women in America. Feng Jian had forgotten what people had said to him when they were trying to persuade him not to get divorced: "It's great to sleep with a woman like that, but don't let yourself get emotionally involved." The love-sick young man decided that Feng Jian was playing dirty tricks behind his back, and sought him out to demand justice. Feng Jian argued languidly. All he said was, "Who told you you could pitch your tent the minute you set eyes on a woman." The furious young man, wanting to teach Feng Jian a lesson, threw the first punch, and got a beating from Feng Jian. Later friends came to Feng Jian's house, anxious to resolve this dispute between friends; Feng Jian, who'd been so worn down by love that he'd become very irritable, grabbed a beer bottle and chased them out. They called the police, and refused to acknowledge him any longer.

The smug girl from the dance hall had been terribly upset when, at the height of passion, she found herself being called Xiao Di. She wouldn't stop crying, pressed Feng Jian to take her to see this Xiao Di, and insisted that he slapped Xiao Di's face in front of her. For her pains she got a slap round the face herself.

"That really wasn't right," I told Feng Jian.

I said that first of all you shouldn't have used another women to take your mind off your difficulties, and secondly you shouldn't have hit her. I said I can understand how you were feeling. "But I still think you were wrong," I said. Feng Jian didn't try to argue back, all he said was that love was a disaster. Even more of a disaster than marriage.

His wounds were quite serious. I looked after him conscientiously, even stayed at his place in the evenings. I kept the pain in my heart hidden throughout. Late, when I felt remorse, it was always the image of this period which came back to me. I had been too harsh towards him: he'd lost all his friends, but all I did was criticize him, never gave him a moment's friendly sympathy. Whenever he did something which moved me, I forced myself to appear calm, not to show it. He said the reason he'd stopped fighting back that time was because seeing me acting so aggressive made him realize that I was a tough man, and in that moment he had sensed that I would be sure to understand his plight. And he also felt a nagging sense of guilt towards me. Xiao Di ought to be with you, he said. When he told me that he'd felt that when I hit him it reduced his burden of guilt, I had to make an excuse and go out to the bathroom. Later, he gave me the tape of "Brothers in Arms".

More than a week before, Xiao Di had told Feng Jian that Bai Guang hadn't been indulging in wishful thinking. Feng Jian had been criticising her for misleading people, said it was irresponsible, Bai Guang was a good person. If that's how she behaved he didn't want to be with her any longer. Feng Jian was just looking for faults to criticize, as he did periodically, and Xiao Di's answer took him completely by surprise. She told him that Bai Guang's impression had been correct. She explained that she really had liked Bai Guang. She found him very interesting, when they'd first met she'd been feeling very bitter and twisted, afterwards he had got very close to her. It had changed her life. But in the end Bai Guang had disappointed her. Feng Jian had made up for her loss. "You couldn't find a better love," she told him.

After that Feng Jian began taking steps to leave her for real. "When you came, I hadn't seen her for seven whole days." He explained that he'd started to find himself unbearable. When he realized that all the possibilities represented by his friends had been destroyed, he could no longer bear himself. "I couldn't make her happy," he said. He went on to say that he was sure that Xiao Di was still concealing things. When she said she was disappointed in you, he said, it was just an excuse she was making because she finds her life uninspiring and doesn't have a lot of patience. "She understands you perfectly."

This resulted in my last trip to the Flavour Garden with Xiao Di. The landlord asked me why we hadn't come for such a long time, I said I'd been out east on business. He also asked when the wedding was going to be. Soon, I answered. Xiao Di sat down in her usual place. To her left was the big window, beyond it the big patch of grass. The winter sun was still high in the sky, and so the beauty of the lawn couldn't be clearly seen. On the way Xiao Di had said she wasn't feeling too well and asked me to forgive her. "Don't take it to heart," she said. She had seemed flustered, seemed not to hear what I had said to her. Now she was quietly wiping the plates, she looked away from the window and gazed around her. It was that same wan look, that same expression, which made men lose their self-control.

We ordered, and she reminded me not to forget the green Dutch beer. I stopped short, gazed at her for a long time, thinking how incredible this seemed. She asked me what it was. I said I'd lost my job. "Oh, so you're no good either, just like me," she said. When she inquired further, I said maybe it was because of love. "Do you think the two of us could be suffering from the same disease," she said. Her eyes were sparkling, as if she were discussing something joyful with me.

"It's you who infected me," I said.

I could tell that her surprise was very real. "I'm not as sharp as I used to be, could you make it a bit more obvious when you're joking."

I said I hadn't been joking.

She said her intuition wasn't so good any more, and she couldn't tell whether my humour was a means to an end, or an end in itself. She said even if I was making jokes as a means to an end, she hadn't really grasped how to turn me down.

I told her I hadn't come here to do her any harm, I simply wanted to try to understand what had happened. I said, "You gave me a lot, now I want to hear you condemn me." I reminded her of one evening when I'd gone round to her place, and we'd got talking about a painting by Van Gogh. With an effort she remembered. "In fact, it wasn't all that long ago," she said. She smiled gently.

Now she knew Bai Guang meant it when he said he wouldn't be hurt. As I was telling her this story of my heart, she interrupted and said she had been very disappointed in me. At first, she doubted her powers of attraction, but her self-respect had made her forget all this. "I'm an ordinary person," she said, "I can't save you." Back then she had stretched out a hand to Bai Guang, but his inexplicable silence had wounded her deeply. "I curse you." Finally she said: the effort of forgetting about Bai Guang had destroyed her relationship with Feng Jian.

Afterwards, when I'm dead, she said faintly. I'll tell you then.

Xiao Di evaded all questions about Feng Jian, but said, as if to console me, "I don't hate him." As we were about to part, I asked her what she'd been hoping for most recently. She said she didn't hope for anything. She said her hopes had all gone rotten. Then she smiled: "How could I wish for a rose?"

I resumed my attempts to find work. I hadn't wanted to pay the price for interrupting my search a few days before, but it didn't bother me either. Another thing I'd done was tell the big guy that I understood why Feng Jian couldn't get over Xiao Di. Because I'd known Xiao Di for a long time, or perhaps because the big guy also thought Xiao Di was really nice, he agreed that Feng Jian's behaviour was understandable. The fact that he liked Feng Jian played a part too of course. Moreover, Feng Jian had really stopped seeing Xiao Di. At the same time Feng Jian lost his scholarship for the spring semester. He said he was thinking about changing college. We arranged to meet on Saturday to drink spirits. Then, just when my pitiful savings had reached rock-bottom, the clutch on my car went — a complete write-off. A new one would cost more than four hundred dollars. I checked the radiator and the brakes, discovered plenty of faults, made a few calculations, then delivered the car to the breakers' yard, accepted fifty dollars in return, and bought an old wreck of a second hand car for six hundred dollars. On Saturday Feng Jian came over very early, and took me to get the car properly fixed up, which cost me another ninety-six dollars. Now I'd have to go and get a job in a restaurant.

"Xiao Di came to see me yesterday," Feng Jian told me, gazing at me from behind the smoke rings he was blowing. We were drinking strong Chinese liquor, *Wuliangye*, again. I was against him changing college, I said you can't admit defeat, but he gave me another reason. He still couldn't leave Xiao Di.

This time it was Xiao Di who'd come to find him. She told him not to worry, she'd come to ask his help. She said what she wanted was to hear him say those words which she found so upsetting, when he was in a calm state. In the past they hadn't hurt her. She hadn't really taken them seriously, because, at the time he'd said them, he had been driven towards her by an irresistible desire. Feng Jian said the words. He kept very calm about it, until she'd heard enough, got up, said thanks very much, and prepared to leave.

We hadn't drunk very much yet, so Feng Jian was still taking care to protect my feelings. At this point, in the middle of telling the story, he stopped, said, do you understand, I can't leave that woman. I said I did, I said I'd done things that were just as embarrassing. As though unloading himself of a heavy burden, he explained that because of this he'd have to leave Berkeley.

"Have you thought of marrying her?" I asked.

Feng Jian said he hadn't. He said he hadn't had time to realize that things between them had been damaged. That he'd damaged them himself. It was only while he was damaging them that he'd sensed that Xiao Di was the kind of woman he could be with forever.

"You're not supposed to regret things like this," I said, "but maybe this time we could make an exception."

Feng Jian said, it's too late. He said he no longer had the face to confront her emotionally again. I said don't be so bookish. He said it was true. He told me he didn't want to talk about Xiao Di any more, and looked at me attentively.

In fact, the familiar atmosphere of Xiao Di which Feng Jian brought with him hadn't set my blood racing at all. I was a bit surprised at this myself. I assumed that I was now separated from it all by a distance, that Feng Jian had firmly covered it over. Further evidence of this came later, when Feng Jian, liberated by the powerful spirits, began to sink into the flowing waters of Xiao Di.

As she was about to leave Xiao Di had turned back to him, leaning lightly against the door. How come I still can't take it seriously, she said softly. Her words had a distant sound. As though she were resting languidly in a bath she gazed tenderly at Feng Jian as he walked towards her. Do you want me to open the door for you, he asked her, standing in front of her, in his last moment of calm.

Xiao Di's eyes were particularly radiant, her warm body was enclosed in figure-hugging clothes, she came closer, opened her arms wide. Afterwards, she caressed Feng Jian with tear-soaked lips, when her soft words paused he heard her voice saying, I really can't understand why you want to drive me away. When Feng Jian's trembling body merged with hers, driving her to extremes of frenzy, she said, if I could die now it would be wonderful.

I opened the second bottle of *Wuliangye*. Amidst the clouds of smoke I had started drinking faster than Feng Jian. I was beginning to feel that I was losing myself too. Feng Jian started to read out loud a part of something he'd written during the period when he hadn't seen me.

I say to her I've lost a lot of friends because of you, you're not a good woman. I tell her, when I sleep with you I'm putting into practice Remarque's theory: it's the best way of leaving a woman. She says that's OK. Afterwards she grants me a morning transported with emotion, then again I'm feeling like I've let myself down. I can't help a feeling of respect when I hear her soft goodbye. She never loses her composure, just looks at me with those life-threatening eyes. I say to her I can tell you've been crying. She tells me it was just for fun, says that if she hadn't cried, then the way I was treating her might have seemed absurd.

Feng Jian handed the piece of paper to me. "If you start to write fiction again one day, maybe you'll think of this. You can use it to show how useless men are."

I told him I thought he was writing about women.

At the big guy's house I'd discovered a record called 'Passion', by an Englishman, whose songs had accompanied me throughout my life. This album 'Passion' was a world of its own. The twelfth song, 'With a love like this', caught my imagination. The sixteenth song also described this kind of love. I told the big guy that things like this were going on all around us. Xiao Di, Feng Jian and a rose. The big guy immediately wanted to go to see Feng Jian, to say, why not go and give her a rose.

Spring arrived. Although, as usual, there weren't too many visible signs, the big guy and I both noticed it. Perhaps it was the season, perhaps it was because the big guy and I had both objected to bookish behaviour, but Feng Jian stopped reproaching himself for a moment and went and bought a rose. That evening, when I got home from the restaurant, half-dead with tiredness, he was waiting for me at the door. I asked why he hadn't phoned first, he said he had nothing else to do, he was perfectly happy waiting for me here. We went into the house, I could tell something had happened.

Do you know what a rose symbolizes, she said.

It symbolizes love, Feng Jian said.

You haven't stopped loving me have you?

You've touched me deeply.

What do you mean by that?

I want to marry you, I'm serious.

It's too late, she said.

"When she said this she suddenly started crying. For the first time she lost her composure," Feng Jian said. His body was almost in convulsions. She had cried so loudly, waved him away violently, then rushed into the bedroom and locked the door.

I poured Feng Jian a drink, wiped my weary face, wondered what to say. Feng Jian asked me: "You don't think anything could happen to her, do you?" I grabbed the telephone and thrust it into his hands. I remembered her talking about dying. Feng Jian dialled the wrong number twice before he finally got through.

There was no reply.

The two of us set off. We drove onto the bridge, before long we were enclosed by the powerful lights of the tunnel, flashing past. Feng Jian said, it's retribution. The brilliant golden tunnel suddenly vanished, and we were back beneath the pale lights of the bridge. As Feng Jian had looked helplessly at Xiao Di's terrifying face, the beautiful image in his heart had faded, and the good fortune he had been seeking to gain through marriage seemed suddenly flawed. "Perhaps it's a good thing if she's gone," he said. I glanced across at him, resisted the temptation to reply. I could see he was in a state of confusion, his words, his expression and his overall manner didn't match, and I didn't want to disturb him. He didn't say any more either, until we set eyes on Xiao Di.

Xiao Di made us some tea. It's Longjing, she said. Feng Jian didn't ask her any more questions, showed signs of being just as weary as I was, and sat down by the wall. Above him on the wall was the print of that picture, with its countless flickering, cooled suns. As we sat facing each other, blowing lightly on our tea leaves, Xiao Di said she was really touched. She said we cared for her so much. She told us not to worry, said life should be a wonderful thing. But I was going through the same process that Feng Jian had been through, I caught a glimpse of Xiao Di's lacklustre expression. She wasn't really beautiful. She never really been beautiful. Her heavy gait, her plain clothes, her sluggish gestures mocked my sensibilities. I did my best to explain it by saying to myself that it was because she'd just been crying.

Later I remembered that although she wasn't beautiful that night, she had been extremely calm. Just as calm as she had always been. For as long as I live I will never be able to understand how it was that, after weeping so uncontrollably, she had managed to regain her composure so completely.

Before Xiao Di left, she asked one of the new officers of the Chinese students' welfare organization to give me a letter. "Are you Bai Guang?" The officer was the soul of discretion, chatting to me for a long time before he came to the point and took out the letter. "I was given the task of delivering this letter to you by hand." In fact I was so impressed with his wide-ranging conversation that we later became firm friends. He asked me who she was. I told him she was a character in a story I was writing.

It wasn't long before Feng Jian left me as well. It was a freak accident. Before it happened I'd told him Xiao Di had already gone, so he didn't need to change college. I said life would go on. Feng Jian's mood swings still bore the clear imprint of Xiao Di, and he stood by his story of what had happened. I told him the version in Xiao Di's letter, and he told me, Xiao Di's got it wrong. "However," he said, "there's no right answer in these matters." Afterwards, the demoralized spring quietly departed. I found a job, and Feng Jian, what with my constant chiding, pulled himself together and began making plans to win a scholarship for the autumn. Life proceeded on its normal course. The last time I saw him was on that small island with the great bridge passing through its middle. It was early summer, a chill evening breeze was blowing.

From the forecast we knew that there could be a high wind. Feng Jian said the wind would be stronger on the bridge. We lingered on the island for a while, then Feng Jian grew impatient and said he was going to set off. On the island you could walk beside the highway, and from there onto the bridge; there was a public order notice announcing that pedestrians weren't allowed onto the bridge. We both knew there was no pavement on the bridge, and it was extremely dangerous. But we shared a feeling that we ought to experience the wind blowing in from the Pacific Ocean. I didn't go with him, I thought night hadn't really fallen yet and there wouldn't be enough wind. I said I'll come in a little while. He set off. The last I saw he was grinning broadly at me, adjusting the camera around his neck.

Xiao Di's letter was brief and to the point, it was because of a promise she'd made. Inside the envelope was a second envelope, on it was written, "If you open this letter, that means I have your word that you won't look for me." I opened it.

What I read was that, back then, because Feng Jian was always telling some anecdote about Bai Guang, it had been impossible for her to forget completely. She'd felt irritated, even angry. Although she kept this very well hidden, she knew that her unpredictable state of mind inhibited Feng Jian's passion. By the time her love for Feng Jian had finally displaced Bai Guang in her affections, it was already too late, Feng Jian was trapped in a vicious circle, and she didn't have the strength to extricate herself either. She cursed me, cursed me some more, said I was the only one she'd spoken to about roses. She didn't want to see me again, she was leaving town.

On that night in early summer, as the strong wind blew, I still had my illusions. My original illusion was that Feng Jian had enough spirit to cope with the impact of all that had happened to him with Xiao Di, and that his life would turn out fine. This was while Feng Jian was walking towards the bridge. Later I had the illusion that he was going to be OK. His will to live was strong enough. In a couple of days I'd be sitting beside him drinking beer, discussing with him what it felt like to be knocked down by a car. This was while he was being rushed off in the ambulance.

On the way I felt a bit anxious, a bit nervous because I was driving very fast, Apart from that, I wasn't worried. As I waited in the hospital my mind was completely blank, right up until the solid middle-aged man said the word death. With a huge, violent crunch I heard my heart crushed within my breast. I slumped against the white wall beside me.

Afterwards lots of people went to look at him. They had once been Feng Jian's friends, now they forgave him all his mistakes. When I was together with them I was very calm, which made seem the same as everyone else, and by simply not talking about this topic I preserved the sense of sameness. Later, sitting alone in silence, I began little by little to realize that he really had left me, it wasn't a misunderstanding, it wasn't a nightmare. And so I started to feel he'd be lonely with no one to look after him, and so I came to his side. I had never touched him. Now that he was lying down, I could make up for this. I cupped his cheeks in my hands: he was cold, he didn't acknowledge me, his silence told me: Bai Guang, why did you do nothing but criticize me?

Now he had no need of anything. His future had been abruptly cut short, brutally forcing me to delude myself about how I could bring him back. Much later, when he appeared before me, glowing with life, I really wanted to leave America. I went to embrace him, but he moved away. I said sadly, I'm not sure when I'm going, I always want to be closer to you; I woke up. It was afternoon, the sunlight was glaring, relentless. Gazing at the neat American lawn outside the window I let my tears stream down again. I told myself I would never see him again. I had lost for ever the opportunity to tell him how much I missed him when he wasn't there.

The big guy told, me, don't be like that, he definitely knew how you felt about him. It was too late, I thought. I had never let it show. I'd been too neglectful, why had I been so naïve as to believe that life always goes on? But there was no way of redeeming my neglect now — I hadn't gone with him onto the bridge on that stormy night. There was no doubt that my reactions, my agility could have pushed him out of the way, or pulled him back. Just by tensing my leg muscles I could have leapt well clear. Or even if I'd just shouted out. Or even if I'd been the one in front of that car and had shielded him.

I felt utterly dispirited. My self-confidence and my resilience were gone. When it came to my career, my friends, the music which filled my apartment, I became humble, cautious, as if I'd lost my right arm.

I gave up my job — it was sapping my energy and my time; I just about managed to make ends meet by doing some translation work and some part-time editing of accounts. And because my resistance was low, I wasn't able to stop the big guy's wife seizing her chance, and so I had a new girlfriend. I soon found myself picking up my pen and starting to write fiction again. In front of me was a piece of writing which had been sent on to me by Feng Jian's parents. It was the big guy who had let them know that Feng Jian had a friend who liked writing. I decided not to alter it, but to let it stand at the end of my story, gazing at my writing from afar.

"This is the year of destruction. You have destroyed your studies. Then love destroyed you. That's your destiny. The things you have cherished will become a small pure space at the bottom of your heart, and no matter what happens to you from now on, you will always be able to find shelter there. Those nights which seemed so real, those leisurely strolls were simple and honest, you learnt how to lie to yourself, and even when you reach the other shore you will find that it has all come to nothing. You have embraced regret; as for your close friends, fate decreed that you would be parted from them.

"Now you can store up feelings of friendship, here everything has been reduced to ruins. When you think back to last summer, to that patch of grass, yes, the one where you met for the first time, you had a taste of love, you will always remember the fresh green grass after the light rain had passed, that's the only trace that remains. There's nothing of you left now, you can throw yourself wholeheartedly into your future, in the summer which will soon be with us again you will be able to bring your destruction to a final end."

My girlfriend soon realized that my degree from Berkeley didn't live up to her expectations. What's more she discovered it wasn't just that I hadn't been able to find work for a while, but rather that I simply wasn't looking, and just frittered each day aimlessly away. She pointed out that writing Chinese literature in America wasn't the most lucrative occupation. No one's got time to read your stories, stop wasting your time, she said. The other thing she couldn't stand was that no amount of reasoning could stop me from listening over and over again to one song, 'Brothers in Arms'. She told me many times that she'd had enough of it. "It's about the Vietnam War. What's it got to do with you?" When she saw me putting it on again, she wept. I was in the wrong, I had evaded so many people's questions. But when that great bridge and the wind engulfed me, I couldn't always keep up my guard, and she could encroach on my time at will. And so, once she'd calmed down, and asked for a reason to explain this contradiction, I told her, "It's because you've got too close to me."

AMERICA AMERICA

Zhu Wen

translated by Zheng Haiyao & Jos Gamble

1 Narrated by the Author

The thing Lao Wu feared most was expulsion by the college. Whenever the end of term examination drew near, his lips would become white and his limbs cold. During that month at the end of term Lao Wu would say he had to be a stepchild. Although he was already exhausted and had used all the strength he could muster to cope with the examinations, even now that he had struggled to become a third year student, he still could not relax his taught string: if he made any further mistakes in two credits, he would have to pack up and go back to Qinghai.

Qinghai is a beautiful place. Ta'er Temple. Qinghai Lake. All the roads there are paved with salt. Lao Wu was passionately devoted while he was saying this. He had a good reason for being so. At any time, Lao Wu might face the fate of returning to his home town. This was something those classmates who were hostile to him knew just as clearly. Lao Wu could console himself by talking like this in front of them. The second reason was to mitigate the attacks on him from his classmates. Lao Wu yearned for America; he always liked to say, "But in America Such and Such." This habit earned him the nickname 'But-in-America-Such-and-Such'. Classmates who were friendly towards him called him 'Lao Wu', but most of them didn't mind taking the trouble to say, "'But-in-America-Such-and-Such', are you going to see the film tonight?" To be precise, what brought the attacks from classmates down on Lao Wu was not his 'American dream', but his weakness and his low academic grades which he could do nothing to improve. In the face of Lao Wu's physical weakness and low exam grades, those guys were fully aware of their superiority. They could sneer wantonly at Lao Wu's ideas, and concentrate on taunting him for its own sake. Lao Wu said, "You lot might try to appreciate a patriot, just once." Most of the time, Lao Wu didn't argue with them in order not to jeopardize the cooperative relationship he hoped for during exams.

The most important thing at present was trying not to be expelled. As far as Lao Wu was concerned, America was only the next step. America, America — the way Lao Wu mentioned it was just the tone his mum had used for years in Qinghai whenever she mentioned Shanghai. Since he was little Lao Wu knew (from the garrulous talk of his mum) that his mum had been duped into going there by his old man. He had cheated Lao Wu's grandfather out of the Zhabei Welding Electrode Factory and his daughter. After Liberation he had donated the Zhabei Welding Electrode Factory to the government and forced Lao Wu's mum to leave Shanghai and go with him to the wild north-west. What a stupid thing to do, his mum said, look at this damn place! You have to walk miles just to buy a bottle of soy sauce! Son! When you grow up you must go back to Shanghai. Go back to Shanghai. Go.

When Lao Wu registered at a technical college in Nanjing on the basis of his 488-mark score, which was high in Qinghai, his mum felt that she had already returned to the status of a young lady from a Shanghai petit bourgeois family. Although Nanjing was not Shanghai, still it was only a few hours away from Shanghai by train. He must definitely try to stay in Shanghai, or somewhere near Shanghai. She indoctrinated Lao Wu with her ten year plan. "When I'm old, I'll go back Shanghai and live with you. If your old man doesn't want to go, he can stay in Qinghai all by himself."

Lao Wu seemed too frail and weak for the mission he had to undertake. In the morning before he went to class he would drink a phial of Royal Jelly, and after dinner he would need to drink another one before studying on his own. He had to hold out in this, his third year, for the fourth year would be better. The Royal Jelly was provided by his mum. Sun God brand Royal Jelly. At the beginning of every term when Lao Wu returned to college from Qinghai, his luggage was always packed full with twenty boxes of Royal Jelly, tied up into bundles of ten. Now Lao Wu didn't have much energy to think of America. In his view, Nanjing was a little nearer to America, at least when compared to Qinghai. Although it was only the first part of his dream, everything had to have a foundation.

It was the second term of the third year at university. Lao Wu was aware that the time had come for him to fight for his life. Apart from the term's classes he also had to resit three classes. The first step he had to take was to reorganize his life. He had to give up lots of his habits due to a lack of energy. Lao Wu cut the Gordian knot and made up his mind up to get rid of the following habits: sleeping late, reading novels, watching films, watching videos, reading newspapers, chatting, nodding off in the study room, staring blankly into space and window-shopping for designer shoes at the 'Merchant' and 'Beauties Island' department stores. Everything went very well for the first week. Lao Wu regained his confidence in the future. In the second week, Lao Wu decided to get rid of the habit of going to the pharmaceutical school every Wednesday night.

Lao Wu's girlfriend was a second year student at the pharmaceutical school. Everybody called her Lao Liu. Because Lao Wu was called Lao Wu, she was called Lao Liu. Lao Liu's mum was of the Uighur nationality. "Uighur girls look just like foreigners, their eyes are blue." Lao Wu also said, "You know, Uighurs are not allowed to marry Han people, it's an unbreakable law of their people. But Lao Liu's dad got through all sorts of troubles and finally married her mum; it was really a rare match." Lao Wu wanted to raise Lao Liu's status up to that of a test tube baby. According to the aesthetic criteria of the technical college, Lao Liu was considered a great beauty. When she was at Lao Wu's side, Lao Liu spoke very genteelly and smiled without showing her teeth. This sort of nicety irritated those classmates who considered themselves superior. In order to avoid attack, Lao Wu modified his method of dating, so that going to the pharmaceutical school every Wednesday night became systematic. Whether to go at another time depended entirely upon Lao Wu's whim. This habit has also been abolished by Lao Wu.

The habit of going to the pharmaceutical school was no big deal — at least not in comparison to Lao Wu's other remaining habit. Lao Wu and Lao Liu's relationship lacked any real content. Lao Liu graduated from the same middle school as Lao Wu. In Lao Wu's life, Lao Liu was the only person who knew the glorious history of Lao Wu's middle school era. Lao Wu went to the pharmaceutical school regularly just to savour this feeling. Lao Wu never spoke of America with her, because in Lao Wu's view, Lao Liu was too far away from America.

Lao Wu's last remaining habit was to take a walk in the sports ground near the Friendship Building in the late afternoon. Foreign students and foreign experts lived in the Friendship Building. Lao Wu hadn't taken any steps to investigate this, but among those white people walking or playing ball in the sports ground he knew which were Americans. He had faith in his own judgement. He could even point out that the blond haired, blue eyed girl was American — although only an American peasant. This kind of feeling was instinctual, in just the same way that Lao Wu was born with an affinity for America. Lao Wu considered whether he should give up this habit as well. Since walking was good for your health, Lao Wu decided to keep this habit for the time being. He decided that in exceptional circumstances this habit would also have to be got rid of.

Once the first phase of reorganization was finished, Lao Wu's changes aroused his classmates' surprise and laughter. They thought that Lao Wu should just continue as usual until such time as he was expelled. That's what should happen to someone like Lao Wu. Lao Wu felt bitterly cold. He understood this to be a coldness peculiar to this land, and that all would be different on the other side of the Pacific. Lao Wu swore silently, using the most malicious Qinghai dialect words, then threw himself into the second phase.

The main point of the second phase was to revise his lessons from the very beginning. Once the second phase was carried out, Lao Wu's mood suffered a disastrous decline. Reality was cruel — far more cruel than Lao Wu had anticipated. Sitting in the first row of the classroom, Lao Wu forced himself to think of America's inspiring and enthusiastic opening up of the Great West. This was rather unconvincing. But Lao Wu was willing to undergo every conceivable difficulty and any suffering in order to do something related to America, but not for any other reason. Otherwise, everything he was doing would be unnecessary.

A whole afternoon of Advanced Mathematics almost killed Lao Wu. He considered Advanced Mathematics and the two other courses he had to resit as three endless quibbling whores. But Lao Wu immediately felt that this sort of metaphor was inappropriate. He believed in mysterious things, such as yoga, and he believed that a vicious idea would receive vicious retribution. He also believed that the concept of America would not always be so distant from him. He need only look forward to it.

At half past five, Lao Wu left the study room to enjoy his remaining habit. It was a long way to the sports ground, and he walked the distance very quickly. This was not Lao Wu's usual pace.

Lao Wu also had to come to the sports ground for his PE lesson. He has been assigned to keep-fit classes (because he had pneumonia before). The south-east corner of the sports ground was where the keep-fit classes took place. Twenty or thirty people would line up in a square and practise *taiji* shadow boxing. This was all there was to the

PE lesson. Lao Wu was now standing at the south-east corner looking towards the grass at the north-west corner (which is the corner nearest to the Friendship Building). He hoped that there would be some Americans walking around so he could feel a little closer to America. This desire surprised even Lao Wu himself. He didn't consider himself a fan of America, simply because he felt he ought actually to be an American himself — that was all there was to it.

There were ten black men playing football on the grass. Offering these blacks a university education was just one of China's many projects to aid Africa. Lao Wu had fought alongside some of them on the battle ground of examination resits. At the time he had felt a bit ashamed. The famous brand name of their American shoes quickly drew Lao Wu's attention. He shook his head. In front of these black men, Lao Wu once again felt strongly that he was really an American.

Do I really want to go to America? Do I really want to be an American? This question sprang into his mind all of a sudden. Lao Wu held a copy of *Advanced Mathematics* in his hand and suddenly felt extremely muddled. To Lao Wu, this question was like asking, "Will my mum really abandon the old man and go back and live alone in Shanghai?" These were unusual times. Lao Wu immediately realised the danger of letting this thoughts wander, and decisively snuffed out the idea in his copy of *Advanced Mathematics*.

Lao Wu's evening was no less difficult to cope with than his over-loaded day. At worst, he got up seven times during the night. Furthermore, the harder he worked in the day, the stronger became his night-time desire to masturbate (the habit of masturbation was not included within the scope of his reorganization). At last, he simply let it go, as though it were simply a necessary compensation for his body, given the second phase.

The development of Lao Wu's masturbation habit went back to his middle school period. Initially he was very nervous. When he saw a short article in the newspaper saying "masturbation poses no great dangers for your health", he at once felt relieved. He cut the article out and sent it to *Reader's Digest*. Masturbation, for Lao Wu, represented sex, and sex was always connected with America. In his first year at university Lao Wu saw a video of Madonna's famous 'performance', which reinforced his ideas. "Madonna is actually masturbating while she is singing." By the second year, Lao Wu talked very frankly to classmates about this habit. This frankness was itself something unique to Americans. Lao Wu had another very famous saying about masturbation, "If you can do something for yourself, there's no need to bother others."

One morning, after the second phase had been practised for two weeks, Lao Wu was frightened when he looked in the washroom mirror. That half-man-half-ghost was Lao Wu. Must hold out, Lao Wu said to himself, just like Americans, from Pearl Harbour to Normandy.

2 NARRATED BY LAO WU

'Might-As-Well-Love-Once' from my dormitory asked me today where Lao Liu was. Had Lao Liu set her sights on somebody better? What a bastard! He seemed to want to remind me all the time that he passed me a note last time we had the Thermodynamics examination. I really wanted to kick him in the crotch. Another 'Might-As-Well-Love-Once' kept calling out: 'But-in-America-Such-and-Such', just because I didn't know which state Los Angeles was in. Does every single American have to know which state Los Angeles is in? It doesn't matter that even a great Chinese doesn't know where Nanjing is, does it?

Forget it. Before going to sleep I flicked through the Pierce's *Devil's Dictionary*; the illustrations are really good. An American imagination. [NB: according to the author's research, the illustrations in the Chinese version of this book were done by a Chinese.] Actually, Americans don't have a so-called 'nationality' or a 'colour'. They are a group of people who are all supposed to be called Americans gathered together from all sorts of directions. America.

Progress in Advanced Mathematics is not very smooth. I've only studied a quarter of volume one, and already have many problems. It's too late, sleep, sleep.

Lao Liu ... sleep, sleep.

•

Today was a gratifying day. For days it's as though I've been living in a damp, dark warehouse. Today I seemed to see, to see for the first time a trace of light. This is a good omen.

At half past five in the afternoon, I went to have a walk as usual. On the way I met a few female classmates. Laughing, they walked past me, it seemed they were still talking about me. Another outburst of uproarious laughter. What makes me so laughable? I'm just a bit thin, is being thin laughable? When I think of them in those artificial postures when they are with boys I feel sick.

There was no point in being angry with them. Really no point at all. I reached the sports ground. Those dozen or so blacks were playing football again. They're not afraid of failing the exams. My head was really muddled, I sat down by the horizontal bar and smoked a cigarette. I know I shouldn't smoke any more, but at exceptional times I have no other choice. God bless me, and don't let my lungs have any problems again.

Just when I was getting a little muddled, I suddenly caught sight of a little blond girl come out of the experts building, wearing a sky blue skirt. She had great big eyes and long eyelashes. — God, I felt that my vocabulary was just too limited. Two snowy white legs just like her eyes were faintly visible in the eyelash-like skirt. She was probably five or six. There were two little pom-poms attached to her socks. She came out, jumping and skipping. Then she climbed up onto the fence of the sports ground and sat down. Using one hand to support her chin she watched the blacks playing football. This adult posture made her even more lovely. She was like a bird that had flown by and alighted on the fence, like a drop of dew.

This was a typical little American girl, healthy and beautiful. Like Shirley Temple. I sat by the horizontal bar staring at her until she left.

That evening my studying was much more effective than usual. I really wanted to see her again. Tonight, I delved into one chapter of *Advanced Maths*. Keep going. I'm really really tired.

After the lights went out, I once again felt that strong desire. In the process of my masturbation, I suddenly thought of that little American girl and instantly felt an intense satisfaction. After I finished this time, I felt that the little girl was still jumping and skipping. Then I did it another time while I was thinking of that little girl. This time it was also very successful. Previously, when I masturbated I had always thought of Old Mrs Xu from our neighbourhood, and later of Madonna. For some time, even though I was thinking of Madonna, it still wasn't very successful. Because while I was doing it, I would suddenly see the words 'Advanced Mathematics' written on Madonna's knickers.

I got up and went to the toilet. I was really surprised, it was hanging down without any strength, swollen like bean curd strung together by a length of grass.

I had to go to sleep.

... That little girl, what's her name? Give her a name, call her Temple? No, that's no good. Call her Jenny, yes, little Jenny, little Jenny....

Must sleep. Must. Sleep.

3 NARRATED BY THE AUTHOR

A ten year old American child's mind is just like a twenty year old Chinese youth's mind. A twenty year old youth's mind is more mature than that of a thirty old Chinese youth, because of this, an American's effective life is ten years longer than that of a Chinese. This is Lao Wu's 'ten years difference' theory. The evidence Lao Wu always uses is a small news report from a digest: "The child star of 'ET' decides to become a person again." This child star announced this to the media when she was fourteen. Before she was fourteen she had been sexually promiscuous (starting at the age of nine), got drunk and taken drugs. What a rich life experience. A fourteen year old Chinese girl is still a fool who understands nothing. Lao Wu said, "There are some who are twenty and still don't understand a thing." By this he meant Lao Liu.

Of course, not everybody born in China has this 'ten years difference'. Lao Wu was one such exception. Lao Wu felt that the difference between himself and Americans, lay only in the difficulties facing him. All he had to do was pass through these difficulties and Lao Wu would no longer feel awkward — he wouldn't feel awkward, he'd be American.

Lao Wu took further steps to rearrange his timetable. Lao Wu made plans on a piece of paper. As each item appeared on the paper, he immediately gained more confidence. Attack the extremes. Attack. Lao Wu found the American type of willpower in his own body. With the birth of the new timetable, Lao Wu seemed to regain energy after the exertions of the previous extremely difficult and arduous period.

6am–7am, read English. Morning, go to class. 12 noon–12.15, have lunch. 12.15–3.15, delve into *Advanced Mathematics*. 3.15–3.20, break, go to the toilet. 3.20–5.30, cope with the current lessons. 5.30–6.00, walk. 6.00–6.15, have supper. 6.15–12.00, study. 12.15, go to bed. Everything must be finished by one o'clock in the morning.

"All you need to do is try and you can become president." Lao Wu always remembered this sentence. He couldn't remember now which American had said this, anyway it was an American who said it. The more exhausted he became, the more American blood Lao Wu found that he had. At six o'clock in every morning he kicked off the duvet, giddy and dazed he fumbled his way to the bathroom and put his head under the cold tap until he came to his senses. Sometimes this took a very long time.

Then came the retching. That frightening sound could be heard clearly throughout the building. Lao Wu's classmates regarded this retching noise at six o'clock in the morning as the reveille calling them to get up. One morning, a month after Lao Wu began to implement his second phase, he spat out a mouthful of blood while he was retching. Along the corridor came the sound of footsteps. Lao Wu hurriedly washed away the blood.

The plan was still being implemented without hitch. "Just like a branch stripped of its bark, naked, with absolutely nothing." That's how Lao Wu described his life at the present time. Apart from books, all that he had left in his life was the half-hour walk and masturbation in the middle of the night.

Lao Wu didn't see any more of little Jenny during his half-hour walks. She was an omen, so she might only appear once. In Lao Wu's mind, little Jenny was not even the young daughter of some American expert in the experts' building. She came out of nowhere.

But in the depths of the night, Lao Wu always saw her. Little Jenny, little Jenny — Lao Wu repeated her name over and over in a quivering voice. Lao Wu seemed to see little Jenny's bare foot stepping on his chest with its bare ribs, those little feet, satiny and moist. Once, Lao Wu wanted to catch those little feet, pull little Jenny onto the floor, and then throw himself on her. The next morning, under the attack of the running water, Lao Wu felt deeply guilty.

One day after another. Sometimes in a single day Lao Wu would masturbate as much as two or three times. Lao Wu began to feel a sense of chill, the chill was brought on by little Jenny.

Then Lao Wu started to feel dry. What he held was no longer moist, it looked like a bunch of wheat straw. Lao Wu tried to use water to improve this condition, finally he changed to using Vaseline. He learnt this from an American novel. Lao Wu preferred Vaseline.

There were still two months until the end of term. Dizziness, tinnitus, insomnia and night sweats were the main symptoms Lao Wu felt. He already knew that he was suffering from neurasthenia (he had contracted the disease while at middle school). Every day before going to sleep, Lao Wu calmly took four kinds of medicine inside his mosquito net. Must hold out. Hold out.

Lao Wu held *Advanced Mathematics* in his hand and thought of his third phase. No, better not use it. Lao Wu defiantly lit a cigarette.

4 NARRATED BY LAO WU

(extracts from Lao Wu's notes on *Advanced Mathematics*)

L'Hôpital's Rule:

can only calculate $\frac{0}{0}$ or $\frac{\infty}{\infty}$ types of limit, other undecided forms

have to be changed into $\frac{0}{0}$, $\frac{\infty}{\infty}$ types

the limit   have I reached the limit

not possible not possible $\text{Lim} \dfrac{f(\chi)}{g(\chi)}$

the limit of the ratio of infinity, I

am definitely infinite

damn it $\underset{\chi \to 0}{\text{Lim}} \dfrac{\text{Ln}(1+\chi)}{X^2} = \underset{\chi \to 0}{\text{Lim}} \dfrac{[\text{Ln}(1+\chi)]^1}{(X^2)^1}$

evaluate

little Jenny little Jenny she wants my life can't get it can't get it can't
get it can't get it can't get it can't get it lung lung lung damn the lung
don't recur don't recur I beg you beg you just beg you this once

Fourier's Progression
Taylor's Formula
Lagrange Remainder
Jenny Theorem
blood blood blood blood spit spit spit
beg you beg beg beg you
Lao Liu 666
Jenny theorem Jenny little girl don't move
tell you don't move
you just don't move

5 NARRATED BY THE AUTHOR

Lao Wu's mum sent him a long letter. She couldn't avoid complaining, as she always did, about his old man's stupidity that year. "A perfectly good welding electrode factory exchanged for a just a piece in the newspaper the size of a cube of dried tofu." Then it was her ten year plan. Lao Wu put the letter back in the envelope and did not read any more. What he cared about was America, not Shanghai.

"Do I really want to go to America, do I really want to be an American?" This question surfaced for the second time. The question was complicated and incompatible with present requirements. True or false, Lao Wu answered it like that and left it alone.

At the moment the most worrying thing was whether this body could hold out until the day of the exams. Lao Wu was very clear on this point. With so much hard work to do, he could not afford to relax at all. He sold the guitar and his pair of Adidas shoes in exchange for some nutritious food. Whatever it took he had to hold on for the last ten days. That was all Lao Wu could do.

After another ten days, Lao Wu realized that he was finished. During these ten days, Lao Wu had coughed blood twice, and started to display the symptoms of a low fever. Although he could not get anything else into his mind, not a single iota, Lao Wu insisted on sitting in the study room, carving the table with a knife, continually mumbling something to himself. Ten days before the exams, Lao Wu already knew that the second phase was pointless.

Half past five. Sports ground. Lao Wu sitting alone by the horizontal bar, smoking a cigarette and crying.

Returning after his walk in the sports ground, Lao Wu thought, it seemed that he had no other choice but to start the third phase.

6 NARRATED BY LAO LIU

From my point of view this was a really frightening experience. From the time he came in, I was so nervous, right up until he suddenly slammed the door and went out. I couldn't calm down the whole night long.

As far as I can remember I have only screamed twice. When I was at primary school, my parents once went to work on the night shift and left me alone at home. I was doing my homework at the table facing the window. Suddenly a ferocious ghostly face appeared at the window. I was so frightened I almost fainted. (Later I found out that it was Da Qiang from a neighbour's family who did this.) This time was much more frightening than the time when I was small. I would never have thought it would be because of Lao Wu's appearance.

I hadn't seen Lao Wu for a while. At the beginning of this term he told me that he was going to do something (exactly what he wanted to do, I was never clear about) and he couldn't come to see me. I said, that's alright, it's always better to have something to do than nothing to do. I still think he is different from other people. I believe that one day he will do something.

Lao Wu pushed open the door and rushed in with bloodshot eyes. I was alone in the dormitory at the time, and it was late. My first impression was that something dangerous and horrible had appeared, only when I looked carefully, did I realize that it was Lao Wu. It was already warm enough to wear a T-shirt and shorts, but Lao Wu was still covered up with his thick, dirty denim jacket. His hair was really long, and all sticking up on end, his head looked really big. It was as though Lao Wu had been blown in from another world by a tornado. After he saw me, he just stood by the door, staring at me.

I felt that Lao Wu had become a stranger. Yes, too much of a stranger. Of course, it didn't occur to me just then. Lao Wu had never been as familiar to me as I would have wished. Lao Wu always said that it was as if he didn't have any deep feelings for anybody, on a point of principle, he didn't give anything to anybody, and didn't owe anybody anything. He rarely spoke to me, and even if he spoke, it was always very simple, as though it were some famous saying.

With his body turned away he sat on the chair beside me and smoked a cigarette, all without saying a word. On the floor there were already five or six cigarette ends and big lumps of phlegm he had coughed up. Then there was a fit of fierce coughing, he spat out another mouthful of phlegm with blood. At that time I had a very strange feeling, I felt as though Lao Wu wanted to keep on spitting until the blood-filled phlegm drowned me.

I stood up to walk over to the window. It was too hot and stuffy in the room. Lao Wu stood up suddenly and grabbed my wrist. His hand was icy cold, I remembered the ghostly face I saw when I was little.

"Help me, help me, will you? You must be able to, there is only you, there is only you, please help me, don't let her take my life."

My arm was shaken fiercely. My body froze. I didn't know what Lao Wu was roaring for, so hysterically, his eyes opened so wide, as though the sockets might split.

My whole mind stopped. I sat on the bed like a wooden statue, staring at Lao Wu, who was now yelling, "She wants to take my life, to take my life. Help me." Then he collapsed on the chair as though he'd had an electric shock. I hadn't been able to say anything.

After he'd been quiet for a moment, he threw himself on me, and started to tear at my clothes, repeating, "Help me, help me." I didn't fight back. I was just like a corpse, absolutely like a corpse.

I felt that my top had already been torn open. I also heard the sound of a blouse being ripped.

Suddenly, Lao Wu stopped. He got up slowly from the bed, and standing under the light, kept completely still. After a while, I heard the sound of the door.

In the week after this, I dreamt of the ghostly face every day. One moment it was the one I saw when I was little, then it changed into the face of Lao Wu. Once, I dreamt that something came floating by on the water from very far away. When it came near, I picked it up and looked at it, it was the skin of Lao Wu's face.

7 NARRATED BY THE AUTHOR

The essential point concerning the implementation phase three was whether to use it at all. Lao Wu found that it was not particularly difficult to persuade himself on this point. He thought of the American, Nathanael West. He got the chance to study by forging his exam transcripts twice, and ultimately wrote a great novel, *Miss Lonelyhearts*. To do something by fair means or foul is the American way. No matter what method were used, the real victory would be overcoming the various difficulties which were due to start in eight days time. Lao Wu shifted his slightly feverish body from the duvet to the floor and felt that phase three was actually only a continuation of phase two.

America could only get nearer and nearer, it could not be allowed to become further and further away. Lao Wu went to the study room again. When he emerged he had a set of detailed plans. Everything was under complete control.

The whole plan could be divided into three parts, which Lao Wu called A, B and C. When this plan was implemented, each subject would need five people. One person to deliver it, one person to reinforce it, and the other three Lao Wu called the 'wisdom group'. The author can only give out this much information about the plan, just in case some readers learn it and give today's teachers a headache.

It was extremely difficult to set up this team. After Lao Wu had sold his guitar and Adidas shoes, he sold his calculator, wool jumper, a Crown suit and everything of any value in his suitcase. In addition, Lao Wu collected up all the beer bottles he could find in the dormitory building. Altogether these brought in two hundred *yuan*. As soon as this two hundred *yuan* had been spent on cigarettes, drink, food, lamps and pens, the setting up of Lao Wu's team was complete. Every exam had the right person for that particular exam. A team consisting of some twenty people was temporarily under Lao Wu's command. Lao Wu felt mildly superior.

There were still three days until the first exam. Lao Wu felt that apart from sleeping he had nothing else to do. This really was American style efficiency, Lao Wu said.

But, there was scarcely a single night when Lao Wu felt relaxed. He felt that when the time came he would not even have the energy to sit in front of the exam table. Lao Wu forced himself to do something very mechanical, until he was so exhausted he could bear it no longer and then went to bed. He copied the *People's Daily* in the corridor, until he had almost copied a whole sheet. Then he felt tired enough. The whole building was very quiet, his classmates had drifted off to dreamland much earlier.

He lay down on his bed, and gradually became nervous once again. He knew his mind was like a snake awakening from hibernation. More precisely, it was his soul starting to roam again, but his body had already become too weak to bear it. Lao Wu resisted desperately, but he knew his resistance was already very weak.

"Little Jenny, little Jenny, let me go, let me go!"

"Little Jenny, don't you think I look like, no, I must *be* an American?"

Lao Wu reached one hand under the pillow and found the Vaseline. He used one finger to scrape some out and put it in his palm.

"Little Jenny, little Jenny …"

"Little Jenny, little Jenny …"

Two beams of light shone on Lao Wu. At first, Lao Wu thought it was a dream. When he heard a big laugh, he suddenly realized the truth. The light of the torch was shining on Lao Wu's hand.

Lao Wu threw back the mosquito net and jumped out of bed. One, two, three, four, five, six, seven. Nobody missing, the whole room was standing by his bed.

This was a conspiracy. Lao Wu felt an unbearable shame. The seven were still laughing. He picked up a chair and rushed at one of them, who retreated until he got to the corner. Both Lao Wu's eyes felt like they were about weep blood. They had never see Lao Wu like that, they had even forgotten that Lao Wu could be like that.

Suddenly, Lao Wu raised the chair, and after a while put it down very slowly. He turned back, opened the door and walked out of the door.

In the toilet, Lao Wu wiped his tears with his dirty sleeves, crying, making a sound like a wounded dog.

Endure. Five of them belonged to Lao Wu's twenty-five strong army. Lao Wu could not do anything that would cause failure on the verge of success. Before he got to his destination, he should swallow any shame. Swallow it. What for? Lao Wu asked himself, is it because I am, I should be an American?

8 NARRATED BY LAO WU

I couldn't believe that I had slept for so long. I was like somebody who had just contracted a serious illness, and was about to contract something more serious. I looked at my watch. It was five o'clock in the afternoon. on the xth day of the xth month. Tomorrow would be my first battle.

I wanted to forget everything. It would be best if I didn't remember even a single bit. It was like I hadn't done anything, or it had all finished.

My lungs. My head.

My genitals.

I suddenly felt like an old soldier, yes, like an old soldier, an enfeebled old soldier who just wanted to lay under the sun. An old solider who lost his arm and leg in the war and didn't know what he was fighting for. Old soldiers never die; they only fade away, Admiral Nimitz had said. But I was definitely the sort of soldier who was going to die.

I thought of my father again. Did he count as an old soldier? Now he can only go fishing and play mah-jong. Was he an old soldier?

Do I really want to go to America, do I really think that I should be an American?

Damn! I refuse to answer this question. It's really strange. Who is strange? It is strange.

Forget it, get up and have a walk, then have a good dinner. Tomorrow, *Advanced Mathematics*.

9 NARRATED BY THE AUTHOR

The sports ground.

It was unusually cool for summer in Nanjing. Lao Wu could not tell if the weather was cool, or if it was just him feeling cold. Anyway he felt that his energy was a little restored now. Another night's rest, and tomorrow he would be a little better still.

Those dozen-odd blacks were still playing football in the north-west corner of the field. It was dinner time, and nobody else was on the sports ground. Apart from the occasional shout drifting from the north-west corner, there was no other sound.

Lao Wu stood at the south-east corner. This was where he practised *taiji* in his PE class.

It's time for dinner, Lao Wu thought.

TWO RABBITS —
A MALE AND A FEMALE

ZHU WEN

translated by Zheng Haiyao and Jos Gamble

The rabbit ran away. The female rabbit I bought for five *yuan* ran away. They (I actually bought two rabbits that day, a male and a female, spending ten *yuan* altogether) were locked in my room. Last night the whole block's electricity was cut off and the sweltering heat forced me to sleep with my door open. When I woke up in the morning, I discovered the male rabbit called 'Bandit' nibbling water melon peel in the corner of the room. The female rabbit had disappeared.

The female rabbit had a really ugly name — 'Widow'. The name had been chosen by Turtlehead Lee. 'Turtlehead Lee' was also a very ugly name, it was chosen by me. Turtlehead Lee's original name was Lee Gang. He was the sports teacher at the Ji An Company School. I guess you could say he was one of my friends. Whenever he wasn't with his girlfriend "Hero", he was with me.

"Hello, Bandit! Eh — where's Widow?" Turtlehead Lee walked straight in. He was stripped to the waist. The muscular Turtlehead was supremely confident when he was stripped to the waist.

"Run away," I answered for Bandit.

"Run away? Damn! I've said it before, that Widow was bad news. She couldn't be tamed. Bandit's a good boy. Bandit's a good boy." Turtlehead Lee tried to stroke Bandit while he was saying this. Seeing that huge, rough five-legged monster attacking him, Bandit hurriedly hopped away.

"Why isn't Hero coming?" Yesterday they said they'd come to my place for lunch. Early this morning I went to the market specially to buy meat and fish. I only bought one fish to make soup. I also bought one and a half kilos of meat. Turtlehead, Hero and myself brag about being able to eat half a kilo of meat in one go.

"Let's have three quarters of a kilo each." Turtlehead Lee grabbed Bandit's two back legs and in an instant pulled him out from under the table.

"Hey, don't waste your energy on him. Bring me that basin, over there."

"There you are, Spare Parts ... Do you think it's possible that all along, you've made a mistake? I reckon, it's very possible."

I was 'Spare Parts'. I'm the person known as Spare Parts.

"What do you mean?"

"I mean ... Bandit must be Widow, and Widow must be Bandit. It looks more and more the case." It seemed that Turtlehead lacked any common sense about rabbit genitalia.

"Do you mean I might have mistaken Hero for Turtlehead?"

"Fuck off. Hey, nobody can deny that Spare Parts' cooking is really delicious."

Lunch was over. Turtlehead had eaten three quarters of a kilo of meat. I only ate one quarter. We started drinking tea. He had a habit of picking his teeth. It made me feel really uncomfortable.

Turtlehead was fated only to drink tea from a big bowl, and when I got him to drink tea from a small cup it was really very difficult for him. "Hey, can you change this for a big mug? Or just give me a bowl. Spare Parts, you're pathetic, boasting you can eat half a kilo of meat in one go."

"Just because I can eat half a kilo of meat doesn't mean I have to eat half a kilo of meat at every meal. What do you reckon, can Hero really eat half a kilo of meat?"

"Sure. If she's hungry she can even eat a pile of dog shit — she said so herself." With a single "glug" Turtlehead drank the whole bowl of tea down in one go.

"It wouldn't make much difference if she ate half a kilo or three quarters of a kilo. How come Hero's still so thin?"

"The way she chops and changes, even if she ate a kilo of meat at one meal she still wouldn't put on weight. I still don't think it's right, are you really sure Bandit is a male?"

"Have you ever heard of this saying: 'A male rabbit's feet scratch the ground, a female rabbit's eyes look dazed'? Look at this rabbit...."

"That's not certain. I believe that some female rabbits are definitely more active than male, much much more."

Turtlehead picked up the teapot tried to pour more tea into his bowl, only a few drops came out. He shook it and threw it to one side.

"I have to go out for a while." Turtlehead grabbed his coat.

"Now?"

"Yes, now."

Turtlehead left. I started washing the dishes. Once the washing-up was done, I tidied the room. The rabbits had made a real mess on the floor. Turtlehead had made a real mess on the table, the sofa and everywhere else he had touched. I planned to clean and tidy them systematically. Turtlehead said that he was much tidier and cleaner than Hero. I dread to think what Hero is like.

After tidying everything up, I got out the large pile of spare parts to continue assembling my television set. This was my main hobby. The tape recorder, black and white television and four pocket radios in the room were all products of my own fair hands. I now wanted to build a colour television. I had calculated that the price of the tape recorder I had assembled from spare parts was more expensive than the same type of recorder available on the market. It was obvious that I was not doing this to save money.

I plugged in the soldering iron to heat up, and while I was waiting, I smoked a cigarette. I puffed out thick smoke, then looked down to see if the iron was hot. When I raised my head again, Hero appeared in the gradually disappearing smoke.

"Have you eaten?"

"I've just eaten."

"Eh, is there anything left?"

"Yes, look, over there."

Hero first picked up a piece of meat with her hand and put it into her mouth. Only then did she go and get some chopsticks. Hero rubbed the chopsticks on her clothes. She must have seen my expression. I looked at her jeans which were covered in grease stains.

"I've said it before, Spare Parts, you're really very capable. Spare Parts, you're not at all bad." Surprisingly, Hero drank a mouthful of gravy.

She was referring to my cooking technique. I worked out the sense from her tone. Turtlehead and Hero were always surprised at everything they discovered about me at my place. It seemed that they didn't really believe me capable of doing anything. Even the very simplest things. They didn't really give me a second thought. But I wouldn't ever make the slightest attempt to speak up for myself.

"Turtlehead has just left, he said he had some business ... hey, don't give him that, he won't eat it."

Either my words were a bit too slow, or Hero's movements were a bit too quick. She put a piece of meat in front of Bandit. Eat, eat, this is good stuff! Eh — what's he called? Bandit, Bandit, Bandit eat! How can a bandit not eat meat?

"He won't eat it!" The soldering iron was already hot enough, and I could start working.

But, he was eating. I put down the iron, went around the table and walked straight up to the rabbit. Dead right. Bandit was eating meat.

I said to a dumb-struck Hero, maybe there was something evil in this house. Look at the two rabbits I raised! One had run away, the other had become a wolf.

One had run away? It was only now that Hero remembered the rabbit called Widow. Yes, run away.

"Widow? Who chose that name?"

"Turtlehead."

"It's good to run away."

Hero was still eating meat. Spare Parts, have you been out to look for that rabbit? If it she's hiding away somewhere and doesn't have anything to eat, she might starve to death.

No. Seeing that she ran away, she must have had a much better place to go. So I needn't go and look for her. Nonsense.

Hero was not eating meat any more. I want to have a lie down, Hero said. Here? Yes. Can't you eat any more? I don't want to eat now.

I heard the sound of a zip behind me, and then a thud. Hero must have gone to sleep. Hey, Spare Parts, what do you reckon, are those two rabbits a couple?

They should be. Anyway, one was male and the other female.

The inner workings of the television had already been assembled. I was filled with the sense of impending success. Although I couldn't guarantee that nothing would go wrong, it was always very pleasant once this part of the job was over. I started to whistle. The more satisfied I became, the more I whistled. I whistled for all I was worth.

"Hey, Spare Parts, stop whistling. If you whistle again, I'll piss on the bed." It was Hero's voice.

I had forgotten that Hero was sleeping. When I averted my gaze from the big pile of spare parts, I unexpectedly discovered that Turtlehead had appeared from out of nowhere and was sitting on the chair opposite me. He lowered his head. There was blood on his forehead.

"Turtlehead! ?"

Turtlehead nodded his head. It passed for a greeting. Turtlehead reached out for the teapot, shook it around, and finally drank straight from the spout. He could only have had a few drops.

"The thermos flask is over there. Help yourself to some water." I noticed a drop of blood running down Turtlehead's forehead and onto his cheek, "Turtlehead, what's happened to your forehead? Does it need bandaging?"

"Don't worry, I knocked it accidentally." Turtlehead used his hand to wipe his right cheek, and his right cheek became covered in blood.

"Where did you knock it?"

"I knocked it accidentally." Turtlehead didn't look at me any more. He was looking at Bandit washing his face with both his front paws like a cat. To be precise, Bandit was using his paws to sharpen his teeth. A rabbit's mouth has to be kept busy all the time, as soon as it has nothing to chew, it must set its teeth itching.

I got up and went to pick up a piece of cotton and some antiseptic from the bedside table. Hero was facing the wall and seemed to be asleep. Hero, Turtlehead is here.

"Spare Parts, don't trouble yourself, it's nothing I tell you. Eh — still no news of Widow?"

News? What news? I never expected her to come back at all. Turtlehead asked again about Widow, he seemed to be looking for something to say. Widow was just a rabbit that had run away. Actually, it was a rabbit with absolutely no particular characteristics. All female rabbits are exactly like her, with dazed eyes. Her only characteristic was to have run away.

I wiped away the blood on Turtlehead's right cheek with a wet towel. When the wet towel touched Turtlehead's skin, the expression on his face was kind of tender. I thought it strange and felt a pleasant sensation while I was doing this. Hero stood up. I was dipping the cotton into the antiseptic. I thought Hero was going to come and help and I got ready to give the cotton and mercurochrome to her. But Hero went out without a glance.

"Where are you going?" Turtlehead roared, another drop of blood seeping from the wound on his forehead. Hero stopped for a moment by the door, then carried on her way again. She stomped off down the stairs.

When I realized what was going on, Turtlehead had already caught one of Hero's arms. This was Turtlehead and Hero's business after all. I had no choice but to put the cotton and mercurochrome on the table. When I raised my head, I saw Turtlehead holding his groin with his hand, standing on the stairs with his body doubled over. Hero had already disappeared from the foot of the stairs and gone out.

This could be a good idea. At least, it was good idea in principle. But Turtlehead insisted on giving it a try. Early one Sunday morning, Turtlehead and Hero came joyfully to see me carrying a string bag full of green vegetables, aubergines, pork and a pack of beer. It looked like they were coming to exploit my labour again.

Why not? Even an old horse recognises a familiar route. I didn't believe that Bandit could find Widow. Turtlehead's mood was especially jolly today. The wound on his forehead had become a black scab. The muscles of his face moved ferociously when he spoke, I was afraid that the movement of his skin would reopen his wound.

It seemed that Hero was sick of Turtlehead's chatter. She went straight over to the table piled high with spare parts, while Turtlehead continued to prattle away.

"Animals are definitely very sensitive to the smell of their own species, for example, a dog's nose is a hundred times better than a human nose. Right now in some foreign country somebody is making an electronic dog's nose...." I kept on nodding my head, because Turtlehead always tried to emphasise his sentences with overwhelming strength. But I heard Hero mumbling something at the other end of the room.

"You know, you really should know, Bandit, no, I mean Widow is Bandit's properly-wedded wife. How can Bandit be so unmoved by Widow's absence? If I just follow him...." The more he spoke the more complacent Turtlehead became.

Hero said, you're talking crap! "Hey, Hero, don't move anything!" I saw Hero moving the things on my desk.

"No. I must give it a try." Turtlehead grabbed Bandit, and rushed to the corridor outside. He put Bandit on the floor then asked him to lead the way. That's right, that's what Turtlehead said: Bandit, lead the way!

It was my job to prepare lunch. My interest in doing this job was as strong as my love of wireless technology. To do something really systematically, even if it's only some very simple task, makes me feel like I'm alive. For example, fresh aubergines, see, how perfect they are, with their soft shape and shining skin, wash and cut them into regular shapes, one piece after another. It's really enchanting. After the aubergine is cooked, red and green in colour, dish it out onto a clean plate. I know I'll be satisfied before I've even tried it.

I was rather surprised when Hero volunteered to come and pick over the vegetables. She moved a bundle of vegetables nearer to me. Then she kept her head bowed and sorted through them. Her movements were very quick and neat.

"Spare Parts, can I ask you a favour?"

"Put the leaves to one side. Leave them for Bandit to eat later. Ask me a favour? What is it?" I wasn't used to the word "favour".

"If Turtlehead asks you, can you say that I stayed at your place all last evening? Just say that I'm learning how to assemble radios, or learning...."

"Assembling radios? Why?" My vegetable knife stopped in mid air.

"Can you just say it?" Hero still carried on picking over the vegetables without stopping. I knew that she was really hanging on my reply. I looked at her sideways, and for the first time I felt that she looked like a woman. There was no reason behind this feeling, because I, Spare Parts, don't know anything about women. I just suddenly had this feeling.

I carried on slicing aubergines, and used the vegetable knife to scoop the sliced aubergine from the chopping-board onto a plate. I picked up one or two slices of aubergine which had dropped on the floor and put them onto the plate.

"Okay, I'll tell you why," Hero looked up and glanced at me for an instant, "do you remember last time?"

"Last time?"

"Last time when Turtlehead's forehead was cut open in a fight."

"Cut open in a fight?"

"I can't bear it any more, Turtlehead is too much, I'll be driven mad by him. He beats up all the men I meet. He turns up from out of nowhere like a shadow. As soon as he hears about them, he beats them up. My colleague just went skating with me once. Turtlehead appeared by the entrance to the skating rink and beat him back and blue. He's still confined to bed." Hero put the yellow leaves into the basin and left the clean green leaves on the pile of yellow leaves on the floor.

"If you aren't prepared to help me, it means that Turtlehead will beat up someone else ... he might get hurt as well." For the first time I saw Hero looking tired.

"If I help you, Turtlehead might beat me up." I looked down at myself, I wanted to draw Hero's attention to my scrawny pigeon chest.

"In Turtlehead's mind, all the men in the world are his enemy except you, Spare Parts. He believes you." Hero looked straight at me, I turned my face aside.

At that moment my mind was filled with all sorts of strange notions, like some nameless plant suddenly growing through the earth. I didn't know whether I felt honoured or sad.

I continued to slice the aubergines. Hero suddenly threw down the vegetable knife and ran out. I was stunned for a while and then heard the sound of fighting in the corridor, it sounded like Turtlehead's voice. I followed out quickly.

Turtlehead was holding Bandit by the scruff of his neck, in one hand and with the other hand he was fighting with some guy. Even so, by the time I got there, Turtlehead had still got his opponent down on the ground. Hero pulled Turtlehead away, I helped the poor fellow to his feet. My arrival allowed him to get rid of that downtrodden look he had just had. "This is really outrageous, how can you so casually search my house? You even want to search my wardrobe. You probably want me to take off my trousers and search them, eh!?" As he spoke he made out that he was going to rush over. I didn't really try to stop him because I knew that he wouldn't really do it.

An hour later we began our lunch. "Can you believe that Bandit!" Hero slammed down a glass of beer in front of Turtlehead. Turtlehead inclined his head to look at Bandit. Bandit shrank into a ball and, squatting in the pile of yellow leaves, was very carefully enjoying them. I noticed the muscle on Turtlehead's right arm twitch nervously. This might be Turtlehead's most attractive moment.

I drank at least seventeen glasses of beer with the meal. Hero toasted the first glass to my good health, to my uninjured skin and hair, even my appendix which was still there. I knew what this glass meant. Bottoms up! The next toast was for Bandit, then: 'to a beautiful shirt', 'there's not quite enough salt in the soup', 'the colour television will soon be assembled', and so on. It seemed that there were still lots of things worth celebrating in life. After all, life was still good.

As a result, I had no choice but to lie down. I half-consciously remember Turtlehead carrying me like a roll of cotton wadding to bed. My body heaved up and down on the bed several times like a wave, then ceased to move.

Rabbit! A skinny rabbit, like a little white mouse, moving close to the foot of the wall. Ha, too much like a frightened mouse! The rabbits in the middle of the room are so big, with their backs towards you, that fat backside, that squatting posture, what does it remind me of? It reminds one of ... They start to fight, anyway they are fighting now, it's not clear who is fighting with who, all that can be seen is a large snowy white blur mixing together ... "I'm not taking part, not taking part" ... but still get involved ... "Don't step on me! Don't step on me" ... "Bong" the sound of a gong, the horde of rabbits disappears without trace. The room is completely empty, the skinny little rabbit is lying on the floor its bright red internal organs in another place. The sunlight is flickering like a gas lamp....

It was already five o'clock in the afternoon when I woke up. The remaining light in the room seemed ready to leave at any moment. The back of my head was a little painful, like seventeen glasses of beer and a nightmare had been dumped there.

I took another look at my room. What a mess it had become! The little dinner table was turned upside down, plates were smashed into pieces, a soup bowl had left a concave hollow in the wall, and now lay at the base of the wall. Bandit was squatting there licking the bowl greedily.... I would have to spend two hours to clear all this up, or at least an hour and a half. Turtlehead and Hero had disappeared without trace.

I only realised what a precious treasure peace and quiet is after meeting Turtlehead. I was able to live a quiet life again because Turtlehead didn't come round for a long time. Turtlehead only came once since that Sunday, carrying a pile of new plates. He asked a few words about Widow, and said it seemed that Widow really was lost. Apart from going to work, I carried on assembling the colour television and feeding the rabbit. Sometimes I thought of Turtlehead, but I hoped he wouldn't pay me a visit.

Bandit was getting fatter by the day. Under my instruction, he had formed the habit of shitting in the same place. Probably the thing he most disliked was having a bath. The smell he most disliked was that of shampoo. But if he wanted to continue living with me, he had to get rid of his foul smell. I was very patient in my efforts to persuade Bandit.

With his increasing weight, Bandit became cleverer and cleverer. The more I drove him away, the more he shrank into a ball. Occasionally, probably when he was feeling happy, he jumped up in the room once, or at most twice. This was Bandit's idea of running. His appetite had far surpassed my original expectations. Apart from sleeping, he ate and ate. Half a kilo of green vegetables cost twenty cents (and in this area, where there was only block after block of buildings, where could I go to find vegetables?) Bandit's main course was a big bunch of green vegetables. In addition to that, he needed three big handfuls of rice to chew before as a snack. It wasn't unlike the way foreigners chew gum. I wasn't earning much, and apart from making ends meet, I had to buy spare parts. With the addition of Bandit, it was just like having an extra mouth to feed.

I grew increasingly convinced that at the very least it was no bad thing that Widow run away without trace. It was really not worth Turtlehead cursing her every time he came. So she's run away. It was just like when I first saw them, I decided to raise them, so I just raised them. It was just like that and that's all there was to it.

In order to satisfy Bandit's appetite, I asked a colleague to get some grass for me when he went to the park. I would mend his incredibly decrepit tape recorder free of charge as a reward. About one week after I had mended his tape recorder, he brought a small bunch of green grass worth ten *yuan* (the park-keeper fined him ten *yuan* for "destroying the lawn"). Apart from this, he wanted to find out the most recent gossip about Turtlehead and Hero from me.

"I've heard that Hero's with a guy called Wu Gong. The guy is a writer. He wrote 'Three Ways of Getting a Divorce'. Heard of it?"

"No." I lifted Bandit's two ears. Bandit immediately stretched from head to foot, and maintained this beautiful posture. I took a look and put him down by the side of the green grass. This was first grass that Bandit had ever seen.

"Apparently this Wu Gong was the boyfriend of Hero's younger sister. Hey, they're pretty good at making themselves scarce. Turtlehead can't find them at all. Turtlehead even let all the students of his class out to look for them, forty or fifty people were wandering the city, and at last he found them. Now it's really a mess. Turtlehead is very angry. Hero is even angrier.... Is it true?" He looked at me eagerly, with a fixed expression. If I had just said yes, his face would certainly have shown some excitement.

I told him that I hadn't seen Turtlehead for a long time. I really didn't know, really, didn't know. Bandit was shameless, even before my colleague left he had finished the grass completely and still seemed hungry. My colleague smiled awkwardly and said he'd bring some more next time.

The next time was ten days later. I'd almost forgotten his promise. He brought a slightly larger bunch of grass and the conclusion of Turtlehead and Hero's story. They had completely broken up. Turtlehead now usually stayed at home on his own. He was not even willing to teach his class. He looked like he'd been castrated. When he left, my colleague said that, as a friend, I should go and see him.

I went to visit Turtlehead twice, but he wasn't in. At last, I left him a note:

> Turtlehead, The colour television is assembled, come and watch it.
>
> Spare Parts

The colour television had been ready for some time, but Turtlehead hadn't come. Bandit was my only company in front of the television. Bandit was squatting beside me having munched lots of vegetables. He was modest in front of the colour screen. One day, I looked up the entry for 'rabbit' in a dictionary:

Rabbit. Long-eared, short-tailed mammal, with a cleft upper lips, and extended back legs; runs fast.

Bandit matched the definitions of a rabbit except for the last qualification. Looking at his fat bottom, at his unwillingness even to walk, I thought of Widow. I thought Widow was much more like a rabbit.

I saw Turtlehead at last. He came accompanied by Hero. From quite a distance I could hear them calling out: Spare Parts, Spare Parts! Bandit, Bandit! It was not a good time for them to come because it was just time for dinner. Turtlehead said into my left ear, I really miss you, Spare Parts! Hero said into my right ear, I really miss you, Spare Parts!

I immersed myself in preparing dinner. They marvelled at the colour television and said it was even better than a National Panasonic. Then they chased Bandit for fun. Hero held a vegetable leaf, and Bandit stood up to catch the leaf. Why, Bandit really wasn't like a rabbit at all.

Turtlehead was busy saying that he wanted to find a new wife for Bandit, then he was cursing Widow, calling her a bitch. He told Bandit to rely on him for everything, and guaranteed that he'd find him a much more beautiful and placid female rabbit than Widow had been. Hero said, yes we should; after all, our Bandit is an adult now.

"Hey, Spare Parts, aren't rabbits on heat in March or April?" Hero asked me.

"I think it's — March. You two, lay the table!"

Now the time came for them to praise my cooking skills. Three or four dishes, plus beer, and 'CCTV News' on the colour television. The only problem was Hero's piercing voice.

"I can smell something nasty ... really, can you smell it?" Hero picked up the beer glass.

"Probably Bandit peed, it's very smelly." Turtlehead wrinkled up his nose too.

Now I smelt it too. I had stuffed-up nose and hated to disturb our dinner.

The three of us followed the trail of the stench with our noses. We found that the stench was emanating from the cardboard boxes in the corner. Most of my furniture consisted of cardboard boxes. They were piled full of old clothes, books and dated newspapers. I had seven or eight cardboard boxes of family belongings. Turtlehead helped me to move them away one by one.

Turtlehead moved one box and suddenly froze on the spot.

A tiny little rabbit was stuck between two cardboard boxes, the body already decomposed and giving off a foul odour.

BEAUTIFUL LANDSCAPE

NAN FANG

translated by Katie Hill

There's nothing in my life that's particularly worth talking about — I've never even known where I saw this sentence: repeated details bestowed mystery on mysterious things. An arm of this world, which waves exaggeratedly whilst making a joke, yet accidentally whisks away the white-brocade cover of the Gods, I don't even regard as particularly uncommon. But then I am a timid person of no faith whatsoever, and it has never even occurred to me to glimpse beyond the boundless limitations. Nevertheless, my life is always entangled with endless repeated details; in fact, I get utterly exhausted, my weariness measuring the distance between the books which I am gradually losing sight of.

About forty years ago, I came across a volume in a bookshop and it is that very volume which eventually made me decide to write this piece. At first glance, the volume had the refinement of a forger, which was a far cry from the work of a Song printer, and on the edge of the pages there were two collectors' seals, which were neither particularly noticeable, nor would they have reduced the suspicion of someone who had picked it up by chance — so, after studying it carefully, I couldn't control my excitement. I was certain that the Qin style characters of this stamp, which were so ornate as to be excessively refined, were really the elegant name rumoured to be that of the master of the Linglang Esoteric Studio; the two lines of small hand-writing also exactly revealed its origins: it had actually been handed down from the Fei family of the South — the legendary Fei family, renowned throughout the South.

However, the colour of the other stamp was already very faded, the rough Han style seal worn out at the edges of the characters, making it very difficult to recognize the words on it. The seal, rather smaller than usual and not to modern people's taste, occupied an empty corner of the page. The studio name of the owner seemed to hint at some sort of pattern, a kind of terrible symbol. I suddenly had a vague inkling of who it might be. I thought about it for a while, but I still couldn't think of his name. Still, from the sudden beating of my heart, I had an ominous feeling that I had come across something of the highest value. I carefully and quietly put the book into my jacket and took it home.

My poor cramped little study already housed two volumes of Song dynasty editions, which were rumoured to be the only ones of their kind in the country. However, people suspected that they were cheap imitations by Ming dynasty craftsmen. The well-known Xichun Studio began this refined and profitable business several hundred years ago. I don't like to boast about my scholarship, but I stuck firmly to my original opinions, which brought me one or two enemies. The later reproductions of Song dynasty annotated classics, *Liujingzhuan* — those made by the assistants of the Lu family in Jinming county, their eyesight fading in the feeble candlelight of the Baojing Studio — always included brash lines of notes, in small characters; they lacked even the patience or the courage to try to disguise their real origins. Their forefathers of the Wanli reign had preserved the crude, impetuous style of their military background, and it seemed that what they clasped in their hands were not fine, small block-carving knives but the crude steel scimitars of the battlefield. They unscrupulously pilfered postscripts from other people's collections and stamped their own collectors' seal on them. There were always traces — flaws on the fine paper — which made their work a laughing stock. The classics they reproduced met with the open suspicion from scholars. Then they turned to printing unofficial histories and anecdotes, but even these were looked on askance.

The classics published and circulated by the northern Cao family, because of the suspicion that a family member had been involved in cheating during the imperial examinations, were also boycotted by scholars. Before the Lu family turned to fiction, they started to print operas and other trivial little things. What is worth mentioning though, is that, in the reign of Hongzhi, the scholars secretly circulated romances. This was chiefly the bright idea of Cao Bixiu, the second son of the household. A secret treasure in the family collection was a unique fragmentary edition of the *Sanshui Xiaodu* from the Dezong period which was handed down through the generations. In the same way that people enthusiastically swarmed after the family head, a strong, upright character, when he went on his travels, this precious Tang dynasty edition, which was as valuable as several cities, attracted the covetous attention of notorious thieves from all over the country, inspiring thrilling adventures. In the fourteenth year of Hongzhi, it even caused a bloody murder. Some people say that the incident was connected to the southern Fei family. But the mandarin, Fei Jihuai, whose family have been officials for generations, would not be likely to get involved in such dreadful acts, so there are also some contemporaries who disagreed with the idea, dismissing it as idle gossip. Nevertheless, the *Sanshui Xiaodu* is believed to have mysteriously vanished. Besides, what I want to talk about is something else altogether.

In the Winter of 1934, I felt as though I had been infected by scholarship, and became detached and withdrawn. In order to throw off this state, every Sunday afternoon, I would go to the campus of Beijing University. I was a skinny, sickly youth, and there I would meet up with several other similar young fellows who were in the same boat.

The thick snow was dancing in the lonely air above the lake and the light was gradually fading, when someone pointed me to a young man wearing little round-rimmed glasses and called him over. This person was quite unexceptional, with the shiny round face of a university professor and a shrill sharp voice. I noticed his face was also already quite puffy, showing traces of an unfortunate illness. He told me he had heard that I was in the process of composing some writings on logic. Pausing for a moment without expression, he then went on to say that he had also heard that I had in my collection a valuable edition of the Song classic *Dajingzhuan* printed by the Xichun Studio from the Ming Wanli period. He uttered this sentence slowly, pausing between each word.

"In actual fact," I replied, "it's a unique edition from the Song, two volumes of the large format edition, a refined print from the Lanjian Pavilion in the Xining period of the Northern Song."

"A unique example of personal conviction," he said decisively.

He walked away unconvinced. I enquired of the others, and discovered that he was Lu Zhidan of Jinming county, the sole modern human relic of Mr Lu, the owner of the Kuojing Studio. I managed to control my impulse to pursue him and dispute the matter. At this time I had already heard that this fellow Lu had been publicly spreading rumours about me.

On the other hand, I remembered that once when I went to visit the Laixun Studio, the owner had told me something, the kind of tedious gossip which had already reached my ears. I didn't know whether it would be suitable to mention it here, because I had sworn to keep it a secret. It sounded like an obscene juvenile joke. What's more, the owner loved collecting vulgar tales, and this could easily have provided material for his coarse imagination.

However, I did admire his collection of many editions of the famous and wickedly erotic novel, *Jinpingmei,* which took up half his bookcase. Especially the *fully illustrated* Chongzhen edition. It was really difficult to believe that the lifelike illustrations on the paper were simply a series of ancient artifacts; they seemed more like handmade copies, just recently, lovingly lifted from the press by some enthusiastic apprentice. I even imagined I could detect the surreptitious inky fragrance from a secret printing studio. I thought of a good joke. What if my lovelorn romantic friends were to receive letters on paper decorated with images from this book. Imagine the embarrassed state they would find themselves in? How would these self-styled poets manage to maintain their stricken looks, and pretend to shed bitter tears? Worried that my host would not have the generosity to permit this, I used a little knife which I kept with me and, taking advantage of a brief absence while he called his assistant to bring some fresh tea, I stealthily cut out one of the illustrations.

There was no doubt that this was theft. Throughout a whole day of restless misgivings, I consoled myself with the thought that stealing from books was after all the elegant crime of an intellectual. It was nothing to make a fuss about.

The next day, early in the morning, the assistant came to my lodgings and passed on an invitation from his master, asking me to come and share some moments of connoisseurship with him. Naturally I thought this was merely a pretence and that the best thing would be to confess the whole thing to his courteous master.

On the way, I took a detour through a few winding little roads, and eventually confronted his mansion. In order to drag out the time, I first stood on the doorstep and carefully studied it. It was a detached wood and brick house with two floors, a plaster phoenix roosting in the eaves with one of its wings hanging down lifelessly and its head gazing blankly towards the sky. The warped eaves and scattered bits of broken tile, and the mottle of moss and fungus on the whitewashed walls preserved the nostalgia-inducing style of an old Ming printing house. Going up the staircase, I had only a vague impression of the outside view, but a few other details caught my attention. On the steep narrow staircase, the walls were streaked with black tracings of smoke. In the corridor were stacks of dusty bookshelves piled high, and a few pots of withered flowers.

In a poorly lit study, Mr Juchuan got up out of a stiff wooden armchair to greet me. We looked at several very ordinary Jiaqing period block-printed editions from Chongqing, including amongst them a thick volume of the *Shilin Guangji*. He got the books down from the shelves with complete carelessness, handing them to me already open. I had noticed that I was not the only guest to be treated in this manner; he had indeed cultivated a deliberate air of negligence and languor. He pointed to a book at will and spoke to me in an utterly exaggerated, throw-away manner.

"My vulgar library has never been used for scholarship, but for the collecting. One book is the same as any other, or the same as the entire thoughtless circulation of all the literature in the universe. This work, as you can see, is a complete hand-written copy of the *Xufu Gubian* on silk paper."

He pointed to another book, saying, "And that one was originally a pile of tattered, broken pages, but in fact they're a single book. Fate separated them and then got them together again on that tiny little shelf."

"Fate." I couldn't help picking up on what he said. I thought of a proverb, then said it out loud. "The river of Babylon flows along, while on Holy Mount Zion, all is still."*

"Oh, really," he turned round towards me as though it was the first time he had noticed me. "Misleading pagan tales, oh, endless motion and rest, the constant cycle of nature — Master Zhu's ridiculous, obscure, misleading tales."

"No, it's Zhang Zai," I corrected him.

"Oh, Zhang Zai," he muttered, nodding his head, turning to flick through the bookcase. "'Following the spirit to exaggerate expression, glorifying letters to go against the flow' — your love of scholarship has already turned into a talent for words. When the river flows, it just takes its natural course, leading those foot-washers to wherever they will end up."

I didn't waste the opportunity and quickly followed on his words, "Your fine illustration will also pass into the hands of playboys, most suitably, a group of strong bodies who will revive the real spirit of the illustration."

"You're speaking from experience."

* Pascal, *Pensées*, taken from the Chinese translation by He Zhaowu.

"Yes, experience. But not with the attitudes of those Cheng brothers who remain unflustered when pretty women sat on their laps, but in the brothel, in the real bed of a pretty prostitute."

"I can't find it. It's impossible to read the same book a second time. You've got nothing to worry about. No one can find the original or proof enough to accuse another person. It has already disappeared along with the pages which have been turned over."

"You mean ... you can never step into the same river."

"Look, you and your learned eloquence. Books are like rivers, endlessly flowing, overtaking or disappearing into the flow of time."

An orangey-red light from the evening sky seeped into the front of the room. Looking up out through two oppressive high windows, you could see it, a vast expanse of crimson. We were standing in the shadows at the back of the room.

"You invited me to come and take pleasure in your books, now I understand — it's just for your idle amusement or to satisfy your hollow, pessimistic way of thinking. I feel as though it's running through my whole body."

"Not entirely. I want to give you a printed illustration as a present. You'll love it when you see it. Perhaps it'll suit the taste of your playboy friends."

"Oh, they're only rootless seeds floating on the wave of carnal desire — in fact, just nihilists."

What I took home can only be described as shameless piece of erotica. Supposing Mr Juchuan had not told me a story, I wouldn't have been moved by such curiosity, such deep disgust, such violent alarm. I felt cheated that people had been slandering me behind my back and so bringing me into discredit. I carefully put aside his suggestion of using the picture for decorative writing paper, placing ridicule to adorn or show off in the space on the edge of the pages, distributing them to those sad, desperate practitioner friends of mine in the gathering darkness. After just one day, I had lost my enthusiasm for the idea, although I also didn't want to thwart the good intentions of the owner of the Laixun Studio.

Many an evening, I brought the image out under the light and said over and over again: this is impossible — after all, it's nothing more than a bit of spicy, unfounded gossip. Supposing the naked woman with little white feet propped up on the washboard was a latter-day Cao Mo'er, and the desperate, love-thirsty dancing Shiva was really the dandy descended from the Lu family, then the gruesome details of sexual intercourse were most certainly some kind of set-up by an intermediate scandalmonger. What's more, the part with the details was swamped by a conspiracy, which spat out its dreadful silver thread. Who the last victims were, it was difficult to say for certain, whether it was this couple of sluttish sister-in-laws who were rolling about gleefully on a narrow wooden board over a basin of water or the actual rhetoric of so-called "incest" twisting around passionately. Or perhaps it was even an innocent person who was the object of slanderous rumours, since, with nowhere to go, the only way forward is to spread rumours yourself....

This picture was probably the only woodcut print that was not an illustration. I hadn't sworn to anyone that I wouldn't reveal the secret, but I swore to the void that I'd keep it. I nearly said it out loud. However, the silence all around me dispersed my train of thought. Somebody out there was beginning to recite poetry. I moved to a seat by the window and, leaning against the wooden window-ledge, admired the lake outside. Snow covered the surface and embankment of the lake, making it difficult to distinguish the line where the water met the edge of the bank. The snow silently screened my field of vision; a strip of grey light and endless silvery-white dots scurried and danced.

Someone was speaking loudly in my ear. "Vernacular, this year's vogue, with no texture at all." I took no notice.

Lu Zhidan was surrounded by a crowd of enthusiastic female admirers, asking for his autograph. But he was just looking back in my direction. I supposed that if I waited a bit, who knows, he would have taken the latest lucky ones in his arm and hastily passed, stepping through the deep snow along the confusing zigzagging lanes. It seemed to precisely point out the proof of the horrible rumours that had been spread, this reputation of his as a poet, which, combined with the dissipation of a spoilt talent, constructed a mythic yet ridiculous impression. In fact, he wasn't like the ancestors who stole from other people's libraries. He stole for the glory of debauchery, in order to win the frivolous kindness which attracted women's sighs. There was blatant, out-and-out cursing which made him sound like a short-haired dog doted on by women. He certainly had his own reasons for cursing other people, yet everyone sympathized with the real loser: a waiter wearing uniform, bringing wine for everyone on a tray. For a moment my view was blocked. When I saw Lu Zhidan again, he was already standing in front of me. He invited me to have a look at the 'genuine' Xining period edition of the *Liujingtu* which was in their family collection. Since I had already attracted his hostility, of course I refused.

"Oh but please don't refuse, and let me introduce you to Miss Cao."

He almost thrust a girl into my hands. A tall girl with her hair back, wearing earrings, stood in front of me, a slight smile turned towards me. I noticed her long, beautiful slim legs, a pair of dainty feet in glistening silvery and gold high-heeled and pointed shoes, delicately wrought with fine lacework. Lu Zhidan was also to one side, smiling. But I wasn't sure if it was a nasty mocking smile or a friendly, good-natured smile. I had always been a solitary young fellow, and I couldn't help feeling embarrassed in front of everyone, with this girl standing before me. She noticed this and suggested we go for a walk outside in the snow. As she said it, she took my arm with the kind of natural, relaxed manner which led me to fancy that we were already a pair of faithful lovers.

After we had circled the lake once or twice, we started to kiss. I saw our two lines of fresh footprints in the snow. A pair of crows circling above our heads let out a plaintive cry. However, they couldn't be seen very clearly. They were no more than a pair of little black dots. I profited from a quiet moment and said to her:

"I still don't know who you are." But my mouth was immediately stopped and I gradually closed my eyes and forgot about everything. When I opened them again, I found she was staring at me intensely. I knew I had already fallen in love with her. We hugged each other tightly in the snow, stumbling as we ran along. Then we fell over into it. On our way home, I asked her her name.

"Bu Guang," she replied.[*]

I remembered that story and said, "I am the old mandarin retiring from the dangerous path, please sing me a ditty in the tune of Zheng Gong."

We carried on walking aimlessly by the side of the lake. Passing a few trees, and a broken wall, our head and shoulders were covered in white. I saw a thin layer of snow-flakes on the tip of her brow, her fresh red mouth revealing a glimpse of white teeth, smiling mournfully. She quietly spoke in my ear, "I wish you were Scholar Tao, I want to sing 'Beautiful Landscape' which you wrote for me."

This made me think of a fox-spirit story I had once read. But thinking about it at the time, I realized at once that I had no need to worry any more — that evening was the most important night in my

[*] See Wang Jingqi, *Dushutangli Weibiji*, of the Qing dynasty.

life. I had never dreamed of going out with such a beautiful girl. Fate had never taken any notice of me, and now it was rewarding me with the loveliest gift.

"When we get to the post house, then I'll be Scholar Tao. Let's go."

The snow was falling ever more heavily. The world seemed to sink down into a circular movement of silver. I felt as though we had passed through a labyrinth of alleyways. I reached out for her arm and lightly called her name but the only answer I got was a quiet swishing noise. Suddenly, I felt an empty space next to me and all there was left was my solitary figure walking alone in an boundless white world. I stopped and used all the energy I could muster to search the surrounding countryside, and then I saw her ahead, running in the snow. I chased and caught her tightly by the waist not letting her leave me again.

"Sometimes, I feel this world is not real. Now I've found out that you're not real," I muttered.

"Qin Ruolan, please don't abandon me and humiliate me the next minute."

"Look, the moon has come out. Wait a moment, until the moon is at its fullest and then you'll be my Lord Han Xizai."

But the moonlight was quickly engulfed once more by the snowy night. The sky was wrapped in a shroud of ashen light. I thought back to what had just happened and asked her: "Why did my enemy Lu Zhidan introduce you to me? Is it possible that he was waiting at the banquet to humiliate my Han Xizai? Also, he called you Miss Cao."

"He treats me as Cao Mo'er. From your point of view, I am your insecure Qin Ruolan; from his point of view, I am his innocent Cao Mo'er. I hope you two will be friends."

It seemed as though I was looking at that picture. My heart was pierced with pain. I drew back my hands and put them into my pockets.

"Cao Mo'er, people say that's Lu Zhidan's aunt and that they are very close."

She didn't answer me. This time, in a speck of light shining in her eyes, I noticed someone, with his head down, his hands in his pockets, passing through the silent snow all alone, and disappearing into an small alleyway. It was Lu Zhidan. It gave me a start.

I felt her trembling as she held me tightly, her wet hair pressing against my burning cheeks. We had arrived. While I was pulling out my keys I could still feel her shaking like a leaf.

"Cao Mo'er, I don't want anyone to share you. *I* am Lu Zhidan, and the person who has just walked past is Scholar Tao, who ended up with nothing when the feast had ended."

"Quick, open the door, our feast is waiting for us!" She pulled my coat, and said in a muffled voice, "I'm freezing to death."

I don't know with what strength I managed to carry her upstairs. In fact she was very light, like a soft brocade quilt, puffed up softly against my lapels. Many years have gone by, and I still feel ashamed. I only thought about myself at that time. Then, I was an innocent, immature young fellow and I felt ashamed. As for my knowledge of love, apart from kissing, I had no idea about anything else. What I knew of the rest of it I had learned from watching films. That day I was so rushed and foolish. I went up to the bed she was lying on with my face flushed bright red (my whole body was probably flushed). She had already taken off her clothes and was murmuring something with her eyes closed, her body writhing. I saw a circle of tired shadow beneath her eyelids. She called to me in a low voice to come quickly. But she called me Lu Zhidan.

The snow was falling even more heavily, the window reflected the grey light of the snow. The desolate snowy evening seemed as though it would go on and on forever. I carried the basin of clear water, picked up Cao Mo'er and put her on the washboard. That made me sink down, my brain lost in an empty world and I became vaguely aware of something soft rising up and then pushing down on me, two long thin white shadows, suddenly twitching in the void.

When we had warmed up a little after lying under the quilt, she hugged me and said, "Now I'll sing 'Beautiful Landscape' for you, but you must hold me tightly."* I held her tightly, stroking her smooth skin and kissing her breasts, listening to her sing that song in my ear:

"A good match, a bad match,
    all you need is a good night at the inn."

Afterwards, I went to sleep in a haze. I dreamt I saw Qin Ruolan, sobbing, with tears streaming down her face, leaning close against me. I had uneasy premonitions the entire night.

On the second of December 1934, I was suddenly woken by a loud knocking at the door. Sitting up, I felt my head splitting with pain. I fumbled around with difficulty for the shoes under the bed. I banged my shoulder several times on the wall by the stairs. I opened the main door downstairs. There was a person, standing in the snow, holding

---

* *Yuhu Wanshui Qinghua*, of the Song dynasty, at the end of which there is the opera 'Scholar Tao wrote "Beautiful Landscape" when Drunk'.

out his hand to me. I looked at the sky, the snow had stopped. There wasn't a trace of life on the streets, an icy wind blew through my hair. I asked him to come into the room upstairs. When he came in, he tripped over and kicked an empty bottle, sending it rolling down by the foot of the wall.

It was him. The person I could only just see clearly was him, as I had already predicted he would come. It was only after some while that I came to completely. At this moment, he was clasping his hands, as though very patient, or maybe completely at a loss. I asked him to sit down on the only chair in the room. Then I guess I asked him how come he had come to visit me on this freezing cold, clear morning. He looked at me, taken aback. He asked me to recall the arrangement we had made yesterday. I thought for a while. I seemed to remember something, but still had to ask him to make it clearer. "OK, then," he said, "you must see that you have already researched the *real* edition of the Xining period *Liujingzhuan*."

Now I was completely awake and everything came back to me. But all I felt was a boundless sadness. The whole thing was nothing but a warm seductive nightmare.

"Yes, Lu Zhidan, you are no longer my enemy. You let me see the best edition of the *Liujingzhuan*. I will acknowledge this as the happiest memory of my life. However, it belongs to you. And what I will collect is only the scholarly career that makes my face pale and weak like silk paper. We can't afford any more time. I can assure you, they're going to end up at the paper recycling factory which is much more appropriate for them."

He came over to me once more to shake my hand. It was still freezing cold. Then he went over to a bookshelf by the door. He pulled out the volume and put it into his coat pocket, then reached out his hand to take the picture which was leaning against the books. Before going out of the room, he turned around, saying, "See you on campus this Sunday afternoon."

The sound of his steps going down the stairs echoed for ages while I sat still on the edge of the bed, mournful, as if an old tune still lingered in my dazed, lost soul. The words 'campus' and 'Sunday' sounded repeatedly on my lips but I knew we could never meet again.

Forty years have passed. Mount Zion has not been washed away by the running waters of Babylon, but has remained steadfast as a rock, unchanged in every way. My days are steady and repetitive. In the studio, I slowly grow towards old age. But my appearance doesn't show the clock of mankind, cruelly, deceitfully rustling forward. My clock had already stopped for ever, one morning forty years ago. Scholar's little round glasses have already been added to the bridge of my nose. But books, like smoke and ashes, provide me with darkness, desert, a deep river-bed, a truly empty void, storms even. Moreover, everything swirls round more and more quickly, sweeping me up with it, until I can no longer differentiate its distance. I, one of mankind, am in fact no more than a tiny grain of sand, disappearing in the boundlessness of sand.

Then, one day, I came across a valuable volume in a bookshop, which once again brought my memories flooding back, even though it was only for a brief moment. When I went home, I opened the book and a gust of wind (just like forty years ago, a cold winter wind sweeping through the door), blew the pages, dancing and fluttering. A short note on silk paper, dropped onto the ground. That's the tail-end of this story, a ditty to the Zheng Gong tune:

> I recall how in days gone by, with burning incense,
> We made our earnest and sincere vows of love;
> When I saw off his horse and carriage,
> I shed forlorn and dismal tears.
> I've longed so desperately for letters from him
> But he's sent me no greetings at all.
> At the very mention of that fickle faithless man,
> I can't help becoming fretful, seething with anger.
> Oh it grieves me so terribly!
> Oh it grieves me so terribly!
> He's left me behind, so that dawn and dusk
> I suffer all there is to suffer of the flighty singing girl's punishment

Yes, I abandoned you, Cao Mo'er; but in order to preserve my love. I gave my love for you to the devil's platonic soul.

THE DONGLIN ACADEMY

Nan Fang

translated by Chen Yanbing

A poor scholar of the Tang or Ming Dynasty, having affronted the emperor through his search for grammatical and lexical mistakes in ancient books, escaped through history to seek hiding in our time. Such a story is simply unbelievable, yet indeed, it was recorded in an obscure work by some scholars morbidly obsessed by anecdotes. The story can be told another way. Whether it was an indefatigable dream to occupy the university lecture theatre or just pure cynicism, Gu Manzi, a scholar of ancient languages and history, paid no attention to worldly affairs beyond his study. An unexpected incident, however, interrupted his dream. Before the incident, his attitude toward reality was that of general and abstract suspicion; therefore, faced with real and unexpected trouble, he began to feel anger and resentment. With no other recourse, he went to the police station at the appointed time. There he explained repeatedly yet in vain to two ignorant officers, trying to convince them of his innocence; to clarify his point, he even engaged in discussion. But what he said only deepened their suspicion. Back at home, restless and flustered, he found it impossible to confine himself to his desk. Finally, he mustered the remains of his courage and dug out that little article. Shaking his head in dejection, he began to pore over the part that had been taken as evidence. As he read, however, he forgot completely what his purpose had been, and with the meticulousness — or fastidiousness — of a scholar, started to edit the article: a few more details here, a deletion or an expansion of a paragraph there, mistakes pointed out; he even unwisely added his own sad rebukes — the kind that only an obtuse scholar would make when pressed by the darkness of the world and the corruption of reality.

He worked for five days. This unlooked-for labour took up a full five days. He had no food and no sleep, but experienced five days of

* The Donglin Academy: A local study group founded in Wuxi in 1604 by Gu Xiancheng and other members of the Donglin Party, a loosely organized political group of middle or lower-middle class officials during the Wanli Reign of the late Ming Dynasty.

startlingly solid concentration. At dawn on the sixth day, he stood up from his desk. Outside, the houses along the street still huddled together in the city dwellers' only luxury — their sleep. A few sparrows twittered on the eaves and flew away. He rubbed his eyes, not because he was assaulted by sleepiness, but as if he had just woken from a good sleep. He felt relieved, as if he'd just shaken off a sense of calamity and fear that had been crowding in on him for centuries. Life would bring him new hope, for he was now filled with the blinding joy of having overcome himself.

Nevertheless, reality never forgets. It only winks ignobly from time to time at those who are sinking deeper into trouble, and, sniggering, leads them down into a cul-de-sac. Now that the dam of mental exhaustion, which had resulted from his sailing in the dust and the shadow of history, had crumbled under the flood of fortuitous inspiration and blind confidence, Gu Manzi became uncharacteristically officious and boastful. This brought with it a genuine sense of prosperity and good fortune. Several universities opened their gates to him, a few others dropped tempting hints and even made promises. Though a few conservative schools seemed to be still waiting, however, his conquering ambition led him to believe that blind luck sooner or later would find the keys to their locks. In one lecture, he expounded on Zhu Yuanzhang, the first emperor of the Ming Dynasty. He praised Zhu's wit and sagacity, and then with the impartiality of an obtuse scholar went on to examine the cruelty in his nature as a governor. In the course of his exposition, he outlined the view that the relationship between history and reality is not an insinuation between two totally different kinds of knowledge, but a relentless repetition of the same essence. Another morning, standing at the lectern, he saw the quietly approaching spring on the lawn outside, and an unprecedented smile broke out on his pale face. Noticing this unsettling change, a few of his loyal disciples began to be concerned and whispered among themselves. But Gu Manzi paid no attention. He summarized and explicated beautifully the Donglin Movement towards the end of the Ming Dynasty; for the first time making a comparison between conspiracy and reality, and almost reaching a dangerous conclusion. Nevertheless, after he got home, he recalled the inspiration and thoughts he had had that day and felt unnerved. However, up to this point, he was still swimming in the suddenly free and smooth-flowing river of his scholarly reasoning, unaware that a net of conspiracy was slowly closing in on him.

As we know, insubstantial thoughts are rarely the foundation of good judgement, but our judgement may make idle use of such thoughts to explain itself. Gu Manzi's understanding of things and aloofness from them were no exception, it was only that in methodology he mixed thoughts and things together, thereby giving rise to a deceptive sophistry and confusion. He hypothesized that all men were one and that all things could magically become one; the occurrences of history were nothing more than the destiny played out in reality. He spoke of far-fetched stories from lurid unofficial accounts of history as established events; he dramatically brought elements of hero and jester, of human cruelty and generosity into the character of single person. As a consequence, when reading a book, he became one of the characters within it, or his thoughts became but one part of the thoughts that were spun out in the exposition.

So, when he one day stumbled upon a particular historical anecdote and decided that he actually *was* the scholar who had escaped the imperial court, we should find it neither strange nor unlikely.

The city's daytime clamour had relented and the twilight transformed the unpleasantly nondescript character of the neighbourhood. At the end of the day, Gu Manzi felt exhausted from hauling things around in the warehouse of his mind, but he also felt the relaxation of its having been cleared out. He did not follow the disaster of the crowds fighting for a place on the bus, but instead looking furtively about him, walked all the way home. He was now leisure itself. He was the mystery of a street whose setting had been altered by the sunset. Moreover, it seemed that, after a day of introduction, fabrication, evaluation, and worried insinuation, Gu Xiancheng, that Donglin academic who had turned up in his words and exposition, had been injected into his body, and his life had undergone a transformation.* It was as if he were now no longer scholar walking on a hollow street in the 1980s, but had become scholar in a white frock with the unhurried grace of ancient sages and the aloofness of tradition — a resigned official who was sick with the world, who was cynically watching a life to which those eyes far away from him were so accustomed. Turning a street corner, he heard someone calling his name. Looking back, he realized he was mistaken. A middle-aged man with the name his mind had seized upon had already stopped, and, showing on his face the usual delight of impatience of being suddenly called upon, was making small talk with

* Gu Xiancheng (or Ku Hsien-ch'eng), 1550–1612, the most prominent figure of the Donglin Movement.

an acquaintance. Gu Manzi shook his head, as much bemused as he was surprised by his own illusion. But as he passed the doorway of a privately-owned restaurant, someone unmistakably caught him by the arm, pushed inside and forced to a table. He was almost angry, but realising that in the past he had often been respected — or perhaps pitied — here, and given that he was being offered food, something he could perhaps take advantage of in the future, he unhappily suppressed his displeasure. He was utterly sick of the upstart's ignorance as well as the government's connivance. Yet the habitual caution nurtured by poverty restrained him. Eating his usual diet — cabbage, soup and a bit of rice — he swallowed the owner's sarcastic flattery, and put up with his showing-off. He wasted almost an hour.

A seemingly fortuitous shift in the course of events, an unnoticeably small movement, such as the dropping of a button, the appearance of a black mark on one's skin, are, in fact, all indications of fate's determination not to yield to human will. Most people would take the chance and disregard such signs as simply their own wishful thinking. But not Gu Manzi. He would rather believe superstitiously in the mystery of such miracles. For the first time in months after that sleepless, energetic week, Gu Manzi entered the sweet country of good sleep. He dreamed, but as soon as he woke up things in his dreams fled without a trace. Habit forced himself strenuously to try and recall them, but to no avail, leaving him anxious and upset. In his anxiety, he tore the cuff of his shirt while putting it on, and felt a slight pain. He found a faint ring mark on his wrist, as if his skin had been tightly bound by something. The whole day he remained flustered and dismayed. No, it was more a foreboding fear; in his mind which was stuffed with human knowledge and cluttered with useless odd ideas, he could not relinquish a vague sense of approaching doom. But his desk provided with him a temporary harbour of safety and rest. Sitting at it, he closely examined the inappropriateness of his own behaviour, and wondered if his scholastic thinking, for all its caution, had by some chance crossed the boundary of the 'non-political' which he had drawn for himself. It was only later that he realized he had completely forgotten his conversation at the police station. What was worse, he had ignored the unnecessary existence of the two officers and turned a deaf ear to the nonsense of their arrogance and intimidation. He was disheartened and at the same time afraid. But what had been done could not be undone. Fate was about to exact her revenge on the one who lived in the shadow of her power.

Conferences, speeches, writing monographs, preparing for lectures — his schedule was full, and he had almost no time for himself. That suppressed his worries a little. One day rumours spread that he was going to be promoted to the position of professor. The excitement robbed him of several nights of sleep. But then he meditated critically on his own vanity. All this time, however, the anxiety of terror in heart, like a devil, had never left him completely alone. Both in his mind and in his daily actions, he had become two faced: there was this devilish terror and an undisciplined passion which he suddenly felt toward the world. He lived a double life: at night he was an exile hiding in fear, during the day a revolutionary brimming with sudden inspiration. In the classroom, he was Plato, he was Gu Xiancheng, and the classroom became the Institute of Athens, or the Donglin Academy; and his students and friends were none other than that group of cynical, sarcastic literati frustrated with the imperial court; they were the sages, the pitiful creatures equipped with the blind courage and confidence of knowledge but taunted by real life.

Recalling the time when he was summoned to the police station, Gu Manzi felt it was so distant that he was almost lost, but still a cold sweat dripped down his back. He tried all he could to recall the course of events and details of that day, of that conversation and the officers' manner, hoping to make sense of it all. But, alas, all was a blur now. Reality had assumed the materiality of a piece of iron alloyed with all the chance-taking ideas in his illusion. He had thought he could climb out of the bottle of reality behind that glass sheet of transparency, but now only found himself slipping and sliding hopelessly on the smooth wall. He tried every way to get out, plotting strategies, studying their conversation, and gauging the intention of his opponents; he even hoped that he could look upon those two ignorant officers as yes-men with human failings. Finally he grew impatient, and gathered up the death-defying, self-abandoning courage of a victor. Throwing everything aside, he decided to let events take their own course. Nevertheless, the day moved like a slow train on an endless journey. To pass the interminable time, he thought about books, knowledge, culture, concepts and any other escape routes he could take. At that thought, he let out a smile of relief. It would be best if he acted right away; so he stood up and went to the library, glasses in hand.

A girl received him. Obviously, she was tired of her monotonous job. Taking Gu Manzi's request forms, she went inside, but came out only a moment later. Tossing the forms on the long table dividing them, she said in a simple, abrupt manner, "Can't find any of them."

Helpless, Gu Manzi went back to the index-card cabinets, and started all over again, covering the forms with his meticulous and clean handwriting with every stroke of the 'K's and 'T's drawn properly. Another girl took his requests this time, and returned from the stack room with an armload of books. He took a seat close to a window overlooking the lawn. The sun shone silently on the quiet paths lined on both sides with trees. Like a shadow, spring had cast a gloom over the luminous areas in his heart. The books, piled one on top of the other at the corner of a spotless table, obsolete, smacking of the mildew and ethereal fragrance of culture, absorbed his mind at once. Again, he was lost in his reading of that thick tome *The History of the Ming Dynasty*, his eyes long accustomed to the tiny print which looked like swarms of crawling ants. Just as he was beginning to savour the text with great relish, however, the title of another book on the table caught his eye. It was a book of historical anecdotes, unbelievably tattered. It seemed as if it had been left for an appropriate reader, presented to him with the dust, shadows and the unreconciled ghosts of history — a trivial sacrifice in the veiled performance of the history of monsters.

The suspicious collection of anecdotes was cluttered with obscure and mysterious ideas. Yet to understand it was to prove mankind's confidence in the self-proclaiming soberness of reason; it was to prove man's ability to conquer reality through judgement based on analysis and deduction. But not only did Gu Manzi want to exorcise witchcraft with the empty vanity of his heart, he also wanted to extinguish the inherent absurdity of mysticism in his mind, the two of which, eventually, joined forces and formed a thin stream of trust, irrigating his dream and fantasy, comforting his terrorized heart. Yet without his knowing, this theory had already thrown him into confusion. The past was the present, and perhaps the future as well; the book, with its words and characters, had already embraced reality, copulated with its filth and become a ludicrous mask. He was trapped, disappearing in the book, submerging quietly from the crowded, well-lit reading room into vocabulary and grammar, into the labyrinth of distorted meaning; he was led by his delirium from the horror of an evil reality into a past era. With a mind and a heart (as well as the reality behind it) unknown to anyone else, he walked into a group of scholars of the 17th century.

During the day, he could still separate that other person from himself. He listened, but did not take part in conversations, for he had not yet mastered the language of a culture that had long since been lost in time and history. Smiling cautiously, he memorized words and phrases, imitating the rhythm of their speech; and in no time, he could almost use this language to express simple thoughts. Yet he still sat at the table with self-possession, sipping the tea served up by the maids, seeming at the same time perplexed and attentive. At night, however, he shook off his restraints. After drinking wine from the cups of the others (it was a kind of very light rice wine, which doesn't really count in today's world of alcoholism), he traded a few caresses with a woman playing the Chinese lute, and then teased a bashful maid. Someone patted him on the shoulder as a way of showing friendliness. In return, he emptied in one gulp the cup of wine handed him. Afterward, he got more excited and plunged into a heated discussion of politics among a group of literati. Face to face with these white-frocked, fan-swaying scholars with lugubrious eyes and faces turned pallid from excitement, he felt a sense of intimacy and calmness known only after long separation. He began to attack court politics. He analysed the corruption of the current government, condemned the decline of morals and lamented the decadence of public spirit, but in fact, he was directing his criticism to a future dynasty some three hundred years later. But no one could have known. They gathered around him with sincerity and respect, praising and flattering him in the way they would a born genius on his knowledge and methodology, which they found quite unfamiliar. Several people made toasts to him. He wrote down his views in an exquisite hand on a fine piece of stationery imprinted with cloud patterns, and suggested they write a joint-memorial to the emperor. People called him, 'Mr Shushi', and paid their respects. At first he did not known what was happening; only later he found out he was indeed Gu Xiancheng. Praise, acclaim, flattery, and admiration from worshipping disciples — and there were so many of them! It was almost the conquest and intoxication of a dream.

The earth had long been silent, the stars stood still, and the rivers stopped flowing. Gu Manzi, who was now Gu Xiancheng, pushed open a window. A courtyard permeated by the wet fragrance of plants swayed in the shadow of the scholar trees. It led out to another courtyard. Structured like a Chinese box, the yards provided a well-covered shelter for the hostility underlining the thoughts of the Donglin academics. The gathering continued to the small hours. A cock crowed. Eyes, blood-shot, swam passionately in the dim light of flickering candles. Garrulous flaunting of witticisms, revolutionary speech of daunted conspirators, and the learned obscurity of words, like the long river of a text, indefatigably changed or, rather, replaced the mystery of vanishing lives. From a corner, the woman with a sad and sleepy face intermittently played a miserable tune on the Chinese lute. A wild, young scholar stood up, and chanted a line from an ancient poem in sorrow and indignation, "The moon bathes the flower grove in frost-like light," (or was it "Meat and wine go rotten behind the vermilion gates, while at the roadside, lie the bones of those frozen to death"?) Far away, a dog barked. In the dark, a maid screamed involuntarily. With the severity of Zhuzi and his lack of scruples, someone chastened the voice's obscenity. At that moment, a man burst in, his panic-stricken voice, broken with terror, "The imperial police are here!"

That threw the whole place into a confusion. Many jumped out of the window and fell on the brick ground outside. A doctoral candidate who had failed in the imperial examination many times grabbed the maid who had screamed just a moment ago, and crawled under the bed. The lute-player was still plucking out a mournful tune — "Day after day I long for you, my love, but we can never meet" — tears tumbled onto her long tousled hair. Gu Manzi was stunned, and didn't know what to do. A soft, frail hand tugged at his sleeve and led him out through a secret exit. The stars were still sleeping in the night sky. Dark, churning clouds drifted silently above the branches of some dead trees. A few birds made a dim gurgling sound. Death hung over the pond in a pure ethereal light. Before he realized what was happening, Gu Manzi saw a string of red lanterns and heard a barrage of wild shouting, moving closer.

The soft and tender arms wrapped around him, snuggling up to his chest and weeping. A head of dishevelled hair mingled, irritatingly, with his unclear thoughts. He felt at a loss, cranky and helpless, not knowing what to do. Those with the lanterns were near, shouting and cursing, the blades of the long knives in their hands steeped in the cold light of a past era. Absent-mindedly, Gu Manzi let out a deep sigh, and pushed the girl away. In her fleeting glance, he saw, indistinctly, a pair of strange empty eyes, which he thought he had seen somewhere before.

Through the dust of the library and the cacophony of old phantoms, two men walked over to him. Pushing away the female librarian's arms, they took Gu Manzi's hands, and with the satisfaction of successful conspirators, locked those two self-surrendering wrists into a pair of icy-cold handcuffs.

THE GREEN PEACH

Hong Ying

translated by Henry Y H Zhao

When she noticed that the tree in the garden had produced a small peach, her whole body tingled, with a sensation that was so familiar. She supported herself on the fence, and looked up instinctively. When had the curtain been drawn on the bedroom window? She felt sure that there must be someone behind the curtain. She looked down, pretending she hadn't noticed anything.

It was almost ten years since she'd moved to Newgate Street. The tree in the garden blossomed every year, with flowers like the lips of infants, moist and fragrant. But it had never born fruit. Ten years before he had said to her, "You are as beautiful as those flowers." He had repeated it every year until she was sick of hearing it.

She congratulated herself on the fact that this year she would no longer have to suffer the insult. Her heart was full of rancour, covered with enough dust for grass to take root. Often she had dreamed that she taken him on. He doubled over in pain, and from his staggering figure there came the disjointed words, "How could you ... have done...."

And she laughed with joy and said, "You'll change." She stopped laughing and blurted out, "You might change into something inhuman."

He had not been seen or heard from for a year and a half. All possible ways of looking for him had been tried. Time was passing quickly, although the evening paper with his picture in it still hung on the wall of the toilet.

Two or three bees hummed overhead. She picked up a stone and threw it at the tree. The branch shook. She went on throwing stones. All her throws curved wide of the branch.

She went into the house and got out a long bamboo pole. Was it possible, she thought, that he'd been in hiding? She began to be suspicious of him. The green peach was as tiny as a date, almost invisible behind two leaves. She raised the pole high and swung it. Still too low. She turned the pole around, holding the thin end in her hand

and taking careful aim before she swung again. The two leaves fluttered down, but the peach still hung there, quivering.

Gazing up at it, her heart ached. She turned the pole around again and stuck the thick end into the ground. She was very upset.

The sun went behind a cloud and it grew dark. Smoke rose from the chimney of a nearby house. So that was the end of another day. She gave the idea a little though and then went out of the courtyard. A moment later, she brought back a ladder, and smiled as if she were dreaming.

The teacher marks her pile of essays every day. The maths questions are easy; they relax her a little. Afterwards she pins up her hair and begins to undress. The lamplight obscures the wrinkles at the corner of her eyes and on her neck. Her figure in the mirror is not without its attractions, quite apart from the tenderness she usually expressed.

After her bath, she changes into clean underwear. She pours herself a cup of tea and adds two spoonfuls of sugar. It slips sweetly down her throat. She feels sleepy and turns out the light before getting into bed.

He walks up to her, closely, in his usual way, without speaking, just looking at her, almost affectionately.

"Fuck off, you bastard!" He used leave as soon as the curse was out of her mouth. This time he didn't even budge. She opened her eyes wide and saw from the clock on the bedside table that it as three am. The curtain that had been drawn earlier was now wide open. She rose and walked to the window. The garden was bathed in moonlight and seemed to be covered in silver. Her hand pulled back the curtain and then stopped midway. She thought that the peach which she picked that afternoon was still hanging on the branch. There seemed to someone standing under the tree, or was it just the flicker of a shadow? She didn't want to have a better look. Instead, she closed her eyes to shut out the coldness of the moon. What does all this have to do with me?

She turned around — feeling her belly with her hand. The green peach she'd swallowed seemed never to have existed at all.

GAS

HONG YING

translated by Henry Y H Zhao

Another rainy season, with chains of rain-beads hanging on the eaves. Inside there were several basins and bowls, small and large, on the floor to catch the leaks. She had been to see the estate officer in her husband's company, but nothing had been done. She had to move the bed to avoid the leaks, and there was a knocking on the floor from below when she moved the bed. She stamped in answer. How much more fuss could there be over this damned rain?

The lady downstairs was a divorcee who had loads of male visitors. When her husband left on a business trip, he became very insistent. Now that their daughter was sixteen and preparing for university entrance exams, she must be properly looked after. She knew very well what her husband was worried about. Their daughter was to be kept clear of the woman downstairs' bad influence.

"Dad still hasn't come home," the girl complained, working under a desk lamp.

"It'll be a couple of days, didn't I tell you?" She poured the water in one of the basins into a bucket and carried it outside.

The staircase was narrow and it was difficult to carry the bucket downstairs without spilling it. She had always tried her best not to get involved in the frequent quarrels amongst the neighbours. Her downstairs neighbour's door was shut tight, even though it was only seven pm. She frowned and poured the water into the drain. As she went back up the stairs, she was vaguely aware of a sound of music, a waltz of some kind.

She had an uneasy night. When she couldn't get to sleep, she didn't turn on the light in case it woke her daughter. She had to go to school early the next morning. The dripping of the water lessened at the other end of the bed.

There were some noises from downstairs. She cursed herself for trying to guess what the sounds might be.

At daybreak she rose and went out to buy some things for her daughter's breakfast. Passing the door downstairs, she couldn't help feeling a little resentful as she recalled the noises that night, and couldn't keep herself from trying to see in through the crack round the door. It was totally dark inside, and there was a strange smell.

"Gas!" Suddenly she realized. She threw down her basket and umbrella and slammed her body into the door. The door frame was crooked and the lock sprang open easily. She was thrown in under her own force, and immediately assailed by the horrible smell. She tried to cover her nose with her hand. On the bed there were two people, uncovered, but neatly dressed. She rushed towards them, but stopped suddenly, as if she were seeing two ghosts. The room was tidy; the door of the tiny kitchen ajar. She turned and ran out. Before she shut the door on the place, leaving it as it was, she noticed that the pair on the bed were tightly clasping each other's hands.

She climbed the stairs, one step after another. Back in her own room, she covered her face with her hands and tried to suppress the trembling of her body. Outside the window, it was still drizzling, endlessly.

ABANDONED WINE

O

POETRY

SONG LIN

translated by Chen Yanbing & John Rosenwald

THE MODEL AT MONTPARNASSE

How heavy is an invisible being?
like the weariness in a pore on the retina

The sea suddenly wants to go through the fish's eye
and see what waters are on the other side

Before it is drawn
before the fish's eye becomes a peacock stone

Darkness sleeps in a space narrower than the womb
where not even the palm of the creator can fly

The mould awakens, dives to the ground
like ripe pears dropping off stems

Just here, continues, mourning for tears
but with no secret, no sorrow

Fire starting from eyelashes, so terrifying
not leaving even a single freckle

Will she find a bush of black hair
weeping like an ancient harp in a crypt outside the city

Will the icebergs stop floating? will the sensory organs
flee from the wall on a quiet night?

A cherry tree from the past waits in the orchard
while on the portrait a bee nibbles at her golden shadow

THE WRITING MANIAC

he attains ecstasy in his dream
watching, as he buries himself in time
he observes that ships move beneath
        the caterpillar tread of the sea

the brain can also be a sickle,
harvesting useless words sheaf after sheaf
like another photographer
        working overnight in the darkroom

with a suave face, this negative of daily experience
the white of day, the black of night
develops the vanished childhood from an old man

here's a difficult spot, gradually taking shape
the excess of body closely resembles the soul
amplified, trembling, O the weeping of the mosquito

desire is the tool; means — sanitation
pretence, insinuation, and meaning's addition and subtraction
but nomenclature is crowded; lies lost their opposition

he occupies this angle, an angle appropriately dead
as if a monologue read aloud in past tense
On the other side of the negative, death's development
        is bringing him out any moment.

WANG YIN

translated by Chen Yanbing & John Rosenwald

A MOMENT OF THE MASTER

The Master you commend
The clandestine copy you describe
Everything that surprises you
The stiff garden
The lost geyser
The unknown spirits still roaming the winding corridor
Their gloomy but ferocious masks
Riding the Master's sweet voice
Rest by day, travel by night

You send me the long whip
To teach me more
Your ecstasy —
Crime being washed off by terror

All your temptation
All your enchantment
Becomes a brilliant moment of the Master

XI CHUAN

translated by John Cayley

PREMONITION

I hang bright mirrors high on the walls
you let dark clouds in through the doorway

you bring a city beneath the clouds in through the doorway
and the city in the mirrors is plastered with slogans
you bring a village beneath the clouds in through the doorway
and the village in the mirrors burns with torches

eagles in the mirrors, horses in the mirrors
soaked in a downpour, intimate with suffering
my mirrors repel misery
but you lead a lion out of the gunfire

and then you lead the night out of thought
and wind from dejection
and you bring the wind in through the doorway
where it buffets the mirrors: the mirrors of my forebears

carrying the sighs of strangers
and I can hear the immortality of their spirits in these sighs
I bring the spirits in through the doorway
and make up a low bed for them

for you, I make up a heap of ricestraw
I want to capture you in the mirrors
to make you make up before you sleep
to make you bring sleep in through the doorway

no sleep, no sleeper
furniture, ink and tea bowls
the mirrors reflect a last meal
you bring dawnlight in through the doorway

ZHANG ZAO

translated by Wendy Larson

KAFKA TO FELICE
Sonnets

Huete ist wieder niches, liebste, traurig

— Kafka

1

My name is Kafka, if you recall
we met at M. B.'s house.
As you glanced at an album under the lamp
a bizarre fragrance pierced my soul.

My strange lungs face your hands,
like a peacock spreading its tail, seeking praise.
Your shadow trembles on the piano
facing your night, my lungs so strange

a saint from his god cannot part
I long for my peacock lungs always
for them I open the putrid cage,

Go, I say, cleave to that heart:
"Shall I compare you to a red rose?"
Floating boughs fill the room, breathless gaze.

2

Prague's snowy night. From alleys criss-cross
run thieves, gangs, and the sleepless odd.
The earth pricks up its ears. In the wind willows toss,
is it fire quivering? No, that is the angel of god.

An angel has come, they kept saying
in a grey raincoat, so cold blood dripped from his nose.
They said he was not so terrible, staying
by the telephone booth, obliquely peering at power lines.

A sad figure. All want to get nearby,
to touch him. But those who try shall lose
him. A fierce dog's bark breaks open the hedge

and a road shines. His back so big and high.
I hear him open the cellar wine rack
I really want to cry. My hands are frozen numb.

3

Yet fatal is the breakthrough. And the highest of all
are birds. Craning our necks, sensing it below,
birds, just as your name we call
long become something else, your songs fill the streets so.

A day when candy in a child's mouth melts
into the future. On such a day so many things
have happened. I see a coming train
carrying your image. Felice, my bird

I can never go to meet you, fresh flowers wilted, charred
because what we greet is always illusion
the body's morning shadow ahead, afternoon inverted it hangs

behind. And what is illusion? I pray.
Raindrops beat their heads against things,
our breakthrough is infinite change.

4

Night, you are never night enough,
solitude, never enough alone
in the cellar I listen to the gloomy

oak tree (it sucks thunder and lightening to pieces)
and I, never enough myself.
Time, how can there be enough

deer, run increasing on the way —
As if only the wind and moon are used up?
Next to the office building, the cuckoos say:
Living is just slowly losing blood.

I really want something to take me afar
to a place where I'm not;
that typewriter, record and star,
all swirling under a demon's tongue.

5

When do people most clearly see
themselves? On a moonnight, a moonnight in a stone's eye.
All that moves, from splintered years

goes toward a tryst. All is a mirror
I write. Spiders sniff the moonlight's stench.
Words awaken, lift their skirts, face each other,

and start a heavy-hearted dance on the floor.
Who knows if they are the children of god or
belong to the devil's force. I want to cry more.
Something suddenly shatters, they move to hide

slouching back to things, now just shadows remain
to confront that still ringing sound of having been read.
Felice, today again no letter from you.
Alone I ponder my wondrous self aloud.

6

Reading is killing. I don't like it
when lonely people read me, that burning
breathing irritates me; they snatch up the
book, like snatching up their organs.

This boiling night, everywhere pain.
They use me to berate erected blooms,
leaving god no words with which to answer,
leaving the ugly no place to remain,

cruising brothels and pharmacies,
mingling with the neither-sex,
ridiculing the despots, speaking of bad years;

the high stars scream: "Burn me!"
the Prague waters shout: "Give me one wise."
Tombstones are silent: reading me is killing me.

7

A sudden stroll: the blood that spurs us on
a bit darker than night: blood, wearing night's top hat,
throwing on a stinking coat, moving out to
those tiny roaming creatures. Lights like evil owlets;

don't be afraid, this is night. Estranged things rush
into us, smelting us. Withered moths clutch at rays
making final prayers. Life and death suddenly brush
I hear the moths' lost drunken tongues tasting

some limitless opening. A sudden stroll,
they softly call: "This way, this way, not left,
not right, not front not back, this way, fear not?"

If you fear not then you are an angel. Quickly, release
yourself, throw yourself by the road, go forward more purely.
Fear not, this is the wind. Never forget this natural din.

8

Soon it will be fall, and soon I will
use another language to dream; open your palm,
open the tree box, open the sawdust waist,

the world suddenly appears. These are her fallen leaves,
like chessmen, brightened by the player's heart.
They wait by the bridge, sometimes inching forward
a bit, sometimes retreating, sometimes circling, always to insert

themselves in the pattern. Be careful touch them not,
their existence forever played out at home;
a child picking coal bits, from frost-bound gates
comes out, sees the glow, confounded

carrying warmth, the train trembles on the earth
the child thrown off its tail, with his wooden bucket,
as if to leave the pattern. we have no player....

9

They watch it a long time. What
is it? It is god. Then, is god
it? If it is god
then god is hardly it;

like light into light itself dissolves
it appears through the body of god,
already too weak, too bitter, too limited.
It is god: what a process.

The world appears in a Bo tree,
and only the tree itself knows
it is too far, too deep, too unique;

from dense jade leaves watching the ancient castle,
awaiting death, we contradictory
surveyors had best run far away.

BEI DAO

two poems translated by David Hinton

A PORTRAIT

wounded by convictions, he came from August
a mother's perilous love
stolen away by a mirror
he's sideways between the rhinoceros and politics
like a fissure separating epochs

o conspirators, I'm nothing now
but a common wanderer
walking the cavernous museum's chessboard
trading places with strangers

great passion's never outdated
but our visits require secrecy
suddenly I feel the ache of strings
you're tuning, play me a song
somewhere predators haven't yet risen into our history

AT THE SKY'S EDGE

love among the mountains

eternity, that patience of the earth
simplifies our human sounds
one arctic-thin cry
from deep antiquity until now

rest, weary traveller
a wounded ear's
already laid your dignity bare

one arctic-thin cry

BEI DAO

four poems translated by Chen Yanbing *&* John Rosenwald

BACKGROUND

to go home
you must revise your background

rocked by time, some words
take off, and tumble
divulging no news
the sequence of failures: a short cut
past silent grandstands in heavy snow
closing in on the huge gerontic bell

the climax of a family gathering
depends on the amount of alcohol
the woman closest to you
wears always on her face history's grief
watching the snowdrift, space

darkness in which the voles hold their faith

UNTITLED

in the father's plain imagination
the children's persistent cries
finally hit the cliff
don't panic
following some trees' thoughts
I stutter into song

sorrow from far away
is a power
I use to saw the table
for love, someone sets out
while a palace, following the storm loyally
sails across many dynasties

beyond life with
furniture, a flea beats an enormous drum
Taoists practice ascent to heaven
youth reaches deep into the alley
weeping over night's logic
I attain rest

FEBRUARY

night approaching perfection
I float in languages
death's brass
brims with ice

who sings above the days'
cracks? water turns bitter
anaemic flames
leap at stars like leopards
to dream
you need a form

in the morning's chill
a bird, awakened
comes closer to truth
while I, together with my poems
start to sink

February in a book
some movement, some shade

THIS DAY

the wind long familiar with love
summer gleaming in royal colour
in his solitude, a fisherman plumbs
the earth's gaping wound
the bell tolls, swelling
people strolling in the afternoon —
please join the year's implication

someone bends toward a piano
someone carries a ladder past
drowsiness is suspended a few minutes
just a few minutes
the sun studies the shadow
I drink from the bright mirror
& see the enemy in my heart

like an oil tanker
the tenor's singing inflames the ocean
I open a can at 3 a.m.
& let the fish blaze in splendour

BAI HUA

translated by Chen Yanbing *&* John Rosenwald

IN MEMORY OF ZHU XIANG

This is the image that caught my eye
The image in the autumn wind, delirious and wild
But in a book it is so peaceful

A lonely drinker, unassumingly wise
A martyr, incredibly sensitive
One more glass before death
Then bent over to the inevitable sleep

I know you had been rehearsing
the expression of a martyr since a child
And your youth, once homeless among rumours
But your song only belonged to heaven
Why, why only after death did this example become extraordinary
Only after death did it keep us busy, commemorating
Speaking, corresponding
And so on, until 1989.

OLD POET

sunny March, gardens sentimental
in ten days, he'll be fifty

he says there's one line that still tortures him
oh, one word that still tortures him

his hair dishevelled and illegible, like a motherland
obesity once more stirs the table

literature, sloppy literature
motherland, the after-hours motherland in his eyes

but he says
literature should be simple and thrifty
and motherland, therefore, ought to be exported.

DUO DUO

translated by Gregory B Lee

THERE IS NO

There is no one bidding me farewell
there is no one bidding another farewell
there is no one bidding the dead farewell, when this morning starts

there is no border to its self

except for language, facing the land with its lost border
except for this flourishing fresh flesh, facing windows unclosed into
        the night
except for my window, facing my no longer comprehensible
        language

there is no language

there is only my light repeatedly grinding, grinding
that repeatedly worked saw at daybreak
only that restive tulip, until restive no more

there are no tulips

there is only light, stuck at dawn
star light, sprinkling into the speeding train's slumbering
        baggage car
the last light, trickles off a baby's face

there is no light

I use an axe to split open meat, hear the sharp cry of the shepherd
        at dawn
I open the window, hear the yelling between light and ice
it's the sound of yelling makes fog's fetters crack open

there is no sound of yelling

there is only land
there are only land and people who transport grain who know
only the bird which calls at midnight is the bird who has seen dawn

there is no dawn

WATCHING THE SEA

Having watched the winter sea, what flows in your veins is surely
          blood no more
so when making love one should surely gaze on the ocean
surely you are still waiting
waiting for the sea breeze to blow on you once more
that breeze will surely arise from the bed

that memory is also, surely is
false images of the ocean preserved in the eyes of dead fish
fishermen are surely engineers and doctors on vacation
June cotton in the earth is surely cotton swabs
surely you're all still in the fields seeking vexation
trees you brush by are surely bruised and swollen
huge rage surely makes you have a future different from the crowd
because you are too fond of saying surely
as Indian women will surely expose their flesh at the waist

the distance to the place you live together is surely not far
the distance to Chinatown is likewise surely not far
surely there will be a moon shining like a mouthful of spit
surely there will be people who say that is your health
no longer important, or even more important, surely
surely it stays in your mind
just like that square of arrogant bomb-casing on the English face

watching the sea surely uses up your lives
stars preserved in the eyes have surely become cinders
the ocean's shadow surely seeped from the seabed to another world
in a night when somebody anyhow must die someone must surely
      die
although the ring surely does not wish to be long dead on the flesh
shooting hormones into a horse's arse will surely stir it up
so to arrange tidily is then surely to create disorder
when a bicycle chain falls off peddling surely gets faster
the spring wind surely resembles the kidney stone sufferer's fastened
      green belt
the taxi driver's face surely resembles stewed fruit
when you go home that old chair will surely be young, surely.

INSTANT

The instant the sound of the street cellist strikes a chord
in the sky at dusk the last brilliant fleck of sunlight, is dying out
dying over an old train station

a grey intestine opens wide in the sky
besides it there is nothing
except for a weight, still sitting atop the river's surface
that was the weight of the church shimmering
now, it seems there is only silence

after the sound of the cello there is only silence
trees quietly change colour
children quietly drink their milk
the sand freighter quietly sails by
we watch, like tiles quietly watching a roof
we sniff, the air of when whoever and we were together
it's already quietly died out

whoever existed, only light shows no more
whoever left themselves, it was only an instant
who says that instant was our whole life
and this instant, the sound of Scottish rain
suddenly pattering on a basin —

ONLY ONE

      Only one memory is allowed
to stretch in a direction rails are powerless to reach — making you
measure the future with millet, pave the road with cloth
      only one season is allowed
the wheat sowing season — the May sun
from a naked back, tears the earth in all directions
      only one hand is allowed
making you look down — on your palm are furrows
earth's thoughts, slowly smoothed out by another hand
      only one horse is allowed
numbered by the five in the afternoon woman's gaze
making your temperament, tolerate your body
      only one person is allowed
the person making you dead, is already dead
the wind, making you familiar with this death
      only one kind of death is allowed
each word, is a bird with a smashed head
the ocean, still gushes out from a cracked clay pot …

OUYANG JIANGHE

translated by John Minford & Chu Chiyu

AUTUMN
Listening to a Performance by the late cellist, Jacqueline Du Pré

Old dreams haunt, turn toward dead souls, here,
now. But you are deaf to the wild passing of the gale
fading in the light, to a sigh, and then the sounding of the strings dies
and the distant darkness
throws open its tightly closed lips.

Heard: running water arching overhead.
Running water yielding to rotten wood, carving deep traces.
Shadow against the flow, and two eyes in the shadow
looking back
against the flow;
only looking back
can I see how total has been
the annihilation of this generation of aesthetes

Sleepless nights will seize from your ear
that faint torch handed on
a relay to the forging of names —
imbued with grief and nostalgia,
enfolded, moulded anew by fashion. If old age disappears
one morning
one night;
in oblivion no one is alone.

Oh! this generation of romantic aesthetes! these aspirations
of a desperate humanity — for this you sacrifice your flesh;
Hot tears, shed in helpless solitude.
Only the flesh
has warmth, however transient.

IN THE LIFT

The lift goes down; the apple is handed on —
supplement to the imagination. Push through the crowd
and you can enter. Go to work early,
the apple is still on the tree, like the new generation
refusing to grow up.

Do you think they stay in the sky when the lift goes down?
If you're late for work, you might as well be later still.
Next on the roster means two seats closer together, side by side,
exchanging luck, swapping house numbers.

Power has a face that will ultimately be forgotten —
picked out from the marked cards.
The man who makes the most cash is always short;
when he falls into debt, he can start to get seriously rich.

The smile on your face is pasted on with glue;
I can smell the chemical process in it.
Your weeping seems fake;
Do you really believe that tears have no bones?

Bring your daughter along; the beauty parlour
can strip the growing bloom of beauty from her face.
But the residue will continue to grow; senility is merely
beauty trembling as it grows more beautiful.

All this can be explained from the heart.
The whole city descends upon your body, transcends
the illness of the heart. Why today?
The apple suddenly falls. It is too late
for the lift to go down.

DEAN LÜ

translated by John Cayley

THERE WILL BE SNOW TONIGHT IN NEW YORK

There will be snow tonight in New York; but then how will it be?
The darkness will fall first in our eyes
not in Manhattan or on Roosevelt island
and not in any other place.

The hustle and bustle of the day is not yet over
but we let life fall out of our hands
or at least we begin to wait, and we feel
that tonight may be the most memorable night of the year.

We see the birds fly off over the horizon
as if they too know about the change in the weather,
seeking a perch in their flurry and alarm,
falling like the darkness in our eyes,

Where can we find it? Everyone is saying,
there will be snow tonight in New York. It's not a sure thing
but this much is certain: if we aren't covered by snow tomorrow
we'll be enshrouded in our own darkness.

WHALES

One winter's night, a school of whales swept into the village
and quietly occupied half the dry land
like mountains before our doorways. They wouldn't be
           persuaded
to go. What to do? They just didn't want to leave the place,
dark, stubborn, unresponsive. Addressing,
head-on, the vast echoing depths of their mouths
most of the sounds we heard were our own, human.
We shone lights into their eyes: an ocean within glass prisons.
We tried their fathomless weight with our hands,
and lost our strength, became emptied, boundless.
What to do? We didn't want to take even a step away.
They had come to share the same life as we do,
these whales. And although we have different dwelling places,
although we share the freedom of air, movement,
           the village moonlight,
and even half the dominion of the dry land
still they could not give us the power
to summon the tide for them before death.

Huge bodies as if gripped by bouts
of asthma and so caught in time,
staving off daylight, windows opening, the sea
only metres away, and yet their eyes showed
no welcome for it. They had devised a suicide of
historic proportions. Once dead, death added to their heaviness,
long bearing down on the heart of land
like mountains before our doorways. We brought tools
but it was like shovelling earth, and the more we shovelled
           the more the earth fell in.

Or, when we hit a stone (one of those contentious bones)
it was picked out and laid on a wall, where it became another
             unremarkable brick.
It was as if we were tunnelling — from one tunnel to another
always in the direction of the sea. And the whales'
blubber was made into lamp oil, which we offered to the church
and the remainder was given to our families. Everywhere,
everywhere, the stench of fish and a minty scent of truth.
Even today, such actions have their persuasive power,
at least, not like the whales — and their suspicious arrival —
a sudden nightfall, leaving us spiritless.

ZHANG ZHEN

translated by the author

NIGHT VIGIL

Satellites shatter like jade
Dancing shoes on the tightrope
Split in the moon

This music, every note weeping
Curves like the Mississippi
The birds on their return graze my roof
There'll be no more good news in this world

Hair splitting in the night fog
The smallest gesture of life
Calm and pious
When the river bends
I stand in silence, mourning for my friend

The world has stopped entering your picture
I've stopped a part of my life
Stopped a way of speaking
I've closed a channel

Throw the dancing shoes into the river
Wash away the moon
Wash away memory
But your crutches stand against the wind
The night has spread out a mourning flag

Wading into the cold song of spring tide
Galaxies tumble
And among the fish, you rise

(translated with John Rosenwald)

IN AMERICA

In America
Car windows open onto the wasteland of history
Where waves of rocks clash
I arrive at my new home — it has no kitchen

In America, I think of those Japanese cats
Tailless, as if castrated
Playing hide-and-seek with pilgrims
In the temples up and down the mountains

In America I will become a cat
A cat with a tail, but no meow
Roaming about in empty white buildings
Not wanting to return to my kitchenless home

In America all memories of wandering
Are thrown onto scrapyard of cars
        Burning in the wasteland
Learn how to be a mute circle
Under the boundless clear sky

HAN DONG

translated by Chen Yanbing & John Rosenwald

FOG

From all sides the fog oppresses the house
Give it a crack
It sneaks in, crawls along the floor
Gathering and rising where the walls meet
Covering the ceiling. From inside out
It pushes the walls down
The hand of the lantern holder disappears
And the light cannot measure accurately the depth of his lodging
Meanwhile fog elsewhere lifts
As if summoned back into this house

GE MAI

translated by Chen Yanbing *&* John Rosenwald

SEEING BEAUTY IN A DREAM

A tree in the night is a star
A shimmering stone, a nut opening like a flower
A statue in the night, a flute
A song, a small cloud at dawn

This beauty of silence, who can understand?
The sharp ends of the diamond, the shore at the wharf
Peel the skin off a walnut
A prune hits the kernel's rope

Growing in the branches, are Monkey Head mushrooms
A gleaming razor walks into the bird's nest
A grumpy face shrunk to the size of a toe
A precocious girl walks into the soldiers' tent

Beauty is a meteor, shooting across the sleepers
The algae are singing, the reeds are dancing
A sound in the distance plugs the night's ear
Poisonous white flowers bloom on the needle,
          high up, a camphor ball dangles

The refreshing smell of honey consoles the glistening cotton
Sparks from the bullets may teach people better
The blood in breasts, and the river in blood
Just like there're wreaths on the point of the needle, and an ocean
    in the wreaths

YANG LIAN

translated by Brian Holton

THE GARDEN ON A WINTER'S DAY

1

trees frozen red in the snow   as if wearing worn-out wind-breakers
snow crunching underfoot
the hurried night always wears brand-new soles

goats fear loneliness   for every ear
cries become bitter weeping

the path   a cow, just dropped a calf
scarred head to tail by the whip, panting paralysed in bloody mud

streetlamps come on still earlier   lovers dim as stones
stand, faces blurred, by a metal bier
the vole is an exhausted nurse   stealthily
slinking into the garden's wounds to dream
flowers   are preserving their pink flesh below ground
like dead children   straightaway, fresh tender ghosts

underdeveloped stars   lock us up with iron railings

2

in this world the ones who trust writing least   are poets
in the blank snow   roses have been withering since birth
the flame is far away from two cold hands
winter bustles about   like an industrious editor
I   become something spiked by the sunlight
bending to sniff at my death-stench which grows daily stronger
in one man's north wind   the garden long ago ceased to be

existing for the imagination   in the end, as always, returning to
                                        the imagination
the blue music of tree and tree   is played only on silence
so the same heavy snow has twice fallen on my shoulders
when it covers the garden   I am forgotten
stepping on an intersection   I am mistaken
under the lamps the empty street is like a hoarse throat
declaiming   and for years the withered and fallen words look on

3

some people, addicted to corpses   love to stroll in winter gardens
people who salute ruins   can appreciate
a plot to drown a kitten in a ditch
pressing its head down like crushing a walnut
it's definitely children   children running into the garden

children know better than anyone how to trample flowers

even our dying day is unreal   a piece of a charred pole
poking slantwise from the ground like the crocodile's long snout
the sky is so gloomy it seems like daylight sleep
fishbones vomited by the ocean   stab us too
in dreams live fish, scraped clean of scales, are stabbed one by one
alive beneath the travelling knife

all flesh is reduced to a place with no power to look back

touch   all that is touched is non-existent
and cancer swells impalpably in the depths
a black pregnant woman   enwrapping a raped springtime
a treetrunk sliced by sight
swans' necks become pale underwater snares
once we have divided the world with fractured compound eyes
we are all blind   each spectre sets the white snow off
exposed in the dry ice-hard wind
endures the pain of bones budding

until   the garden is shamed into colour
lashed all its life by an unidentifiable season

ZHONG MING

translated by John Minford & Chu Chiyu

TRYING SWORDS WITH THE DAOIST
'GREAT MAN' RUAN JI

Come, Great Man, draw your blade; show your mettle!
There are evil ways whose poison must be purged by the sword!
One ray of that grand light, one stalk of corn,
one quivering ray, and I ride with you into the Nine Heavens;

one single cry from that bleeding throat,
and I gaze upon infinity, let my hair down into the ocean.
Give the little bird a point — let it
flap a few feet further, break another branch or two ...

Don't challenge this trembling of mine, this cruelty —
don't take it to heart;
retire to your forest hermitage, climb to higher ground;
ennui ripples through your sleeves,
while spirits sit in state
against the backdrop of the hills.

This is that other tower of your valour!
Strong-nosed, galvanic,
immune to beauty, ancient ox,
consummate swordsman to the last ...

Tell me, Great Man, that bow of yours,
bent from finest oak,
can it dispel the exquisite ennui
that shrouds your fine beard, your grief —
white blazing sun, pinpoint of fire?

Let me pick up your ivory sword
and learn the phoenix song. Great Man,
Man of Tao,
gone, alas, the singing and dancing,
dulled the fire of desire:
all turned to ashes in combat.

Cosmetic transformation. Great Man,
let the two of us play once more the part of the departed
in a stone mirror,
subdue the disease of ennui, as the disciple did;
come, come, let us cut palms!

YAN LI

translated by Chen Yanbing *&* John Rosenwald

THE DISCIPLINE OF LONELINESS

How great is this loneliness
The merchandise in the heart
The song keeps floating
There is no price for keeping the mouth shut
Complete this eulogy
The pronunciation torn off is immaculate

Spread out — the map, the table's wood grain
Consult each other
I establish the nostalgia of New York
The love buried may have already become a relic
Like the location unbuttoned
The overlapping of East and West implied by nakedness

How great is this loneliness
In the chair the flesh still sits keeping me company
In and out the air still flows
Lines spelling out culture endure gravity on the paper
My feet clenched in the shape of fists
Force my hands to walk on the empty ceiling.

MARGIN

Suddenly loneliness takes on shape
The shape of days
In which I am a side
A principal side

Thinking about things that happened to my elders
But not yet to me
I see everywhere dregs of sugar cane
The chewed-up history
They call it the sweet textbook

From chalk dust the teacher
Rises in loneliness
Linking up this side of mine
And the sugar borrowed by sugar cane
Returns wrapped in this diploma

HONG YING

translated by Henry Y H Zhao

WINTER HORROR

No one knows the truth behind our escape
An accident in the snow. I see the bush turning from purple to
                                                            blue
The snow exchanges suffering with the shrub
    like a torn collection of poetry: Gradually

    a bright spot in the landscape makes the deserted land visible
We are destined to meet here. Oh, tell me, how you became
a charred town at that very moment
Tell me, if snow has not yet drowned the bush —

All right. Let's not talk about it. The bush is an abstraction, yet
it's hung with icicles of fantasy
the inch-long candle, the half bottle of ink, the sheets of paper
are enough to make me happy. If you refuse to leave this
                                                    moment —

that is, if you disappear into this book of poetry book,
                                            please tell me
since I went so far as to have my name changed, seeking a feeling
                                            and myself
would you, and your wit, fall
    under my pen and freeze my ink?

The way you deliver me, I know, is to make me get on
someone else's carriage — too soon. But the snow,
                                    Oh the snow —

183

BUTTERFLY AND BUTTERFLY

I draw a pattern on your body
Every time I move, you call out, and the garden,
    sculpted by your body, expands.

The day comes, as long expected. I am still surprised, though
the theorem and the disaster are a couple
embracing. Every point of your beauty
is pierced by a sharp stone
The reflections of your peculiarity refuse clothing
    however light: Shadow upon shadow, like butterfly

and butterfly. The phrases that I have stored up
become sentences for you: A single encounter must be swift. Special
encounters require the pleasures of maltreatment

Dawn. It comes without mistake however slight
and the grass under you —

ZHU ZHU

two poems translated by Chen Yan bing & John Rosenwald

SANDY BEACH

Less than islands in winter.
Less than days beyond memory.
Less than my shadow; less than that among the rocks,
Which is your shadow.

Such moments are rare,
I walk through the wind, walking through
        a whole afternoon's latitudes
And sea — language, the tail of language
On which the shrieks of the peacock grow.

EARLY SPRING

Drowsy under the sun
I rest in my body, like a late
Greeting, longing for a similar wind

The air this afternoon, fresh and clear
Hides so many possibilities
For the sake of this moment, someone's taking a walk in Fuzhou

From these two streets, you cannot see the boats come and go
As evening falls, I come to fill the absence
Of the vanishing day. My body's stretched out
The window. Ivy entwines my fingers
A spring of your own, sensitive
Like the drop between clouds and the earth

The clouds cast grey shadows on the earth
Not the earth, but my earth-coloured limbs
The breath coming from the nostrils, trots like

A horse in spring grass. Sitting up, lying down, sing
A song, listen to a song, so far away
From the sun above your own shadow

HU DONG

translated by Wendy Larson

H. D.[*]

In my dreams he shuts the Venetian blinds.
Each night chilly. Alive to rail against
the dark garden, those two hands,
their crashing waves awake me,

and make an ocean of my life.
My veiled peaks, resisting,
I hide Neptune's trident, yet
in quirks he finds a Caesar.

Nowadays he is aged as a craggy rock.
The Rome in his face praised to me
by flattering clamshells and oysters.

Saying his smiles' dregs were removed by me
and in due time he would call my barren
mind's barn, once tangled blooms and weeds.

[*] The American poet, Hilda Doolittle (1886–1961).

HU DONG

translated by John Minford & Chu Chiyu

SEDUCTION

See, the blood strikes me!
Cold, feeding a tree in its dream of love.
The branches make me coy. Oh! I
would have remained asleep but for you, bumping into
the shy day I hung on your chest — I would have stayed silent
but for your beauty —
I'll spit it all out: all that stuff in the pitchblack kitchen
in the front of the house, those cumuli of maudlin wine
in the back
struck with a whiplash of lightning. You called out,
you can drive — fast, horse, sewing-machine,
you know the pedals;
while I wrapped the earth like a highway,
and stumbled on you, cool as ever,
tender as the blue of disaster; from the carpark came the sound
of your never-to-escape-me heart; apple eaten, 'apple'
intact, and me willing — to spend my days a stinking insect, crawling,
singing the graveyard of your desire,
and the late-blooming dragon-orchid …

1993.5

GU CHENG

translated by Chen Yanbing *&* John Rosenwald

GHOSTS: HEADING FOR THE CITY

The ghost
Of zero hour
Takes only baby steps
Fears it will slip *&* fall
turn into
A person

(Monday)

Ghost is many people
They sleep Wake up, they
Check the bulletin board   Swim
Stand so tall by the water
Underground swim a school of gold
Flip fish   Turn somersaults   Blow notes from wine bottles that
have wept

They like to look at things above
With one grasp grab the golden
Leaves

Ghosts sometimes read:
"After all they knew each other"
Then put their hands under the document
"This old rose by the water"
With one voice Puff out a cloud of smoke
People in the evening say
"Should be back by now"
On their way Lanterns Shadows Hazy
Ghosts do not speak   All the way, the wind blows
At the station it says   Eat grass   The face turned blue
A gust of wind churns the fog

189

(Tuesday)

Whenever the ghost closes its eyes
It sees people   With eyes open
It sees nothing

A giggling kite
In the dream sometimes looks at it
Now along the balcony railing
It tumbles   Carefully the ghost comes up
All along the corridor the giggling
                      Kites

"Half for others Half for you"
He unfolds a piece of clothing
Looks inside   Nobody   Unfolds another
There's a short blue skirt
"The   sick   's   mander   Kept in water"
    fifth   room   sala
        He's startled
He sees a large red fish staring at him

The fish is sick   It says on the plaque
From one side the fish slowly slaps his hot palm

(Wednesday)

Heading for the city on Wednesday
The ghost thinks a long while
& steps on its own shadow
                      "Thump"
The ghost finds a big hole in itself
Rice pours out
        Five cents for grownups   Three cents for children
        Two cents for anyone smaller

The ghost crouches to mend its clothes
Then mends the road
"Thump"   A big hole in its Self
          Songs surging up
Never again hears of the Spring Goddess
Everywhere demonstrations erupt
The prince starts collecting his winter clothes
You stand on the bridge
                        Where the cars move the trains stop
"The definition of Lovesicknessism is
I've been wanting to fight for a long time"
                        Children

Bottles thrown all around

(Thursday)

Ghost judge   Ball-point pen
          Coil flowers
          Three cents a blossom
The ball-point skirts some adults
Keeps them tied up   Rolls a ball
Eats them up
              She changes her name without leaving a trace
The ball-point refill eats up one word   Writes again

          Family name   Single
          Given name   Fat lips
          Volcanoes cold   Those from the north
Simply talking won't do
One person spits one person   Whoever is taller speaks

"In three minutes the flower will blossom"
Who asks   The air turns transparent
One person   In the study builds clothes
Into piles   Opens the collar
The strokes grow fewer & fewer ...
One person draws   & the ghost loses several strands of hair

(Friday)

(He grows more *&* more fierce)
    Pushes people   Up the glass
    The ghost backs up
& the person turns into a big-mouth fat-face
Pancake   He dares not ask himself if he's
Fallen   Pry open the mouth to see the license number on the side

The ghost reads
          One horse
          Five clouds   Five soldiers
One horse pressed in a book barks in a frenzy   Meanwhile he
                              notices
The pointy-chinned author *&* on top, a head of dishevelled hair

      Five horses   Five pawns
               Move back   Check
Pin   Ping Ping   Pin   Five armies
   (He has no hope no matter how he moves)

That is a northern endgame
Grapes yellow *&* dry   Soldiers brave *&* true   Flowers rich *&* full
For the first time he does news broadcasts in a film

(Saturday)

The ghost
Once more acts in a film
          : *Popcorn Revolution*   Intro
Several people beat him
He says   Division or brigade commander's all right
   Army commander no way   Army commander I still want for
                           myself
   Don't put me on
   A troop of soldiers offers gifts on the ground
   Who doesn't know   Red plum trees blossom
   Turning red from green she's the other side's
   Dignitary   If you want that we'll negotiate
   Why are the flowers so   Red

First: marriage registration
    If changing names change the nickname   Use ball-point
Second: students lift stools   Into the sky
    Throw   Not that way
    Need three people standing on stools throwing ropes into the
                                                          sky
    Done   Count them as kites

Third: gig•gle•gig•gle
As soon as he laughs   The director makes everything full of smoke

(Sunday)

"The dead are beautiful" the ghost says
& looks into the mirror   In fact he's only about seven inches
    Held down by a pile of glass   Glass
                         Wiped clean
"The dead are all pretty"   Like
             Shadowless glass
                   Silver screen   Lit up
                   Show the slides   One layer after another
The dead are behind the safety door
A pile of glass cards

He plugs one nostril
The light comes up Plugs the other
Lanterns Shadows Hazy   The city stretches forever
•Still she can not see•
You may hear bricks hitting the ground
The dead make the air tremble

In the distance, stars   Further
More stars   Only after a long time
Does he know there's a transparent poplar above the smokestack

(At the Time of Qing Ming*)

The ghost does not want to do the backstroke
                                        Bulletin
The ghost does not want to slip & fall
                                Bulletin
The ghost does not turn into a person   Bulletin Seven   Ghost

                            Plays piano   Relaxes
Ghost   Ghost
    No faith   No honour   Writes letters   Turns lights on
    No love   No hate   Eyes
Ghost   Snap
    No father   No mother   Open
    No children   No grandchildren
Ghost
    Not dead   Not alive Not crazy
                  Not stupid   The raindrops that just fell
                            Are gathered in a bowl   He looks
                            & knows they are eyes that just blinked
    The ghost swims underwater
                            Dripping wet
    Conclusion
The ghost slips & falls only on the diving platform

* 'Qing Ming' (literally 'Pure Brightness') is the annual Chinese ceremony in
remembrance of the dead.

194

ABANDONED WINE

◯

CRITICISM &
BELLES LETTRES

I CANNOT DWELL ON IT TOO LONG

GU CHENG

translated by Simon Patton

ONE

I cannot dwell on it too long; everything that comes from the unfathomable returns to the unfathomable. In between there is a life of flowers and trees. I sit back on a bench, switching off the sound of the world. I say, this time I want it to last a little longer. I take your hand. I know that this time has not yet turned into a shade.

I am a spirit, looking out. I know that time is short; flowers equally beautiful; they do not know me; resembling the heavens; invisible unless they turn into people; when they see me, I have already been looking for a long time; ever since the Spring, they have all passed by.

This is something of the little I know; life is blind; shades drift back and forth, and yet the world is full of 'sound and fury'.

TWO

This is something that never was; those who obtain a shade can become as beautiful as the flowers. 'When the ormosia blossoms in the South, Spring puts forth branches' — this is one of the most beautiful things in the world; while watching the flowers, he suddenly becomes one himself.

When the flowers wither, he is not broken-hearted; life desires repose in death; purification; this is the same thing — a flower is a 'gene garden'.

THREE

It's Spring again, band after band of Springtimes, bringing festivity with them.

I know the secret of life; I laugh, and taking up the over-abundant water, I sprinkle it amongst written words, which then take root and blossom; it's as if I've worked a miracle; but no, it is soon too dark; like a lamp I give out light, and in consolation I say to myself: 'I am man of understanding;' come here to this place through me.

We all die, in the instant we obtain our material bodies; this is already foreordained. While alive, we can turn into shades and continue our wandering or, together with every leaf, we can be covered over by the ice and the snow; this is the fear of every shade in the moment of their transformation — they somewhat resemble people; shades feel no fear, of course.

FOUR

He gazes at the Unfathomable and asks: Will you take me? The Unfathomable does not reply; it has never responded to such human questions.

He gazes at the flowers and asks: Will you take me? The flowers do not respond either; they are daughters of the Unfathomable.

He gazes at a pile of stones, he jumps into it and dances; he allows cities to prosper, and then to crumble; he lets the feet of the earth stretch into the sea, lets flags and flames flutter across the North.

A painting is painted, and he is locked outside.

Shades are unable to die, but at the time of death, they turn into flowers as before.

FIVE

When we enter the boiling water, the spirits appears; they toss and we tumble, and a long time passes, before a transparent heart become visible; this is the hope that they were unable to hold onto.

Did you see it? Yes, I did. Then let's go.

Life is both flowers and demons, and both are invisible, when we have forgotten love and death.

REINCARNATION IS DIFFICULT

FROM 'A SECOND LIFE' BY LIU ZAIFU

translated by Sean Golden *&* Laureano Ramirez

Living in a foreign land is like being reincarnated in another body. It forces you to undergo unreal transformations you would never have imagined.

Even today I am still invaded by the claustrophobic sensation of being reincarnated in another body. From East to West, from that far-away but familiar shore to this near-at-hand but alien shore, from the great yellow-skinned black-haired masses to the great yellow-haired white-skinned masses. This earth is not the earth that I belong to, these streets are not the streets that I ever walked; even the weeds and the wildflowers and the wild ducks are not the same. This world is a different world in its very essence. I really have been reincarnated.

At the same time I must doubt my reincarnation, because reincarnation implies living in another body, and I do not inhabit another body.

Once I was an embryo in the womb of my homeland, an irreproachable embryo, were it not for the fact that I could not stomach the stench of ferocious gunpowder in the womb, that I liked to expose open wounds in it, that I liked to tell the truth and could not stomach lies. In the end I became a freak. Once a freak, they censured me, they expelled me, they would not let me speak. Of course I could not change my fate.

An embryo expelled from the womb should be reincarnated in another body, but I have never fully been able to achieve this. The new womb has walls as hard as iron. Nothing inside is soft or warm. Some Taiwanese friends who have already been totally reincarnated here, tell me not to fear confronting the metallic hardness of the walls, because at the beginning we all have to bash our heads until they bleed. But I cannot compare myself to them, because I know that their reincarnation took place when they were still very young, when they were still 'infant spirits'? Infant spirits can be reincarnated naturally and easily, in strict fulfilment of divine will. But I am an old man of fifty years, without a 'spirit' and still less 'infant', whose tongue, hands and brain have started to bloat, who can see how truly difficult it is to enter the linguistic and psycho-cultural world of a new womb. And this new womb stinks of money; it makes me want to vomit. Entering this world would surely make me scream, "I can't stand it," and I would become a freak once again.

In the end I took on a very strange form of life, detached from the eastern womb on the one hand, but unable to enter the Western womb on the other; a vagabond, wandering in a crevice between two wombs. My reincarnation did not take place in another body, but in a wasteland. I subsist amid the barrenness that stretches between the two wombs; and what was once a freak is becoming a monster. My thoughts and my writing are rank with the stench of freaks and weeds of the crevice.

Because I could not be reincarnated in a new womb, I want to return to the old one, and nostalgia constantly engulfs me; the moon of my land is rounder, even though I never noticed it before; the applause of my land is louder, even though I never heard it before. But when I remember the stench of gunpowder that that uncontrollable freak smelled in his mother's womb, I repress my nostalgia and continue to live in the crevice, continue to wander between two fronts — the two fronts that Lu Xun evoked in his image of a lone warrior, the only survivor between two fronts, wandering aimlessly and alone, shouldering his lance, although his were battlefronts, while mine are wombs.

Wandering is not the same as falling, however. There are many things to do in the crevice, as the ants, those long-time inhabitants of crevices, know well, untiring workers from sunrise to sunset. A body recently expelled from the womb is still wet, impregnated by maternal waters, and must be washed. I can still remember the washing I got after my first birth, fifty years ago: the water was so hot that I screamed. This time I have to wash myself, calmly, reflecting on the past, freeing my body of the stench of gunpowder, of the spirit of the shadows. What is more troublesome is that there are quite a lot of blood stains, and for some unknown reason I cannot wash them away, and they hurt: maybe I am wounded. All I can do is lick them, late at night.

I pace the crevice, washing myself and looking about, and I discover many flowers, plants and fruits that grow in the waste land between the two wombs, the deer and the squirrels indifferent to time and space that keep me company. And when I manage to free myself from mental barriers, I observe the absurdity of both worlds from the crevice between them: I can see it clearly. Yes, I can see it clearly. There is nothing beautiful about these worlds that act as hosts to embryos. The womb is a muddy pond full of snobbish eyes and serpent guts. Fortunately, some embryos emerge unsullied from the muddy pond, like solitary lotus flowers.

A FAREWELL TRIBUTE ZHAO YIFAN

Yi Ping

translated by Jacqui Adu-Poku

Yifan was a straightforward sort of person, but, living in times such as these, he became quite a complex phenomenon. Yifan was also a pure person. Now, as Qingming comes round again, I think of him, that huge head of his and that slight, well-meaning smile. Outside, rain drips gently from the sky onto the wet grass below.

I met Yifan relatively late in his life in around 1980. A friend asked me to seek him out to give him some material. I went to Qingdao in search of him. The Democracy Wall had been ordered to move to another location, and Yifan was there gathering underground publications just at the time when things were at their most tense. My friend had told me that Yifan was a 'career revolutionary'. But, he was wrong.

What used to be number eleven Guaibang Lane was a large, densely packed compound of houses, and it took several circuits before I managed to find his. I remember going in through the back door. Yifan's parents occupied the front room, and he lived in a small room at the back. It was a tiny room and very cluttered, with all kinds of bits and pieces, books and writing materials taking up more than half the space. It was a warm day and Yifan was hard at work. A small electric fan that he had made himself hummed as it turned on the table. Yifan had a very broad and prominent chest — a consequence of always being seated, and common among those unable to walk. His head was huge — bigger than any head I'd ever seen before — and he had an absolutely amazing memory. I felt sure there was a correlation between the size of his head and the sheer capacity of his brain. His forehead was broad, too, and shiny, reflecting all the glory of his life. Having suffered from scrofula, his lips turned inwards, and his voice, when he did speak, was very faint. He didn't say very much to me the first time we met, but then there were so many people coming and going all the while. I told him why I'd come. He leaned forward in his chair, and sorted through some papers he had taken from a cupboard. I was struck by the obvious strength in his hands and arms. He fished out the material I was after, put it in a bag, closed it and wrote a few characters on it. A methodical man. When I made to leave, he dispensed with the ritual encouragement for me to stay a bit longer, he just nodded at me and smiled. A sincere and unaffected smile.

The next time I saw him it was already autumn. I asked him to look over the few articles I'd written, and also gave him back the books he'd lent me — Ehrenberg's *People, Years, Life,* Freud's *The Interpretation of Dreams* (a xeroxed copy). After *Today* ceased publication, it was from this source that *Literary Material* obtained the articles it distributed. It was at that time that Yifan moved from his cramped little room into a bigger place in the outer courtyard. It was quite a nice room, although the light was none too good. Whenever I went to see him he was invariably sitting at his desk working. He had fewer visitors then, so we had the chance to talk.

Yifan did not have a job as such, but kept himself by proof-reading for a publisher. He did the final check on the dictionaries *Xinhua Zidian* and *Xinhua Cidian.* Yifan had been a child genius, reading by the age of four or five. At ten he had read the classics, and at thirteen had already published a book of his own. In China in the 50s, he edited the largest anthology of children's literature. It was actually through this work that he became sick with exhaustion. Regrettably, Yifan never had any other literary successes, but he didn't live in a very good time. Nonetheless, he willingly dedicated himself to society and to others. Had he lived in a different time, he might have been one of the greats of the literary world. I can to this day still remember dozens of volumes from a Russian encyclopaedia lying on the floor of his poorly lit room. In fact, huge works like this must only have come to be published through Yifan's efforts.

Yifan's father was a founder member of the League of Left Wing Writers in the 1930s. His mother joined the cause early on, so you could say he was born into a family of literary revolutionaries. Revolution and culture completed the tragedy that beset Yifan all his life. When he was two, Yifan was injured in a fall, but his nurse didn't dare tell his parents. Consequently, he contracted tuberculosis of the bones and was bed-ridden for a number of years. It was from his sick bed that Yifan first began learning to read and write. Later, when he'd recovered, he participated in physical labour and built the District Primary School, where he applied himself to such an extent that he wore himself out and fell ill again. He was admitted to hospital and spent many more years confined to bed. He eventually lost the use of his legs.

In 1981, the novel *When Sunset Clouds Disappear* was published and was for a while the most popular book around. Initially distributed underground, it cost 1.20 *yuan* and was printed with Yifan's help. During the previous winter, I'd visited Yifan once and found him busy binding copies of this book. His single bed was almost completely concealed beneath stacks of printed paper. I'd felt a little anxious on his behalf, wondering how long it would take him to get through so much work. I decided to lend him a hand and took about twenty copies to bind. The following spring, Yifan invited a few friends round to discuss the book and not long afterwards it was officially published. I managed to get hold of a copy and noticed it had undergone quite a few changes. Later I heard that the writer had been none too happy with Yifan, probably because publication of the book had been delayed. This brought a wry smile to my lips.

From the end of the 1960s, Yifan had been at the centre of Beijing's underground literary circle. Many people visited his home to borrow books, chat and exchange literary works. Yifan had been a catalyst for literary enlightenment to the extent that he altered many of their lives and destinies. Yifan was also a collector, and had kept practically all the old Red Guard newspapers. He also collected letters from the rusticated youth, underground literature and philosophical tracts. It was for this reason that in 1974 Yifan was arrested and imprisoned. He was charged with propagating reactionary literature, with the Security Bureau accusing him of belonging to a non-existent organization (the Fourth International). Using a pair of crutches to prop himself up, he spent two years in jail, and was freed only in 1976. While in prison, Yifan had continued to explain *Das Capital* to his cellmates. After his death I came to see the list of his belongings that had been drawn up by the Security Bureau. Among the items listed were Bei Dao's *Strange Beach* and what appear to be works by Guo Lusheng and Mang Ke. After leaving prison, Yifan went on with his business. In 1978, he played a major part in the publication of *Today,* contributing a number of the manuscripts he'd collected, some of which even the authors themselves had lost. I don't know exactly what Yifan did for *Today*, he never said anything. He had collected together a huge amount of literature from the Cultural Revolution, and in 1979, when Yu Luoke's was exonerated and no one in Beijing could find any copies of his essay 'On Class Origin', it was Yifan who provided *Guangming Daily* with one. Yifan once said to me that if ever anyone wanted to research material from the Cultural Revolution, he would happily hand his whole collection over. Sadly, this precious collection did not survive. After Yifan's death, the material was sold as waste paper by the family servant. When I got to hear about this and hurried over, there was already very little of it left. I am still unable to reconcile myself to the tragedy.

After 1981, many changes began taking place in society, and Yifan's visitors gradually fell away. I had the feeling that Yifan became quite lonely. At that time I was working in the outskirts of the city and everyday caught the bus to work near the entrance to Chaoyang market. Yifan lived only a few minutes from there and sometimes, when I had some spare time I'd drop in to see him. Yifan was always something of an innocent. Whenever he came across something new or strange he became as excited as a child, much in the same way that scientists and artists do. It seems a pity to me that he didn't walk this particular road.

With great interest he talked about a man who, in the 1950s, had presented the State with a prescription that would allow people to go without food for a very long time. He spoke so earnestly that I became interested. Yifan himself told me he had invented a new way of reading. This involved reading with one eye open and the other closed, then switching eyes. The idea was that this lengthened reading time. When Yifan was running a printing business, he came up with a new way of typesetting. It had taken him several months to develop. I remember watching him working with those densely packed characters beneath the dim lamp in his room. He admitted that the efficiency of this new technique could do with a lot of improvement. He had done some research on the Chinese writing system and had written an article on the subject. He'd had the idea of a new system of characters, and when he described it to me I was both amazed and excited. The pity is that his paper on this new system of his was never completed and people will never know the wonderfully creative and remarkable writing system it described. I am unable to speak particularly highly of Yifan's ability when it came to literary appreciation, but when it came to the written language, he was truly a genius. With that immense head and startling memory, together with his imagination and dedication, he could have been an outstanding language specialist.

When Yifan was young, he used to daydream about being an ant and going to Ant Land on holiday. Indeed, Yifan was the sort of person who would distance himself from the affairs of everyday life and let his mind roam to some magical mystical kingdom. It's a shame he lived in a time such as this, where everything has been unceremoniously elbowed aside in favour of the politics of greed. Yifan confused the real world with the imaginary one that was his.

Yifan was a devotee of communism. He really believed in it. In his lifetime he'd worked as secretary of a Party League branch; had been a Red Guard; spent time in jail, took part in the democracy movement, collected underground literature and later he went into business....

However, he was no philosopher, no politician. Neither was he a revolutionary nor a businessman and, above all, he was no realist. Yifan had a great number of friends: some from the literary world, some who were dissidents, some who were members of the Communist Party, young unemployed people, even some of the servants in his household. Everybody and anybody who visited Yifan's house was accorded respect. There were times when I even began to wonder whether Yifan was perhaps the embodiment of some new kind of religion, one transcending the boundaries of kindness, honesty and love taught in all other religions. I was never one for harbouring illusions, but I clung to the idea that mankind would probably benefit a great deal from adopting common ideals. Yifan helped so many people. It was he who helped me print my first pamphlet of five poems. In 1986, a friend of mine went to Japan, and it was with Yifan's help that I printed his collection of poetry. That was his life in those last few years. It still makes me feel guilty. Yifan was so incapable of refusing a request for help that more often than not his enthusiasm exceeded his capabilities! Unfortunately, not everyone is blessed with such a free-giving spirit, and so I could not always approve of the extent of Yifan's kindnesses. I was not aware of him ever having made demands on other people, or ever having disliked or hated anyone. He'd been jailed, yet even then he never railed against the society or even the system that had put him there. I have said that 'hate' was an emotion that Yifan simply did not possess. The concepts of interest and ideology had already been buried beneath his love, kindness and ideals. Against the backdrop of all that is fashionable today, Yifan was something close to a miracle, in whom all those discarded qualities had come together. For so long I had shunned such words as 'love', 'kindness', 'gentility' and 'morality' because they had been tainted and vulgarized by the power-hungry. Today, I give these words back to Yifan in order to cleanse and completely restore them to their former meanings.

In 1982, Yi fan started up a mimeograph service. His family and friends tried time and again to dissuade him from it, but Yifan's stubbornness was such that their effort were in vain. He eventually got the venture off the ground relying on his two crippled legs and a handful of money. I helped him look for typesetters and pull together a small number of orders. In the beginning, business was very slow, so we still had the opportunity to talk. Yifan's energy was extraordinary — he managed on just a few hours sleep a day. When he used to talk about his next big idea, his eyes were calm and bright. No sooner would he start than he was off in fantasy land again, where he would be publishing the collected works of his friends and hitherto unpublishable literary works, imagining that the arrival of a democratic China was imminent. Although I tried to persuade him otherwise, I didn't even begin to imagine the tragedy that would later unfold. Yifan's business gradually increased. He took on more staff and got a bigger stall. However, when I went to see him again he didn't have time to talk, and with me having been transferred to a different area, I wasn't often able to go back to visit. I occasionally got news of Yifan through friends. His mimeograph service had become March Ltd.; his business was growing bigger and bigger, as was the number of his staff. There were all kinds of people involved in all sorts of projects and dealings, and he had even taken out a big loan. I remember not liking the sound of this since I didn't believe it was the sort of business someone as guileless as Yifan should get mixed up in. By my next visit, his mother, a half-deranged woman in her eighties, who used to spend her day causing havoc around Yifan, had died. His old place had been torn down, and another house had already been built in its place. He and his father had moved into a four-room house, which was turned into the company's office. When I saw him he looked so tired as he held up that huge head of his, his eyes lacking their former brilliance. We didn't talk much. The buzz of people and the ringing of the telephone made a din like gunfire. It was as though we were strangers. It was only the familiar nodding of his head that gave me a glimpse of the old Yifan. I felt quite concerned and wasn't sure whether to say anything to him, afraid that it would increase his burdens still further. It seemed that he was completely immersed in a chaos from which he could not extricate himself. There was no night and day for him and he slept very little. I said to Yingzi, his assistant at the time, that he could not continue like this and would literally burn himself out. She said she and the others working for the company were trying to come up with a way of protecting him. But our words were empty ones. Some time later Yingzi came to see me. Yifan had put up the money for some underground poets he knew, to publish a collection of their work. She'd brought along a dozen or so names and asked me what I thought. Yingzi had gathered together a bundle of manuscripts. I understood Yifan's enthusiasm and good intent, but I didn't believe the venture could turn out well. Yingzi kept very busy for a quite some time, and I ultimately heard no more about it. I went to see Yifan again and found that things were more or less the same. There was just one occasion when we had the chance of a quick chat. He told me he was no longer as busy as he had been and was getting more time to rest. He seemed satisfied with the way business was going. He also began talking of his plans for the future again, like building his utopian village, where enterprises, science institutes, writers and artists could all go about their business in peace....

The old sparkle was back in his eyes. Yifan was a man with great imagination. However, it's only now when I think back on it that I realize just how dangerous it was and how much it cost him. These ideas of his were the last thing Yifan and I ever talked about together. It was not quite two years after that conversation that I heard of his death. His business had run into a terrible mess, his staff having cheated him continually. The company had huge debts and the creditors had pressed him incessantly for repayment. There was nothing Yifan had been able to do and he reached the point of indifference. I heard that when Yifan had fallen ill he began haemorrhaging and by the end of the week he was dead. After his death, those who'd been working with him grabbed his possessions. Soon afterwards the State television news covered the story that someone who'd worked for March Ltd. had embezzled 600,000-odd *yuan* but had turned himself in. Yifan had never been able to understand the ruthless and corrupt side of human nature. He was a worshipper of the temple, but had unwittingly brought the sacred rites of the temple down into a dark cave.

I sometimes visit the little lane where he used to live. It is a bleak place now and I wonder if the people who used to live there have all moved away. I don't know if his father — now in his eighties — is still around. Yifan had never married and his only brother lived abroad. He had amassed neither property nor money. The only thing he'd had was that precious collection of writings from the Cultural Revolution, and that, too, had been pulped. Yifan's ideals, kind-heartedness, warmth and generosity followed him to his grave. This is an era where quality of character, morality, conscience and ideals are not required; he was their last resting place. I have no faith in society, but neither do I resent it. This is simply unchangeable history. The thought of Yifan puts me in mind of Durrenmatt's *Der Besuch der alten Dame*. Human progress and morality do not come about because of civilization, but rather through the uncivilized experiences of prostitution, murder and robbery. I didn't always support Yifan and his way of doing things, but sometimes when overcome with sadness, I look up at the sun suspended in a haze of blue sky, and I think of Yifan, of his spirit, of his smile, and the memory soothes me.

When I decided to write this piece, I had thought it might be quite relaxing. Little did I realize that writing it would actually plunge me further into the dark as if into the snow of another world.

SWAN BY AN ENDLESS STREAM

WRITTEN ON THE TWENTY-FIFTH ANNIVERSARY OF ZHU YULIN'S DEATH

CHEN JIANHUA

translated by Angela Geddes

> Paris change! mais rien dans ma mélancholie
> N'a bougé! palais neufs, échafaudages, blocs,
> Vieux faubourgs, tout pour moi devient allégorie,
> Et mes chers souvenirs sont plus lourdes que des rocs.
>
> Aussi devant ce Louvre une image m'opprime:
> Je pense à mon grande cygne, avec ses gestes fous,
> Comme les exilés, ridicule et sublime,
> Et rongé d'un désir sans trêve! et puis a vous, ...
>
> — Beaudelaire 'Le Cygne' *

It is hard to pinpoint the precise time, but I am fortunate to have a piece which Qian Yulin wrote as a preface for an unpublished anthology of my poetry, in which there is a passage that reflects both our general circumstances and Qian's ever-precious sincerity:

"I first met Chen Jianhua in early spring 1966. The weather was bitterly cold and our surroundings bleak. We often met together with a group of young friends to share our common love of poetry and literature. It was a kind of immersion in one another, sitting there back to back on those dark winter nights as if warming ourselves by a fire while waiting for the sun to rise. Our fire, our source of warmth was literature and poetry. Cherishing love, cherishing hope, and even in

---

* The original article, of course, prints samples of Zhu Yulin's *Chinese* translations of Baudelaire. Here we give the original French of Baudelaire's verses, to fill out the context. Those readers with Chinese are invited to consult the original article in *Jintian*, in order to properly appreciate Zhu's translations as such.

the midst of our despair, refusing to give in to it, we sang songs in our suffering. And we suffered deeply — for the lives of others."

I came to know Qian Yulin, Wang Dingguo, Wang Shengbao and various others in a second-hand book shop on Fuzhou Road, Shanghai. We used to run into each other there nearly every Sunday, as we had ascertained that this was the day when all the newly acquired books went up on the shelves. As soon as the doors of the shop were opened in the morning, everybody streamed in and headed straight for the few shelves of literature. I would have given anything to be hawk-eyed and deft of hand. I would be scouring the shelves desperately, not knowing which books were the best, when they would be snapped up in front of my eyes by someone else. After a few hours, the shelves would be in total disarray.

It was easy to strike up a conversation with both acquaintances and strangers alike. You had only to mention a few revered names, or poetry that was special to you, to reveal your innermost self. The shop was set back seven or eight yards from the alleyway, creating a square between it and the pavement. Those waiting for the shop to open completely filled that space. We stood there immersed in pure passion, immersed in our common dreams, acquiring and proving our enlightenment through the prism of literature. My memory is of the sun always shining brightly, reflecting off a high plaster wall on the right. How could we naïve, would-be 'literati' possibly understand the profound sadness about which we read and wrote?

Directly opposite was the antiquarian book shop, which was another of our favourite haunts. The table in there was covered in bargain books; copies of the texts and explanatory writings for the imperial civil service examinations. The cheap prices of these books were like a gift from heaven. Qian Yulin's home was down a narrow street only a couple of hundred yards from the book shops. His family of six squeezed into a tiny, windowless annexe at the back of the wool shop. Yulin, Dingguo and the others went to a key upper-middle school in the heart of the city, whereas I was a student at a part-study, part-work technical school in the suburbs. I felt like an outsider from the back of beyond when I joined the clique.

Qian was the eldest amongst us. He had suffered from asthma since early childhood, which had caused him to miss much of his schooling and fall behind. He had a round face, and a generous mouth. He wore a pair of black-rimmed spectacles and had a permanent shadow of stubble on his chin. Talking away ten to the dozen he would frequently produce a small bottle and take a few swigs of medicine with a well-practised movement.

There was also a small attic in Qian's home, and this piece of private territory was where he kept all his books, and where he wove his romantic poems and dreams. He wrote all his poetry in the same uninhibited style. Among his role models were Tao Yuanming and Xin Qiji, Pushkin, Heine and Whitman. We all shared our poetry with each other, and expressed mutual admiration, regardless of the style. Qian continued to write poetry until 1976, and it is still being read today.

The intense, pithy frankness of his poems startled people, as they were not written in the popular style of the time. He did not have the 'correct' family background and was rejected as a child. In addition, he became ill, but despite all this he never stopped singing songs about love and hope. His kind of individual, unreserved and ardent poetry really did express a brightness which could only be found in the world of dreams. Under the brilliant sunshine of socialism, however, this brightness became somewhat pallid and sombre.

From the spring of 1966 until June 1968, when the ruthless attacks began, we talked and debated incessantly. I do not know if anyone had planned it this way, but everyone seemed content to pursue this one, single interest: it seemed that we all shared the same attitude. When the Cultural Revolution suddenly broke out, this way of looking at life through literature was made to look naïve, but we genuinely did value individual perspectives on literature, perspectives shaped by experience. When Zhu Yulin joined us, our interest acquired a certain refinement, and we began to know the decadence of nineteenth century Paris, as well as eighteenth century romanticism. Our interest formed a stark contrast with the bloody, malodorous Cultural Revolution, and we found ourselves in a distressing predicament.

It is possible that it was a feeling of separateness from the rest of society, and weariness of the popular talk of the time, which actually brought us together, although we were not consciously aware of it at the beginning. We were unanimous in our praise of classical and Western literature. We could all argue vociferously about *Anna Karenina*, as if we would never exhaust its spirit, but if the topic of conversation turned to the contemporary Chinese literary world, there was only silence and sighing, as though we had encountered a stretch of wasteland. Those doggerel songs and worn clichés about the 'fervour of life' failed to arouse our interest. If indeed some contemporary writer's name was mentioned it would be met with sharp criticism. It is not surprising therefore, that we were overjoyed to discover we had all written poetry — sonnets or candid lyrics — using the ornate and flowery language of a bygone era. Seen from another perspective, our strivings in this direction concealed a need to separate literature from public authority. In the short 'golden era' before the Cultural Revolution we chatted contentedly, laughed unreservedly on the streets, in the book shops and in other public places. In Mao's words we "gave instructions to the mountains and rivers, and coaxed the written word." It was as though we wanted to proclaim to our dull, steely surroundings, "Look, we're special!"

Our study of the arts was confined within the borders established by the political and moral propaganda of the day. It seemed the only thing worth discussing was Western literature, because when we did pass judgement on contemporary or earlier Chinese literature, art became our weapon of criticism — and so we subconsciously avoided turning our critical weapon to politics. Despite the countless shadows cast over our innocent minds by the political movements between in the fifties and mid-sixties, we empathized with Deng Tuo, and we still appreciated his romantic love of the classical Chinese woman with long hair. We passed around Tian Han's novel *Guan Hanqing*, admiring him more for his moral integrity than for his literary talent. Our critique of the writers of the twenties and thirties was entirely different again. We held Wen Yiduo and Dai Wangshu in high regard, and, with the exception of *Thunderstorm*, we bemoaned the demise of theatrical writing in the period following. We had much good to say about Yu Dafu, but not on the subject of 'His Lordship' Guo Moruo. It was difficult to distinguish, in these critical appraisals of ours, the fine line between art, and politics and ethics. No doubt also the traditional classifications of 'elegant' and 'vulgar' influenced the way we looked at literature.

Our interest served us in our strivings for status and recognition, and we were content throughout to concentrate on the early part of the Aesthetic Movement. Cherishing our impetuous and ill-formed aspirations, striving with every sinew for new sources of inspiration and new language, and wanting only to escape from the parched wilderness that surrounded us, our drinking from the poisonous springs at the same time terrified us. The second hand bookshop was our Mecca, where the 'poisonous weeds', the undesirable writings which had managed to escape censure, were there to satisfy our secret desires and feed our imagination with fresh stimulants. I can remember when we came across He Qifang's *Picture of a Dream* and

Prophecy, and we returned again and again that summer to pore over those books.

Our 'secret desires' were, for the most part for 'forbidden amusement'. The official propaganda criticising writers' works only served to arouse our curiosity. When we procured a copy of Ai Qing's *On the Cape*, we could find nothing wrong with it.

Zhu Yulin's arrival on the scene made us jubilant and excited. He was much older than the rest of us, and we generally acknowledged him as our mentor — he was so learned and accomplished. Qian Yulin and the others knew him before I did; my first meeting with him was through Baudelaire.

It was an unusually hot day, and there were quite a number people in the second hand book shop. I was browsing, not having bought any books nor seen either Qian or Wang, and I was feeling quite downcast. Zhu Yulin came over from the shelves towards the counter and we stood face to face. Even though we had never spoken, we always went for the same kinds of books and I already felt a rapport with him. He asked casually:

"Found anything?"

"No, have you?"

I had noticed that he was holding a copy of the translation of a highly desirable Symbolist work. "Dai Wangshu translated Baudelaire's *Les Fleurs du Mal*," I offered, somewhat hesitantly, implying more of a question than a statement, and intimating that I was looking for a copy.

His response was casual again. "Mm."

I came out with it. "Do you have the book?" I was sure that he did.

"I have seen it — actually the translation is not brilliant."

These words were earth-shattering to me and I blurted out, my eyes widening, "Have you done some translating yourself?" He was non-committal. He simply smiled, taunting and enigmatic.

The following Sunday we met again in the book shop and he handed me his own translation of some poems from *Les Fleurs du Mal*. There were four altogether: the first, 'Le Guignon':

Pour soulever un poids si lourd,
Sisyphe, il faudrait ton courage!
Bien qu'on ait du coeur à l'ouvrage,
L'Art est long et le Temps est court.

Loin des sépultures célèbres,
Vers un cimetière isolé,
Mon coeur, comme un tambour voilé,
Va battant des marches funèbres.

— Maint joyau dort enseveli
Dans les ténèbres et l'oubli,
Bien loin des pioches et des sondes;

Mainte fleur épanche à regret
Son parfum doux comme un secret
Dans les solitudes profondes.

The other three were 'Sonnet d'autome', 'Tristesses de la lune' and 'Parfum exotique', all great literary masterpieces. Zhu Yulin was a highly gifted translator, and he attained perfection in his translations of Baudelaire, not only because he was fluent in French and fully conversant with French literature, but also because of his turbulent background and his aesthetic accomplishment. I believe he regarded translating Baudelaire's works as a mission; since he died in July 1968 at the hands of political persecutors, the eight translated poems of his which have remained in my possession have become a little cultural 'jewel'.

It seems laughable now, but at the time I did not really know much about Baudelaire, nor did I know that the literary newspaper *Renmin Wenxue* had carried Chen Jianrong's translation of excerpts from *Les Fleurs du Mal*. It was only through a book, translated very early into Chinese, on the modern literary trends in Europe, that I knew he had been dubbed the original 'demon poet' in Western literature. I subsequently learned from Ai Qing's preface to an anthology of poetry by Dai Wangshu that the latter had published a book of selected poems from *Les Fleurs du Mal*. Nevertheless, I did seem to be attracted to 'demons' at the time, probably because I had been deeply affected by the harshness of the campaign against capitalism and feudalism.

I was studying and working at a technical school in Pudong, Shanghai. The school belonged to the central communications department and many of the teachers were seconded from the army. They kept a tight rein on us politically, talking all the time of class struggle. Dormitory life was like being in the army. I did not have the 'correct' family background, and so encountered political discrimination. I was not interested in my subject either, and had become bored with the training, so I was utterly despondent. Unsociable by nature, I became even more cold and silent, and it was thus that I stumbled into the realm of literature, seeking solace in writing poetry. To begin with I emulated the style of the barking-mad, boot-licking Emperor's pet, Guo Moruo, then went on to write a sugary, philosophical poem in the style of Bing Xin. My next infatuation was with the insipid style of Xu Zhimo and Wen Yiduo; then I delved into Symbolism, and then Modernism. All the time that I was friendly with Zhu and Qian, it was as if I was trying to craft something approximating a cross between Zhu Jiang and Dai Wangshu. 'The Legend of the Embroidered Shoes' was, it may be said, written with desperate sadness, mourning the fact that our country's history was being trashed for the proletarian revolution:

> Remember all those lush and splendid years
> in overflowing wine from feasts and banquets steeped,
> as waiting concubines would fill the night with tears;
> from whom, now weak and old, the last remaining rouge is stripped,
> gone, like the bells which once adorned the land with chimes,
> like willow shadows on imperial rivers cast,
> which, with the setting sun, are fading fast.
> Do the Tang masters see with sorrow from their tombs
> that o'er the river now the rain clouds loom?
> Remember those years, as you hear the camel cry
> who treads on thorns that in the desert lie.

Although I began with such naïve imitations, in all those different styles I tried, I wanted not only to experience the joy of expressing beauty, but also to forge a link with immortality. In fact I still had no clear idea of what to write about. I made no conscious attempt to treat the important topics of life. Take, for instance, 'Song of Falling Blossoms', where I wrote about comforting the "sweet skeleton, wanting to keep its lonely soul company", or 'Dirge of the Man on the Frail Donkey'

> Riding alone his frail gaunt donkey, sobbing slowly
>   a plaintive muse,
> Hearing death's drear, cruel laughter deal its blows....

Perhaps these primitive scribblings demonstrated an inner need to stay apart from the hostile world around me, and envelop myself in innocence and harmony through an aestheticism of death. But it was impossible to attain originality in this way. The inherent connection between this type of art and the subject of death was also influenced subconsciously by political thought, presaging a literary crisis. However, for the time being, I wallowed blissfully in these tinkerings with style and the language of death, which meant that my first encounter with Baudelaire was like meeting an old friend, not because of the modern feel to his work, but more because I already had an empathy with hellish.

'Old Zhu', we called him. In the fifties he had studied foreign literature in the Western Languages Department of Beijing University, later transferring to Shanghai's Tongji University to study architecture. He had worked for a short time after graduating, but when we met him he was out of work and single. This was all we knew about him — we did not know where he had come from or where he was going, nor was that important to us. He was tall and slim, and wore a pair of run-of-the-mill glasses. The expression in his eyes was alert and profound, and full of suspicion. His lips were flat and serious — when we talked and joked he was often scornful and sarcastic. He dressed casually, but he spoke with great authority. The way he smoked was reminiscent of the literati of the thirties, with their long shirts and queues. Under the dim light, he would draw deeply on his 'Brave' cigarette, the cheapest brand, at thirteen cents a packet, and would joke about being the 'hero consuming brave', whilst at the same time delving into the intricacies of Dostoevsky's *Notes from the Underground* as if he had been there himself. He looked slightly ill. The furrows on his brow looked like the scars of old wounds.

Old Zhu opened up a whole new literary world to us. In Dostoevsky's books were to be found the humiliated and scarred characters that were closest to Zhu's heart. He talked about the freaks in Balzac's novels, and loved to speak about satirical writings such as Daudet's *Sapho*. He had a fascination for literature which expressed the complexity of human nature, especially qualities of strength and independence. His tastes were strange and macabre. The writers he plainly most admired were Baudelaire and Edgar Allan Poe. He translated the latter's poem, 'To the River' as 'By an Endless Stream' *(Zai yitiao yongheng de xi pang)*. He did not speak lightly of these two eccentrics. One day, when we were talking about Baudelaire he asked, "What is art?" The question startled us, and he went on mysteriously, "Art is opium." He quoted a poem by Baudelaire, saying he felt that the joy which came from art was "more penetrating than ice and steel."

He was also fond of talking about "letting one's imagination run wild" and praised the kinds of writers who could create the most aesthetic and imaginative works. We did not really understand his outlook on all these things; we simply responded with amazement and admiration.

Old Zhu was by no means decadent. It is impossible to put one's finger on what exactly his character was. He had a deep understanding of human nature, great insight into humanity. When we talked about Pushkin or Heine he would smile benignly, always astounding us with his knowledge of classical literature. He once memorized Longfellow's 'In Praise of Life' in English. He was passionate about the 'three Li's' (Li Bai, Li Shangyin and Li He), and compiled and hand-wrote a booklet of their selected works. Then, untiring, he went on to compile a small collection of poetry by Du Mu and Xu Hun. His diligence was evidenced in his repeated translation of *Les Fleurs du Mal*, aiming constantly for perfection. When we discussed his translation of 'Sonnet d'automne', there were endless deliberations as to whether he should transliterate the French name Marguerite as 'Meiguirui', meaning rose stamen. As the Cultural Revolution progressed, his political ideals came increasingly to the fore. He wrote a thirty line poem of political satire, using literary quotations from classical imperial anecdotes, scourging the villainous men and women in the poem at every opportunity. He was quite clearly making an oblique attack on the current political situation.

The Cultural Revolution arrived like a rushing torrent, and when we had picked ourselves up, stunned, sorrowful and shattered, we met our situation with bitter smiles. The number of friends congregating in Qian's home grew, with people coming from further afield, and coming not only to talk about literature. The revolution broke down our barriers and tossed us all into history's great wave, enjoying our secret pleasures, but at the same time constantly aware of the battle raging outside. We discussed the rumours, talked about the situation; we cursed Mao's vicious malice, and the cunning, fawning madness of Zhang Chunqiao and Jiang Qing; and at the same time we circulated books and writings. Both my home and Qian Yulin's were ransacked, and the antiquarian book shop was also closed down. The revolution made the 'poisonous weeds' emerge from the woodwork and disseminate rapidly. We read Fu Donghua's translation of *Gone with the Wind* and *Forever Amber* — favourites of old Zhu's. Still, we had to meet cautiously, changing our meeting place frequently.

The most indelible memory is of one day in Autumn 1967 in Changfeng Park with old Zhu, Yulin, Dingguo and Shengbao. We had rowed a boat over to a grassy patch of land, feeling as if we had found our Utopia. There, we sat in a circle and Dingguo read out the translation that Zhu had brought of Baudelaire's 'Swan'. We were so moved by it that we became quite serious. We rained praise on Baudelaire and on Zhu's translation. That day, eating, singing, taking photographs, we were happier than we had been for a long time.

The winter of 1967/68 was particularly cold and particularly long. It seemed as if spring would never arrive. We could not summon up any enthusiasm for writing poetry, and our spirits were in purgatory. I felt the current situation closing in on me, forcing me to relinquish imagined death and face the real thing. The poems of 1967 had been like dreams, empirical and quaint. In the April I had written "I love my dream-world as a tender, sweet lover / As the moon rises, I softly call her name" ('My Dream'). In July of that year I wrote a piece of prose called 'Dream Fragrance', a soliloquy that came of a perfume which I smelled on a tram seat in the depth of night. Indulging in the memory and the mirage of that fragrance, the prose depicted a kind of dreamlike beauty. The style of Baudelaire and Zhu Yulin influenced me little by little. I began to relinquish my use of colour and dreams and started to look for things in real life which moved my spirit. I wrote a few poems about the suppressed sexuality of the masses. Then I wrote 'Terror of the Dream': "I opened my eyes to endless darkness: / a net overlaying my fear / Limbs benumbed, as though severed; / flogged and left deep in a crevasse." It seemed I had found my own style, brought closer to the horrors of reality, approaching its dark cavern, afraid that I would be swallowed up at any time. Then in 'Sad Singing on a Rainy Night' I wrote about "the spirit that awakens in the night," singing a sad song "like prisoners chanting in a dim cell, like a stretch of turbulent sea, with countless heads awash, floating so pale and wan." Towards the end of the year, I found myself cursing the "Sun hidden behind dense fog, candle burning to the quick." I was ecstatic and electrified.

I despised the reality around me in which death and hate were constant. When my aesthetic method met up with reality's ugliness, what resulted was far from beauty and happiness, but pleasure at being able to vent my hate, my heart-felt sorrow and revulsion. But I could not return to writing about dreams; I could only suspend myself in front of the cavern, looking back at the broken dreams, looking forward and trying to escape real death. There are recurrent images in my poems of incarceration, of beatings, expressing the sorrow of a spirit that was being tortured, as in 'The Deserted House':

As I murmured to myself, alone,
A lion sprang out from hell ...
He wanted to escape, to roam,
In his forest free, where wolves
Bowed down to him on bended knee.
But the fearsome turnkey
came and lashed him till he fell,
unconscious in the corner of the cell.

Art did not enable me to overcome my terror of death, and at the same time I felt another kind of moral compulsion which seemed to say that only by using the weapon of writing to pierce the enemy through the heart could we prevent art becoming a pretence, an escape; only that way could we sweep away our timidity and weakness. But to follow this compulsion would mean the death of my artistic ideals, and I was faced with a tormenting conflict for which I found no resolution. My only choice was to be silent and to hope.

In June 1968 our 'counter-revolutionary' clique was exposed, and one by one, the members were taken by the Red Guards of the Guangming Middle School, where they were locked up and forced to admit to their 'crimes'. Zhu was also taken as an abettor, and after several days of brutal torture, he was killed, reported as having committed suicide. The Red Guards then publicized his counter-revolutionary history. He had criticized the Communist Party in 1957 in the 'frank airing of views' trap and had been labelled a 'rightist'. After graduating he had been sent to Xinjiang, where he later became ill and returned to Shanghai.

The other members of the 'clique' were interrogated and forced into submission one by one. Up until the beginning of 1970 I was labelled a counter-revolutionary by my work unit. I was kept in solitary confinement and interrogated. When they asked me for the two booklets of poetry which we had circulated, I lied and said that we had burned them. In the dark room where I was held, I turned death over and over in my mind. I imagined being taken to the execution ground, kneeling on the ground with my hands tied behind me, the bullet entering my head from the back. This time art was victorious over death. After six months the police declared their verdict and bestowed on me a conical hat inscribed with the words 'political errors'. I was a branded a lesser 'devil' for the next ten years.

In October 1979 a funeral was held for Zhu Yulin in the Longhua Crematorium. From the eulogy I learned that he was originally from Baoshan County, Shanghai. He was only thirty-four when he died.

This, then, was how a quarter of a century passed. I often think back to Zhu's death. He died so needlessly. At first the Red Guards had not known where he lived, but then someone had seen him going to visit the doctor and had found out his address from the doctor's records. I now often reread the poems which he translated, particularly the ones, like 'Le Guignon', which rank as poetic masterpieces. There is something also which has plagued and perplexed me; I have thought about over hundreds of times. Several months before Zhu's death, at a time when I also had the feeling of being in the greatest danger, he often surfaced hazily in my mind, an ominous premonition, haunting me. I wrote a verse, 'Untitled', the first line of which is, "I think of you, like an insect", quoted from the beginning of his translation of 'Swan'. In this poem the insignificant insect "forms an image of mystery and beauty, / filling and smoothing the cavities in the road." The last section runs:

> If some day I find you 'mid the dust and dirt
> and see your open eyes unwittingly reveal
> your love, your hate that goes on still unhealed,
> unheeded, but by me, the truth of your past;
> do not worry, friend, for I
> will hold the black war banner high
> for you to smile and close your eyes at last.

I do not know whether hate still keeps Old Zhu's eyes open, and neither do I know how he really died, since, to this day, there has been no proper investigation. When I read my poem 'Black War Banner' it seems very naïve — I often remember the scene in Changfeng Park and think how none of us really understood the true essence of 'Swan'. There was so much of Zhu's turbulent life, his misery and loneliness contained in that poem. We were blissfully unaware that day of how cruel our laughter must have been for him.

If only he were alive today.

BLUE-AND-WHITE, REMEMBRANCE OF BLUE-AND-WHITE

LEE YU

translated by Foster Robertson and J J Zhao with the author

The blue-and-white porcelain bowl was kept, among various other things for sale, in a roughly-made glass display case three feet tall and two feet wide.

A simple piece, its air of nobility seemed out-of-place among the cheap knick-knacks.

The shopkeeper ended up dismantling the whole glass door before he was able to take it out.

The bowl was from Macao. The man's Portuguese or Spanish accent explained why a bowl made in China was being sold in a shop for handicraft items from Latin America.

As you know, Macao, in China, is still being governed by Portugal.

He smiled and showed off his well-made false teeth of an attractive, natural-looking white like two strings of pearls. They made his smile graceful and this man of Spanish or Portuguese descendant wistfully expected that the friendly smile contained an apology from the colonist to the colonized.

The white background of the bowl, compared with other white porcelains, had a warmer feeling to it. The mineral blue which only the Chinese know how to apply, had been used to draw the God of Longevity with deer and clouds on the inside, and the Eight Immortals around the outside. The quality of the porcelain itself was not very fine; there were some imperfections in the glaze. The subject matter of the painting was commonplace. However, one could see that the brush work was excellent.

The fine line drawing was exquisite, a sensitive brush had touched in the folds of the robes. In places the lines appeared and disappeared, making the folds of the robe look like ripples. The portrayal of the figures, particularly their facial expressions was simple, archaizing and a bit clumsy on purpose, a fine example of the distortion that yields a subtle sense of humour.

It did not seem to be the work of a hack painter, but the light-hearted brush play of a master painter of the period.

The shopper returned the bowl to the velvet display cushion on the table. Turning it upside down, she saw the four imprinted characters spelling out an inscription in the cursive style of calligraphy: made in the Guangxu period.

It is not easy, within the Guangxu period, to tell the difference between the work of craftsmen who painted for a living and that of cultured artists. There was a tendency among them all to be skilled in a wide range of themes, subjects and styles. Ren Bonian was the master among them.

Ren Bonian's brush work is remarkable, both powerful and delicate. He could use the sophisticated, apparently effortless, *wenren* brush; and he could use the ordinary nail-head-rat-tail method, both at the same time, bringing together high class and lower class art. His eccentric and whimsical figures display an excellent sense of distortion. With a quick grasp of the immediate moment, no one was better than him at catching the essential characteristics of his subjects with a bold incisiveness which at times verges on caricature, a feat of no ordinary skill. And then there was Wu Changshuo, a master of fluent lines; there was Su Liupeng, a painter known for the carefree spirit of his bold Zen figures. And also there were Sha Fu, Qian Huian, and Ni Tian, who all painted beautifully.

Could someone actually buy a Ren Bonian work in a Latin American crafts shop? Could a realistic novel have a magic plot? If the painting on the bowl was indeed by a folk painter, his or her technique was not a bit inferior to the accomplishments of the established artists of that time.

Calculating the unreasonable price of the bowl for a while, the shopper finally made up her mind and said, "Double paper bags, please."

I, a person who rarely shopped for antiques, was driven by an indescribable urge at that moment, and bought the bowl. The French novel, *A la Recherche du Temps Perdu*, called in Chinese 'Remembering the Past' after its well-known English title, could be better translated as 'Searching for the Past', that is 'zhuixun', not 'zhuiyi', as most people think. Early in the novel, and again near the end, a much-discussed incident is reported in the life of the author, Marcel Proust. The elderly Marcel recollects his youth as he drinks a cup of lime-flower tea. In the first volume, *Swann's Way*, it is a winter's day when Marcel comes home and his mother offers him some tea and sends out for some of those short, plump little cakes called madeleines. As soon as the warm liquid, with the bit of madeleine soaking in it, touches his palate an extraordinary sensation overcomes him.

"At once the vicissitudes of life had become indifferent to me, its disasters innocuous, its brevity illusory." He puts down the cup and casts his thoughts back to the circumstances of a moment in his life.

It was on a Sunday morning, in Combray, when he went to greet his aunt Leonie in her room. She gave him a little bite of a madeleine, first dipping it in her own cup of lime-flower tea before he tasted it. Now Combray has changed, and the gardens and houses are all gone. Nothing remains.

> Taste and smell alone, more fragile but more enduring, more insubstantial, more persistent, more faithful, remain poised a long time, like souls, remembering, waiting, hoping, amid the ruins of all the rest; and bear unflinchingly, in the tiny and almost unpalpable drop of their essence, the vast structure of recollection.[*]

Grandma has a blue-and-white porcelain bowl. On the white background two pines are painted; one is taller, the other shorter. Under the trees, sits a faceless man on a big rock, fishing. In the distance are hills and the full moon above them. Beside the moon is some poetry, 'Fishing beside the Wei River and the Qi Mountains, entering into my morning dream'. There are said to be some mountains named Qi both in Fengxiang County of Shanxi Province, and in Jiexiu County of Shanxi Province. Since there is a Wei River flowing through Feng Xiang County, one gathers that these Qi Mountains are probably the former. At any rate, what the poetry seems to say is that early in the morning, one sees only the river flowing by softly, while the moon, reminiscent of night, still hangs in the blue or white sky. The drawing is very simple, conveying a kind of naïvety and humour, rather similar to the style of Feng Zikai. Used only by Grandma, the bowl essentially belongs to her.

According to Marcel, his aunt Leonie's lime-flower tea is made of dried petals and green buds plucked before they mature. The fruit of the lime tree is certainly greener, and smaller than that of the lemon

[*] Quotations are from Proust's *Remembrance of Things Past*, translated by C. K. Scott Moncrieff and revised by Terence Kilmartin (1981).

tree, and its skin is thinner. But it does not really grow in China. So it is called green-lemon in Chinese. This green-lemon is often used in cocktails, a foreign influence, and in food decoration, rather than cooking, while lemons are used in cooking, also a rather foreign usage. Both have very fragrant, whitish flowers. In the Chinese version of the novel, lime-flower is translated as grapefruit-flower, which grows on a much taller tree, and its colour is rather yellowish than whitish. Whatever the translation should be, luckily all belong to the citrus family, related to one another.

If aunt Leonie does not feel quite right that morning, the job of making the lime-flower tea would fall to Marcel, instead of the maid, François. Then it would be Marcel who would shake out of the chemist's little package onto a plate just the amount of lime-tree flowers needed to steep in boiling water.

> The drying of the stems had twisted them into a fantastic trellis, in the interlacings of which the pale flowers opened, as though a painter had arranged them there, grouping them in the most decorative poses.... marking, as the glow upon an old wall still marks the place of a vanished fresco.

They give out the fresh fragrance one can still smell when taking a walk on a warm evening in spring.

If Grandma was making soup or other main dishes with lots of sauce or gravy, she would surely be using her bowl. From Marcel's tea cup rises the lime-tree flowering in spring, while from Grandma's bowl, emerges a variety of dishes: Bean Curd Stewed with Fish Head, Salty Fish with Pork, Roast Chicken with Anise, Preserved Bamboo Shoots with Mushrooms, Pickled Vegetables Stewed with Pork, Stew with Dried Scallops and Eggs, Steamed Breaded Pork, Cabbage Stewed with Dried Shrimp, Vegetables Braised with Sliced Pork Stomach, Shredded Meat and Vegetable Soup, Vermicelli and Meat-ball Soup, Radish and Carp Soup, Soy Bean Sprouts Stewed with Spareribs. From Marcel's lime-flower tea cup, a fragrance like spring flowers would affect one's senses. From the blue-and-white porcelain bowl, the scents of crushed garlic, sliced ginger, and diced green onions, or thick sauces of fennel, star anise, mustard seed, or sweet cinnamon would whet one's appetite. The names of different dishes prepared in their due seasons flipped through my mind, all those which had been spread out by time across the varied seasons of my life, adding up to a sequence of menus and creating a sumptuous banquet in my memory.

Grandma was really good at stewing. After various kinds of materials were rinsed, soaked, cut into appropriate shapes and added to seasoning, how cleverly she would blend them together, put the pot on the fire, and patiently wait for their transformation. When dusk came, imperceptibly, the atmosphere of the whole house would become milder and warmer, the scent of the stew which was coming into being would permeate the whole house. As for the food, all the ingredients and spices had by this time mellowed and melded their flavours, the stew would melt between one's teeth in every mouthful without even chewing.

At one side of aunt Leonie's bed stood a large yellow dresser and a small table. On the table were a statue of Our Lady, a bottle of Vichy-Celestins, her prayer-book, and her medicine. The other side of her bed was bound by the window. Looking out from beside the small table, one could read "the daily but immemorial chronicles of Combray."

Grandma's blue-and-white bowl was used for all kinds of purposes and appeared everywhere. Usually it was set out on the dining room table, at times it would be on a small wooden table, or on the cutting board, or beside the sink, or on the coffee table in the living room, or on a mah-jong table in the sitting room. If it was in one of the last two places, it would hold candy or watermelon seeds for guests. When evening came, it was washed thoroughly, dried, and put back in the most handy spot in the kitchen cabinet.

Its place was on the bottom shelf of a cupboard that had two shelves. On the same shelf there were chopsticks, plates, spoons, enamel dishes, and ceramic bowls. Beside these were the tins keeping sugar and salt safe from rats and roaches at night. On the top shelf of the cabinet lay a few pots and pans, a few basins, a couple of bamboo sieves, and a rolling pin for pastry and noodles. The dried daylilies, mushrooms, and the ginger and garlic left over from the day's use were stored in plastic bags. Every object began to spread out in front of my eyes. The bowl returned to its place in the cabinet, everything else resumed its place. What had been gone regained life.

Next to the cabinet is a small, old table, its wood grain etched out. On it is a worn cutting-board, slightly concave in the centre. On top of it lies a well-washed, shining kitchen knife. Next to the cutting-board is a sink where a bright green plastic hose is connected to the faucet. Dripping out of the plastic hose, onto the green vegetables soaking in an aluminium basin, is the tap water. The running water, so crystal-clear in the rice-white daylight, is immensely valuable and expensive in the post-war years.

The rice-white daylight comes in from a small window. Through the window one sees, not the alley itself, but the stucco wall of the opposite neighbour. The back door of the kitchen is open; a beam of light slips through the narrow alley and rests itself in a leisurely way on the kitchen floor. And Grandma loves to move a small stool to be by the threshold, to sit in the oblique light, and to shell beans.

Snap beans, spaghetti beans carefully cut to half-inch lengths, green peas, young soy beans, or Navy beans troop into the blue-and-white bowl beside her feet, shining green.

It is just before time for dinner. Underneath the fragrance of the stew, you can faintly smell something coming from the back alley that seems quite interesting. So, you stick your head out of the window. Looking out, you see the drain opening between the two stucco walls. Waste water flows gently and cheerily though it. Where the current is slow, blood worms cluster. Looking up, you can see a few twinkling stars around a new moon pale as a trace of water colour.

When the fragrance becomes faint and the image of the flowering lime tree fades away, the "vast structure of recollection" rises up; the white kitchen wall begins to recede, it blurs, boundless, unrestrained and inconceivable.

Grandma was married young to the son of a prestigious family whose ancestors were said to be related to the Ming imperial family. The family inherited wealth and property, and had been granted permanent exemption from punishment by decree of the Emperor. Their garden was as fancy as that in *The Story of the Stone*. The stronger the power, the bigger the shadow it casts. So it is said that this family had been responsible for many awful things, such as the occupation of land, exploitation of peasants, internal family intrigues, greed, extravagance and promiscuity, all of which were extraordinary enough to produce another book like *The Story of the Stone*. Treachery lay in wait for Grandma as soon as she stepped into the household. She was deprived of her human rights. She suffered an oppression both subtle and open, delicate and rough, the kind of oppression that only sophisticated Chinese know how to create.

Such stories sound as if they come from a novel, yet I did not learn of them from Grandma. Everyday she simply got up early, washed, dressed, and began to use her bowl quietly and contentedly. She was diligent, invisible, and selfless, like the faceless fisherman under the pines, living a life without complaint, no longer touched by the harshness of life. Concerning Marcel Proust's magnificent reconstruction through memory, his biographer André Maurois writes:

> On the vast landscape of his sentiments, an oblique and golden radiance from the far distance of his lost paradise shines on all existence, touching every form of poetry. He orchestrated this rich melodic material, turning out a great work of art from thousands of fragments.

And so it is. The beams of pale golden light from the back alley continue their oblique radiance. The red worms continue to flaunt the bright curves of their splendid silky bodies in the current. As evening falls, the deep glow of the late sun illuminates the sky in ever-changing rhythms and colours; sentiments become intense. Truly, it is a glorious landscape unequalled by any work of art.

RUSSIAN SAGE·

D J LIU

translated by Diana Liao

A sunny day at last. He thought about cleaning up the border of perennials in the backyard.

The border was started a good three or four years ago, but was still not much to look at. When he first plotted it out with the help of some books, he figured on three years before its reaching 'maturity'. After three years of tending, he expected every specimen to fill the space planned for it, that no unsightly gap would appear between plantings, that the shape and style of leaves and stalks would complement each other, that each flower would shine in perfect harmony with the colours and patterns of the others: all a testimony of the fruits of his labour on paper.

Yet what struck him most now, especially in the pale light of fading summer, was the terrible lack of order and balance before his eyes.

Take the cleomes and shred-leave coreopsis as an extreme case. It was then thought that plants of that height would help fill the gap between the front and the back rows and that, because of their bright colours, two or three would be more than enough. What happened three years later was that they practically took over the place through self-sowing and self-propagation. In the back row, the single-petalled hollyhocks, purple delphiniums and mustard-coloured yarrows, robbed of their already precious sunlight, never quite reached their proper stature. Meanwhile the vigorous cleomes and coreopsis, unchecked, snatched up the sunny spots instinctively and overran the place. They not only overshadowed the tall plants at the back, but blocked the semi-ground cover in the front, such as the English lavender and various dianthuses, depriving them of the sky above.

To hack out some eighty percent of the coreopsis and cleomes should be the first chore, so he told himself. He brought over a wooden bench, set it down overlooking the border, sat on it and

---

Russian Sage, common name for *Perovskia Atriplicifolia*, a flowering plant originating in Asia Minor, was probably first introduced to Europe by the Russians, hence the name.

pondered the weekend ahead. The thought of putting aside all other urgent matters and devoting his time to sweat and labour already filled him with a sense of happiness. Of course, the work should have been done in spring. To delay it till now was in itself rather absurd. What was more, he knew that frost would be here in a matter of two or three weeks. So why this sudden urge for a complete overhaul now? The temptation to leave everything till next spring began to tug at him.

Before he knew it, a large human shape had settled itself at the other end of the bench.

"Dad, how could you have let the weeds grow so tall!"

The large human shape lurched forward, followed the stepping-stones to the back of the flower bed, and pulled up a bunch of thin, stiff, silvery blue sage.

"O dear.... easy, son!"

His son was standing in front of him, his precious Russian Sage in one hand, and a silly grin on his face.

The very first time that he set eyes on this plant was some four years ago, one day in early summer, when he was seeking inspiration from the Botanical Garden. The place was styled after the English garden, its perennial borders displayed in full glory between the bright blue sky and the luxuriant lawn, graciously relaying the rationality and elegance of the Victorian Era of the British Empire. The clump of Russian Sage, originating in the grasslands of western Pakistan, bloomed furiously from the back rows of a border of mainly pink, white and lilac. Hundreds of stalks of verdigris Russian Sage soared above the rest, spraying forth clouds of tiny blue flowers which, from a distance, resembled wisps of grey mist.

The plan was rational; the dream it spun was seamless, and pure romance. This was what inspired him three years ago to turn his backyard into a garden. This remnant of an aborted dream, now clutched in his son's palm, was ordered, after much research, from a nursery in Oregon which specialized in rare specimens.

Silently he brought out a pair of secateurs from his dungarees, clipped off the wilted leaves and rotted roots, and replanted his dream in the ground.

Maybe the son felt something, maybe not. Anyway, he sat down again on the bench and, without looking at the father, began to talk, almost to himself.

"I'm skipping college. I sent out the application yesterday. The minute I graduate next year, I'll report to the Marines...."

All joy vanished at this instant. He turned and looked his son straight in the eyes for the first time. He wondered why this particular late summer afternoon had to be so different.

Two weeks ago he met with Dr. Perkins, the school careers and further education counsellor, and discussed his son's future.

Something in the eyes of this white man from a small town told him that his son, academic excellence notwithstanding, could not escape the fate of a discriminated minority.

"The S.A.T. scores alone are not enough," explained Dr. Perkins. "The schools you picked have their own standards of selection. That includes proof of leadership quality, record of community service, achievements in sports, etc., etc...."

There was no choice but to compromise. Finally a second-rate State University was included as a safety measure.

Yet from the secret just revealed by his son, he realized how absurd his worries had been, his years of hope nothing more than a feeble romantic dream, like those clouds of blue mist which never rose before his eyes.

"What went wrong?"

He was still sitting on the bench. His son excused himself immediately, leaving no room for discussion. This decision was not to be changed. That was the message from his son. He also knew that his son deliberately played it light — the silly grin and the clumsy gestures formed a curious mix with the underlying deliberateness and decisiveness. At seventeen, his son was like a snake coming out of its first moulting, venturing gingerly into his bewildering world.

A scene from four years back suddenly came alive.

The tall young officer asked him, "Mr Lu, could I have a word with your son alone?"

He nodded in confusion, overwhelmed with self-reproach and frustration. His son, like a criminal caught red-handed, was led away to a room he could not see. Half an hour later, he watched his son come out, his head hardly reaching the chin of the officer behind him. Against the officer's black uniform, his son's face was ashen, as if he had had cramps.

He was not conscious of anything seriously out of line. Still overwhelmed with self-reproach and frustration, he thought whatever the officer did was reasonable enough. "Take this as a warning," said the officer, "Should the same thing happen again, he'll have a criminal record, and there'd be no way to talk the parents of the other side out of pressing charges." Nor did he pay much attention to the shock his son was going through. His own upbringing convinced him that his son got what he deserved. Still, he remembered asking: but what happened inside that room that he could not see? His son would not answer. When pressed, he only blurted out, "That son of a bitch! He thought he could scare me into selling out my friends ... that son of a bitch...."

Whatever truly happened, he never did find out. The police simply notified him one day that the parents of three female students were bringing charges against his son and three other thirteen and fourteen year-olds for chasing their daughters with a B-B gun, that one actually went off and almost hurt somebody. Luckily it was winter. The pellets only pierced the coat, sparing the body.

The story from the boys' side was all the same: that the girls led them into the woods to chase away some racoons. But what racoons? There were none in sight. So what did the girls want? Only they knew....

And the bullet hole through the coat — how did that come about?

Again the boys gave the same story.

The girls demanded to see the boys nude. When they refused, Jeanie took off her coat, shot a hole through it, and threatened to use it against them.

There were four days between the incident and the interrogation at the police headquarters, enough time for the boys to put together the details of their version. Yet, did 13 and 14-year old boys actually have it in them to deal with such fine points?

It was impossible to come to a judgement, even for the police. One thing noteworthy was that all girls involved came from a grade above.

Thus the case was dropped.

But he came away with a knot in his heart. Of the four boys, only his son was singled out for one-on-one interrogation. The only possible explanation was that his son was the smallest of the lot. Were smaller-built yellow people easier targets for intimidation?

He felt the knot inside, but he never gave the whole thing much thought. He was inhibited by his own upbringing, felt that he had not brought up his child properly, that his son would surely go from bad to worse... He was overwhelmed with self-reproach and frustration. With time, the knot loosened — until now.

"Why the Marines? Why was there no sign all this time? How come I never realized that my son had drifted so far away? Why? Why?"

Why had he not noticed, until now, that the Russian Sage, which needed much light, could not grow because the cleomes and coreopsis took away its light?

His rational and elegant dream burst right here in this upside-down, topsy-turvy perennial border.

When his son most needed his care and protection, he was wallowing in self-reproach and frustration. So his son chose the Marines.

On this rare fine day, he finally made up his mind. Not spring, but now, now he would dig up all the plants in the garden, clean them, prune them, then replant them in their proper spaces according to their individual needs. The Russian Sage was finally granted the sunniest spot in the yard.

Still six months to go before the deadline for college applications. Maybe, he told himself, maybe he would be given another chance.

ALSO ON DEATH

TANG JIE

translated by Yang Yunqin

The topic for this essay rose to my mind when a friend of mine called together a few people, including me, to seek our opinions on a play he had written. It was a story of love between a black man and a Chinese girl. The man was as worthy as could be, but the girl held back from any commitment because of his colour. Under pressure from her parents, she left him, but only to go back to him later against all the odds, for the separation made her appreciate his good qualities even more.

Among the first critiques offered was the comment that the denouement was as unconvincing as it was banal, and that the play should end with the black man's death, to the readers' chagrin and the girl's eternal regret, for such an ending would not only enhance the dramatic effect of the story, but also elevate the man's image to a sublime height, since a dead man errs no more.

I looked around to find the speaker who, surprisingly enough, turned out to be a pretty girl with refined manners. I marvelled at her lack of fear of retribution for killing, so flippantly, a black man brimming over with the vivacity of life.

I never readily condemn my novel characters to death, not out of the goodness of my heart, but out of fear of death.

I have given much thought to the source of my fear of death, if not for the mere description of death. Is it because, as Christian priests say, fear of death stems from the aura of mystery over death, for no one has ever returned from death to tell the living about it? This explanation might be valid, but it still leaves much unanswered. Probably the most likely reason, in my case, is that all four deaths I have ever witnessed — of people close to me — were untimely, violent deaths that left me with not only the usual pains of bereavement but also bitter memories of the tragic circumstances.

The first death I saw with my own eyes was that of a colleague named Lu Zhiyun who worked in the picture-mounting section. He was thirty years old at the time. I knew this because he had trouble finding a girl friend, and his age was constantly on the lips of his brother-in-law, a colleague in the oil painting section to which I belonged, who took it upon himself to ask acquaintances everywhere to find Lu Zhiyun a match. Lu being an only son, getting himself a wife was more than a personal need, for he was also charged with the mission of continuing the family line. That was why his brother-in-law ran around on his behalf, more anxious than the party directly concerned. Of medium height and fair complexion, Lu Zhiyun was not bad looking, nor was he the talkative sort. Through the huge glass pane of the mounting workshop, I often saw him working with rapt attention by the vermilion-coloured table, wearing an apron, stiff with starch. He lived frugally. When listing his merits, his brother-in-law never failed to mention his sizeable savings account. But on the other hand, he also had a fatal weakness. He had had an attack of schizophrenia when in college. It was after he was dismissed from the college on the grounds that he joined our company after the recommendation of his brother-in-law. In fact, there was no lack of people in the company who had daughters, but none of them was willing to offer him one. A person with a history of schizophrenia is of no more worth than a broken bowl which has been glued back together.

To everyone's astonishment, Lu Zhiyun suddenly found favour with destiny in the realms of romance and got himself a most lovely wife. It was also said that she was the daughter of some chief-of-staff in the army. For all the revolutionary austerity of those years, the occasion was still celebrated, at the insistence of his aged mother, with a decent banquet attended by dozens of guests. At the sight of the bride and bridegroom radiant with happiness, those colleagues with daughters to marry off looked none too sure about their decisions.

Three months later, a grave incident occurred in the picture-mounting section. A portrait of Chairman Mao five meters long by three meters wide, mounted for the Party School of the Province was found with a foot-long slash on the left cheek. It was the work of a special kind of knife used for mounting purposes. Needless to say, this was as good as slashing the face of Mao himself. With all speed, police and army men had our entire company surrounded. The picture-mounting section was cordoned off with yellow ropes. The incident became listed as one of the major cases of the year at the municipal level. But all attempts to track down the perpetrator were baffled. In the end, Lu Zhiyun was arrested on the sole clue that he held the key to the office on Sundays. In the process of the interrogation, Lu had another attack of schizophrenia. He filled the sheets of confession paper with senseless inanities. Along their route of circulation, the horrible confessions also came into my hands but the handwriting was barely legible. Soon thereafter, he was sentenced to death.

On that day, the sky was overcast and hung so low that it appeared likely to fall down on our heads at any moment. By order from above, two hundred employees in our company stood at the intersection of Zhujiang Avenue to, in the words of the authorities, "receive an education." After the public trial at the Wutaishan, six or seven large trucks slowly rumbled down the street. Right by the railings in the first one stood Lu Zhiyun for all to see. His hair was all shaved off. Against his back, in much the same way as with convicted criminals in ancient times, was a two-meter long tablet bearing his name. That was the first time I ever witnessed a death or, to be more exact, a man on his way to death. I kept my eyes fixed on him. There was not a trace of any expression on his face, though it was drained of all colour. The eyes, however, were wide open, giving me a sudden unaccountable feeling of hollowness that engulfed my whole being until I was no longer conscious of my own existence.

It was widely said in the company that it was his newly wedded wife who represented the evil star in his destiny. Being a man scarcely blessed by fate, he lacked the strength to withstand the sudden marital boon. This speculation made all bachelors in the company apprehensive of beautiful marital candidates, so much so that they would be wary of any girl, sight unseen, about whom they heard too much praise.

The second instance I have in mind is the death of Zhu Shuizhao, a famous Yue Opera singer as well as director of the Yue Opera Troupe. She played Liu Yi in the movie 'Liu Yi Marries the Dragon King's Daughter'. Though I had seen her no more than a few times at conferences sponsored by the Bureau of Cultural Affairs, her beauty left a deep impression on me. Not only were her looks impeccable, but there emanated from her an air of deeply imbued refinement. Indeed, she was one of the very few people who had looks of such perfection that the slightest change in whatever way would mar the otherwise immaculate proportions. Just as is the case with geniuses, to produce such rarities takes generations of harmonious union between supernatural, natural and human factors.

I had a colleague whose mother was the Vice Director of the Yue Opera Troupe and also a well-known singer who sang the role of the Dragon King in the same movie. I often went to play cards in her apartment, located one story underneath Zhu Shuizhao's home. The night it happened, I was there again playing cards when, at around twelve o'clock midnight, a woman's scream was heard from outside the door. "Zhu Shuizhao is dead!" I remember how that scream shook me more than as if I saw death with my own eyes. My heart went cold—it was but a long-drawn-out scream heard somewhere down the alley. The world of the living was diminished by one human being, and such a beautiful human being, too.

Zhu Shuizhao died miserably. It was suicide. The idea of death did not occur to her though she had been put through a good many 'struggle sessions'. It was when her daughter slapped her face to exhibit a determination to break clean with her that she collapsed and lost all faith in life. Being illiterate, she stabbed herself with a knife right in the middle of her chest. Little did she know that she was to hit only a bone. She pulled the knife out from the bone only to lunge it again to the right. That was where the liver was. To make sure that she would not survive, she twisted the knife around violently, mangling the entire liver. I have used this detail in a story of mine, but the character of the story was sent by ambulance to a hospital and brought back to life in the nick of time, for, I believe, that none of those who had seen her on stage could have borne the thought of letting her die.

The third death happened to a college classmate of mine from Xuzhou named Liu. He was the son of a deceased revolutionary honoured as a martyr. He was quite a handsome young man with a head-full of curly hair and it was as 'Curly Hair' that he was popularly known.

In the first two years at college, he was the class president. Later, he resigned with grim resolve, saying that he had had enough of it, but others attributed his resignation to his romantic involvement with a girl in the Department of Music, majoring in the zither. Curly Hair's forte was not in colour but in sketches. He could draw a person from head to foot in one unbroken line. His sketches were mostly nudes, emphasizing the breasts and the hips. We jocularly called him a pornographic artist. He was not among the best students in the class because he did not do well in oil painting. At the time, oil painting was taught exclusively in the unimaginative style of the Soviet Union. However outstanding he was at sketching, it was but one of the minor courses where the grades did not carry much weight. I remember having sometimes seen him all curled up by the window-sill of the classroom, singing in a slightly melancholy bass voice.

In the summer vacation of the last year in college, he hitch-hiked his way to Xinjiang probably to seek sources of artistic inspiration. As it was a steamingly hot day, he sat on the top of the rapidly moving truck. All of a sudden, a tree branch cut off his head. News about his death plunged our whole class into a despondency that lasted for the entire semester. No more promising artists emerged from our class thereafter. Many classmates changed careers. I wouldn't say that it was unrelated to Lu's death. I had never really paid him much attention, but for a whole year after his death, my thoughts were on him constantly. I even recalled that he had once treated me and another girl in the class to dinner on his birthday. How could this have happened? I remember all too well his beer-flushed face, the thin childish crack between his front teeth when he smiled, and his booming, slightly pretentious bass voice. No amount of thinking could shed light on what occupied me. Is death sometimes indeed dictated by the Will of Heaven? Throughout that year, I suffered from insomnia.

The last death I shall relate happened to a man I loathed—my instructor. He was only fifty years old when he died. It was considered an untimely death because in the Chinese government, those at this age were still counted among the junior ranks of the so-called third-echelon. He himself would have wished strongly to live on, if only for the sake of his greatest pride and joy — his savings of a lifetime in the amount of approximately ten thousand Chinese *yuan*.

His stinginess was a well-publicized fact in our company. For instance, when working on a summer's day, he would take off his undershirt so that it would not be damaged by the sweat. His shoes were often on the wrong feet so as to prevent the heels of the shoes from getting worn down on one side. At first, we thought it was a mistake and reminded him that the shoes were on the wrong feet but he dismissed our remarks with a conceited smile. For a time, the company put him in charge of the distribution of materials. Getting painting paraphernalia from him was a painful hassle, for he begrudged us whole tubes of oil colours and would only squeeze out a strip on our palettes, advising us to apply more mixing oil to dilute the colours. During the time he was in charge of materials, the oil paintings from our company were no less transparent than water-colours.

All too suddenly, death descended on him, catching him off guard before he had a chance to enjoy the savings he'd taken such pains to put by. Colleagues in the company all felt sorry for him. On the day of the memorial service, his wife complained tearfully that he had hidden the money in a place that the entire family had not been able to locate after days of searching. She said in a tone that was not without some resentment against the Party that he might have offered the money to the Party as Party membership dues. The director of the personnel section was present at the time and immediately denied having ever received anything of the sort. Could he have taken the money along with him? How? Needless to say, his body must have been searched goodness knows how many times. Someone commented that there was only one way he could have taken the money with him: he had swallowed it. At these words, his wife burst out into bitter wails of grief, for this was something he might well have done.

These four people all died against their will. Death not only brought pain to themselves but to the living as well, more enduringly. Lu's mother, for example, lost her mind. At the mass assembly held to announce rehabilitation for her son, she screamed, "What's the good of rehabilitation? I want you to put his head back on!" Zhu's husband used to be a very handsome man. It was said that when the couple walked down the street together, everyone would cast a glance at them. After Zhu died, her husband aged rapidly until he looked like an over-used rag. My instructor's wife must also have suffered much mental anguish over the lost money.

For such reasons, I thought differently about the ending of that play, but I kept my thoughts to myself — I know they are based only on my personal experience.

AN INTERVIEW WITH THE RUSSIAN POET GENNADI AIGI

CONDUCTED AND TRANSLATED BY ZHANG ZAO

Zhang Zao: It is a great honour for me to have this opportunity to interview you here. I am doing this interview both in my function as an editor, who fulfils a task for the literary magazine *Today*, and as a young poet, who uses this opportunity privately to ask for advice from a great living master. The day before yesterday I read some Chinese translations of your poems; this morning I saw some more translations in English. I have noticed that almost all of those poems touch upon the issue of 'Silence', although the content of silence has undergone a profound change since your earlier days. In the poem 'Road' written in 1959 you said "We speak because silence is terrible." The silence there was a kind of self-protection, a youthful sensitivity toward oppression from the outside, whereas the silence in your latest works is a kind of remoteness. Do you want use poetry to reach a state of silence?

Gennadi Aigi: Yes.

Z: What is that silence actually?

A: You have just correctly observed the development of that silence. I became silent before because I feared the world as a young man. Later I reflected much upon silence as a phenomenon, and I obtained a different imagination of silence, a different way of accepting it, or if you like, an agreement with silence, a kind of longing for silence. I was thinking of writing a book not long ago, which I would have liked to call 'Poetry as Silence'. Let me put it this way. Nature itself is in the end silent, all noise and clamour will finally return to silence. Noise disturbs the essence of things, whereupon silence brings people back to themselves. Only in silence can people talk to themselves and think about their existence and the meaning of creation.

Z: Is silence also an agreement with loneliness and death?

A: Yes, but it is first of all an agreement with life. What is life as a phenomenon? For me life unfolds through reflection upon life itself and death, and through accepting death. I have always said that life and death are one. He who agrees with life must also agree with death, and who does this, must first of all be silent. In this sense, silence is surely loneliness. The silence of the word originates in the silence of God.

Z: I was just about to ask about the transcendent aspect of silence. No doubt in your later poems silence has been treated more philosophically and religiously. What is interesting is that, that deepening process is accompanied by suspicion of language. I remember you saying in a poem that without that one word there would be no words. Actually 'that one Word' refers to the verse in the Bible, "In the beginning was the Word". Do you want to teach us a fable: silence is looking at us, but we do not see silence?

A: Quite correct. The fact that we can not see silence is owing to the fact that we are too weak, too timid and totally unable to accept loneliness. I really believe if we have a family, we are satisfied, however I believe at the same time that everybody should have a small piece of silence and loneliness in order to understand himself and confront the world. We are lonely only in the sense of writing and creation, which mean a dialogue with God. We must endure silence and loneliness with will and gratefulness, and teach others to do the same. That is the obligation of the poet.

Z: To put it other way: silence speaks, because poetry speaks, because the Word speaks ...

A: Sure. That is a paradox. It is only through words that silence is created, and God creates speechlessness and silence only through words.

Z: Reading your poems, I can not help but thinking of a great Russian film director, Andrey Tarkovsky. Are you a friend of his?

A: No, I did not know him directly, but we had common friends. His father, Arseny Tarkovsky, one of the greatest Russian poets in our century, was a friend of mine. The films of Tarkovsky also teach us about silence. In silence people live together, in silence people come and go.

Z: It is well known that Russian poetry written in rhyme belongs to one of the most beautiful spiritual adventures of human beings. However, you use almost no rhyme. Is that a deliberate opposition to orthodox poetical discourse which attempts to beautify life?

A: I never use any rhyme. You know, a dictatorial ideology always requires systematization and identification, binding every word into armour. In fact systematization requires lifeless words and people. The heart of a poet is free, and the things and people he wants to express are lively. In other words, using rhyme is just like playing chess: although playing methods could have a thousand variations, there is an ultimate end to the numbers of variations, and when this happens, there will be nothing left but repetition. The rhyme and rhythm of a poem stem from its inner structural requirements. Meaningful rebellion happens only when those formal things become absolutely necessary, but generally speaking, they always blindfold thinking and oppose freedom.

Z: Our life is being fragmented by everyday occurrences, allowing no more inner consistency and unity. A true story-teller has no more stories to tell, a director has no more plots to dramatize, a painter has no more objects to paint. As early as in the beginning of our century, Malevich, a great Russian painter, advocated the art of Suprematism. Is it true that a poet uses no rhyme because he has lost life?

A: Malevich wrote in 1919 a piece of poetics, in which he criticized the poetry of the whole age. He said poetry was making a dangerous mistake by only paying attention to the world of objects and neglecting the spirituality of the world. I think it is very important that a poet should try to convey the spiritual energy in himself to the world, and that kind of energy is abstract, it is only through abstraction that we are able to precisely express our inner states. I agree. We humans have no more stories to tell.

Z: At the same time, the form of art only exists in a kind of non-form, which means every poem sails to a unknown form, a form that only comes into existence when it is found, and it exists only once for the author as well as for others.

A: That search means the rebellion against categorical thinking I have mentioned just before. The world is multifarious, we perceive intuitively and subconsciously that a poem would be satisfying if it could be taken as a small model of the world.

Z: Shall we return to the topic of the transcendent aspect of poetry? I feel the religious intensity in your work appear as a sacrificial readiness. In the poem 'The Birch Rustles' you say that we all rustle in this world, and then you mention the resurrection. Do you want to tell us this: if the cross is empty, everybody should be prepared to sacrifice himself on it?

A: What a terrible question, what a terrible question! Only people like Kierkegaard would give an affirmative answer to the question. No, we are too humble, too weak to be crucified. What I want to do is to teach people to weep, because our 'rustle' will stop before long. We are mortal.

Z: After Nietzsche, at the outset of Modernism, artists lament the departure of God, but today the post-modernist is accustomed to, accepts and even plays with that vast vacancy. How do you feel about this?

A: I am still lamenting it. When I work and write, I feel God stays with me. Sometimes I do feel that God leaves me, so my poems are filled with words like 'leave', 'abandon'. You can do nothing against it, if God wants to leave you, so far as I am concerned, what I can do is wait, wait patiently. But I do not agree with the post-modernist compromise, you know, that is a compromise of the soul. Artists substitute God with vacancy and other people substitute God with computers and electronic buttons. People mistake the pressure on the button for the coming of a beautiful life. That is illusion. The German poet Gunther Eich says, "All of your dreaming is nothing but deception."

Z: You had hardly published anything back in your country until recently. Were you unwilling to publish things or did that political system not allow you to do so?

A: It is of course not only a problem of politics. You know, uncommon words displease people everywhere, that is very simple.

Z: You have had private contact to Boris Pasternak. Would you talk about your spiritual relationship to your Russian forerunners?

A: Mayakovsky has many characteristics which Malevich and Apollinaire have. His genius, his thinking are marvellous. It is important to note that his way of thinking is sculptural, which has brought about a tremendous breakthrough in the Russian language. Like a true sculptor, he shapes words in such a way that they become five times weightier than usual, and words just change their size to be bigger or smaller in his hands. However, you can not require intellectual reflection of him, which is a strong point in Pasternak, and which turns into tree, bread, nature, so vital and lively. Pasternak is a great phenomenon. And Mandelstam—his spirit endures incredible fate, and he cries sharply from his soul. That cry unites the Russian word and the Russian soul perfectly.

Z: Can a poet as political creature write pure poetry, for example, like Tsvetayeva?

A: Tsvetayeva is a wonderful poet, but in terms of ideology she is very naïve. One day she wrote a poem called 'To the God of the White Army', a work that advocates a monarchical system and showed it to her husband, an officer of the White Army. He said, oh, Maria, you understand nothing, you do not understand that the God of the White

Army is a disaster. Actually, politics and pure poetry do not hinder each other. Today in Russia, a five-year-old child is already a politician. He knows what to say in school and what to say back at home. You see, politics has already penetrated everyday life, but in spite of that, the soul which experiences everyday predicaments is higher than politics. The soul must speak in the name of the human being, in the name of freedom and beauty.

Z: The last question: in this broken age of ours, is writing still possible?

A: Post-modernism is a disunion, although it functions as a cultural and spiritual horizon, it has no roots. The root is love, which turns out to be history, tradition and future. Here I can not help thinking of a sentence of Jesenin: poetry is not difficult, what is truly difficult is to live an integrated life. Humans should learn to live with others, should try to understand each other's misfortune and sorrow. Humans should try to live together with nature. When a tree suffers, we suffer too. Anyway, humans should live their lives and give their lives meaning. Life is never so one-sided and short as the post-modernist presumes. Life lasts as long as the cosmos lasts. So speaking in that sense, writing is not only possible, but also absolutely necessary.

DANCES WITH THE OTHER — WRITING AT A CRITICAL MOMENT

HUANG ZIPING

translated by Mei S Chang de Huang

SHADOW I

In the past hundred years Chinese literature, literary criticism and literary theory have always lived in 'the shadow of the other'. The most sincere Chinese contemporary literary theorist Liu Zaifu writes as follows:

> The rather influential standard formulations of twentieth-century Chinese literary theory have indeed an alien source.... The debates and quarrels in Chinese literary circles are often the quarrels of foreign theorists ... and are not the academic debates of actual Chinese theorists. This has given rise to various fatal weaknesses in modern Chinese literature: (1) lack of original, non-stolen fundamental propositions; (2) lack of an original, non-borrowed system of categories and concepts; (3) lack of original, non-transplanted philosophical positions (or lack of one's own philosophical standpoints). In summary, there has been a lack of creative transformation of imported theories and a lack of independent formulation in our own theoretical language; there has also been a lack of propositions of our own and a lack of theoretical narratives that belong to ourselves. In other words, in its development over nearly one hundred years, Chinese literary theory has often lived in the shadow of the other, shrouded within the concepts and categories provided by the other.[1]

---

[1] Liu Zaifu, 'Bidding Farewell to All Gods — The *Fin de siècle* Struggle in Contemporary Chinese Literary Theory,' *Twenty-First Century*, No. 5 (June 1991), pp. 126–27.

After describing these conditions, Liu Zaifu states sadly that "the *fin de siècle* struggle" dogging contemporary Chinese literary theory since the 1980s has been to "walk out of the shadow of the other."

This struggle is indeed sad, perhaps even tragic. However, it is also a continuation of the great effort initiated by Chinese men of letters at the end of the last century who had to face "a momentous change unprecedented in the past 3,000 years", in search of a renaissance amidst the cultural crisis of the decaying era. One can get a flavour of the 'decaying era' from the rhetorical style of Liu Zaifu's statement. If the cultural borrowing had taken place in the prosperous Han or Tang dynasties, one would have been bold and confident in 'taking it' as Lu Xun states in his essay 'Looking in the Mirror'. One would not have felt uneasy about borrowing, or worrying about becoming a cow just by eating beef or a sheep just by eating mutton. One would not have worried about using such pitiful terms as 'borrowing', 'stealing' or 'struggle'. However, such a state of affairs would not have been improved merely by repeatedly yelling, "Take it." Our decaying era happens to correspond to a prosperous era of the other, or as a currently popular expression states, one may see it as 'an impoverished culture encountering a powerful culture', or a Third-World culture being governed by colonial discursive hegemony. Nevertheless, we should note that changes have occurred in the last hundred years.

SHADOW II

The term 'shadow' is a concept 'borrowed' by modern psychology and psychoanalysis from optics, and later adopted by literary criticism; however, the term more often used in literary criticism is 'anxiety'. Western scholars such as Professor Steven Owen of Harvard University and Professor Bonnie S. McDougall of the University of Edinburgh, who represent distinct approaches, happen to concur in their use of titles such as 'Anxiety of Global Influence' and 'Anxiety of Out-fluence' when talking about contemporary Chinese poetry or the Chinese literature of the 1980s.[2]

---

[2] Steven Owen, 'The Anxiety of Global Influence: What is World Poetry?' *The New Republic,* (19 November 1990), pp. 28–32; Bonnie S. McDougall, 'The Anxiety of Out-fluence: Creativity, History and Post-modernism,' presented at the 'Symposium on Modernism and Postmodernism in Chinese Literature,' University of Aarhus, 11–12 October 1991. Also see; Wendy Larson and Anne Wedell-Wedellsborg, eds., *Inside Out: Modernism and Postmodernism in Chinese Literary Culture*, Aarhus: Aarhus University Press, 1993. Chinese version translated by Zhang Zao, *Today*, Nos. 3–4 (1991), p. 86.

The expression 'Anxiety of Influence' comes from the eponymous book by Harold Bloom (New York, 1973). Professor Bloom uses psychoanalytical patterns to explain literary history. He thinks that budding young writers have some kind of Oedipus complex towards their older generation. The new arrivals do everything possible to bring down the tall figures of the older generation: all changes and innovations in their creative writing stem from this anxiety. Extending this pattern to the domain of cross-cultural interpretation, it is natural that all the Third-World's modern literary writings are considered as a response to the threat of Western imperialistic discursive hegemony — either to follow the trend, to write for 'universal readers' and produce poor replicas of an original model, or to retreat to a native position, clinging as die-hards to cultural conservatism. By taking the offensive, one envisions that "the better a national literature is, the better chance it stands of becoming world literature." Therefore, isn't it precisely this strong desire to "walk out of the shadow" which explains the anxiety of Eastern sons desperately wanting to 'kill' their Western fathers?

Obviously, this anxiety is not uni-directional; it is also experienced by the other. In her paper Professor B.S. McDougall talks frankly about the difficult position assumed by Western scholars when commenting on contemporary Chinese literature:

> If well-intentioned Western scholars appear to praise Chinese writers (whether living at home or abroad) for adopting post-modernism (for example) in their own work, then we are open to the accusation of being patronizing in assuming that Chinese writers should follow trends defined predominantly by Western literati.

> On the other hand, if we urge Chinese writers not to follow the path of modernism –> post-modernism, we are being patronizing in assuming that Chinese writers don't qualify for the mainstream, and must forever paddle in stagnant backwaters instead of bravely setting sail for the unbounded ocean.

> If we give the label *post-modernist* to works by groups or individuals (for example), on the basis of a few surface similarities, we are being perhaps culturally chauvinistic by ignoring all the features which are not consonant with the practice of post-modernism in London and New York. If we withhold the coveted label, we also offend by our parochialism in assuming that only the London and New York products are entitled to set the fashions.

She concludes, "There are so many ambiguities and tensions here that all parties end up being damned whatever they do."[3] Following the suggestion of Lu Xun in his 'Wild Grass: Argument', one can only say, "Look at this baby... How ... Ha, ha, ha...!"

Perhaps it has never been considered, at least by the Western scholars who try to explain it, that contemporary Chinese literature is also such a dark 'shadow of the other'. The intertwining of the two shadows reveals a certain 'universality' in the contemporary Chinese cultural crisis: Chinese literary works which 'resemble' and at the same time 'do not resemble' their Western original texts do not only disturb native discourse with their chaos and disorder of symbols, but also disturb the 'universal' discursive order. They do not fit well into established explanatory structures. Would it be some kind of inspiration to the *'fin de siècle* struggle' stated by Liu Zaifu? — We have eventually produced some UFOs that ominously sweep past the interpretative sky of the other.

PATTERN

If there were only one shadow, we would be satisfied with clear-cut interpretations. But the overlapping of a second shadow provides us with a richer feeling of gradation when we perceive things. 'Shadow II' has cast a shadow on 'the theory of shadows'. The intertwining of shadows provides us with an opportunity to ponder on the explanatory pattern itself. The cross-domain use of patterns often inspires or enlightens, but at the same time it leads to perplexity and new predicaments.

To use the language of international trade, there is one kind of critical discourse that has turned comparative literature into statistical operations of 'favourable or unfavourable balances of payment'. This is an age-old academic practice. Lately it has been transformed into a political-economic mode of discourse. People talk about the post-colonial local production and reproduction of imperialistic macro-narrative patterns. These fruitful discussions draw attention to the complex power relations in universal discourses. The psychological and psychoanalytical models show that the relation between one text and another is not only a relation between languages, styles, or concepts, but is also a relation between individuals, generations, sexes, and desires. The complex application of these models makes us aware of the 'worldly' text — whenever we talk about a text, we fall into a net

[3] Bonnie S. McDougall, op. cit., p. 87.

inextricably implicated in the thick of political, economic, psychological, sexual, social, and cultural relations.

An interpretation without a model doesn't constitute an interpretation. But if one fails to consider the limitations of the models which one uses, one loses an alertness to the misinterpretations and misunderstandings caused by these limitations. We may use an example from modern Chinese history (including literary history): Western scholars either use the 'Challenge and Response' model, attributing the motive force of the development of modern Chinese history to the Western challenge and the subsequent Chinese response (J. K. Fairbank); or the 'Tradition vs. Modernity' model, distinguishing two antagonistic elements inside modern Chinese society — traditional and modern, and showing that the way to get rid of traditional historic cycles is to identify with Western 'modernity' (J. R. Levenson); or a third model which on the surface differs from the first two in that it attributes all Chinese sufferings and misfortunes to Western imperialist aggression. These models share a similarity: they overlook the internal traditional crisis of Chinese history. Only when we place ourselves in the internal context of Chinese history in order to analyse Chinese problems, circumstances and historic desires, can we further discuss the Chinese Story within the universal context, the participation of Western discourse in changes undergone by China, the Chinese mode of response, and so forth.

The formulation of the 'anxiety of out-fluence' is an instantiation of the above mentioned models, especially the third one. In its analysis, the internal crisis of Chinese literature and culture has been treated merely as the result of external pressure and enticement. Besides trying to catch up with the world trend, it seems that Chinese writers and critics do not need to face indigenous problems. By crudely comparing their work to certain foreign trends or techniques, they have, in effect, written off their several decades of experiences in Chinese cities and towns, as well as those artistic expressions emerging from meditations on history. The complex discursive relations within Chinese literature are not taken into account, since it is relatively unimportant from the perspective of Western discourse.[4]

[4] You Yi, 'The Westernization of Chinese Literature in the 1980s,' *Undersky and Underground*, (London: Wellsweep Press, 1994), p. 172.

COMPLICITY

A careful reading of Liu Zaifu's quote at the beginning of this paper will reveal a subtle 'misplacement'. The period in which Chinese literary theory is governed by the 'aesthetic despot' under 'the other's shadow', corresponds mainly to those years in which mainland China closed its doors most tightly to the world. However, it is precisely in the 1980s, when Western schools of thought, theories and writings are again flowing into China, that people talk about struggling to walk out of 'the shadow of the other'. During the time when slogans such as, 'Be self-reliant and work hard for the prosperity of the country' resounded through the skies, 'our own story' remained silent. Only when different 'voices', including those of Western discourse, were 'allowed' (though in a limited way) did 'our own story' let out its first cry at that time of upheaval. Liu Zaifu's apparently unintentional 'misplacement' indicates the most specific personal experience of Chinese writers, revealing the power relations within Chinese literary discourse and the means by which a foreign discourse participates in consolidating the power structure.

Why has the obvious application of the 'patriarchal laws' in our own household been considered bitterly by Liu Zaifu and his contemporaries as 'the shadow of the other'? We know that since the nineteenth century the global industrialization process has brought a certain grand narrative concerning 'universal history' to the whole world, so that global spatial differences have been merged and reduced to successive links of a one-dimensional time chain. Western discourse, positioned at the very end of the arrow-head of time, proudly regards the imitative efforts of the late-comers, and builds up this hegemony of a grand narrative pattern relying on its political, economic and military strength. Hegel's historical philosophy is the classical exposition of this monistic and hierarchical ideology of time. It is easy to understand that the doctrine of 'socialist realism' or 'the combination of revolutionary realism and revolutionary romanticism' is obviously the clearest expression in the literary domain of the power structure and value standards contained in this ideology of time. In the name of 'proletarian discourse' (the discourse of the most advanced class in history), the discourse of the State relegates all 'non-proletarian discourses' to the role of the mute. Simply attributing this set of theories to 'utilitarian Chinese peasant aesthetics' would definitely blot out certain aspects of its 'modernity', revealed as the power of centralized control and total uniformity. And the other who shadows the literary discourse is no other than the 'Father' of Revolution that has been built up in the course of modern Chinese history.

The introduction of Western modernist literature and arts for a second time in the 1980s (if the introduction done by such as Lu Xun and Mu Dan could be considered the initial introduction) is generally considered as a complicity between Chinese writers and the capitalist mode of production. There is no 'Chinese literature' as a whole, or 'Western discourse' as a whole, and no singular relation between the two. In a sense, modernist literature and arts constitute a kind of protest against capitalist 'modernity' or alienation. While Chinese literature is in the process of 're-writing poems', 're-telling stories', re-building discourse spaces and new discourse relations on the ruins of Cultural Revolution, the circumstances of how modernist literary discourse is reproduced have always been muddied by pseudo-formulations and have never been clarified. The discussion concerning the problem of 'alienation' raised in the 1980s in Chinese academic circles, despite the use of Marxist language, has been suppressed high-handedly. It is no accident that the discussion's sad ending coincided with a violent attack on Western Modernism, revealing a complicity between Eastern and Western dominant discourses. It seems that this complicity remains a narrative blind spot of some critical discourses.

Some non-incidental instances may illustrate the point better than theoretical argumentation. In the early 1980s, an American scholar visiting mainland China saw that the People's Literature Press was publishing the Chinese version of the American novel about World War II, *The Winds of War*, not only in a huge edition, but also using the best binding and design. (Later, the Chinese version of its sequel, *War and Remembrance*, was also published on a similar scale.) Rather surprised, the American scholar commented, "This book is soaked with the most conservative American capitalist values. You welcome it only because it is a work of so-called 'realism'. But the Modernist literature that you very much dislike is precisely what challenges this system of value standards!" Years later when Herman Wouk, the author of *The Winds of War*, visited China, the Chinese Writers' Association assigned a military writer, Qu Bo, the author of *Immense Forest and Snowfield* (a 'revolutionary historical novel') to accompany him on a tour to different parts of China. Throughout their journey, both writers often drank toasts to the great friendship between the peoples and armies of both countries. (Let us imagine what the author of *Catch 22* would say to his Chinese hosts if he were to visit China.) Incidentally, this also explains another event which is astounding, but seems to have astounded nobody: when the *People's Daily* took delight in commenting on a report that "the West Point Military Academy learns from Lei Feng." Why was the inappropriateness of this entirely ignored since the 'spirit of Lei Feng' implies 'the spirit of Communism'? Another instance is the American film 'First Blood', which was very much welcomed when shown in mainland China. Favourable articles were published in *Literature and Arts Journal*, the organ of Chinese Writers' Association. The only voice of criticism came from an American-Chinese writer Dong Dingshan who sent an article to *Literature and Arts Journal* from far away New York. Another even more complex but equally interesting instance is how one listen to the feeble voice of the 'Hong Kong Story' through the gaps of the dominant discourses, the discourse of complicity between the Chinese and British authorities. Hong Kong literature of the 1980s is without doubt the best material for a study of how 'post-colonial discourse' would function in a peculiar historic circumstance.[5]

George Orwell's *1984* uses an anti-utopia to describe the modern man's nightmare as a perfect combination of Stalinist totalitarian politics and the advanced social communication system. It also seems to indicate that there is a fundamental inclination of the hegemonic discourses from both the East and the West to confront and at the same time compromise with each other. With the spread of a growing cynical materialism, the geopolitics at the end of the twentieth-century will further highlight this possibility. This will show more clearly how the modernist and post-modernist discourses will participate in narrating the Chinese Story.

PERFORMANCE

I would therefore suggest using the concept of 'performance' to replace the concepts of 'stealing', 'borrowing' or 'transplanting'.

Only within a homogenized and hierarchized ideology of time could one long for heroic 'originality', and turn a blind eye to the ironic parody and 'performance' of the cultural practices and texts that one finds in a given pluralistic space. And only within this ideology could the generations of fathers and sons be arranged in the order of arrival, and the Oedipus psychological tragedy be directed on a universal scale. This would serve to consolidate the one-dimensional plot of the son

[5] See the short stories Sih-Sih, 'A Story of Lime Circle at Fertile-Soil Town' and Ziping Huang, 'The Narration in Lime Circle,' *All Directions*, (Hong Kong, November 1990) No. 12.

succeeding the father or the son usurping the father's throne, totally ignoring other ways of exploring the space of discourse, such as the 'evading mode' or the 'guerrilla mode'. Only within this ideology can one depict a structural drawing of universal discursive power, in the form of a pyramid or as two armies pitted against each other; and use the concept of administrative or legal power to explain submission or rebellion between discourses. This would totally ignore the complex strategic circumstance shaped by the confrontation, compromise, conflict, coordination and manoeuvring among infinite points in the discursive network.

Let us take a look at the spatiality of 'performance'. Performance comes with an occasion, a scene and an audience. Performance is imitation, reproduction, as well as interpretation and creation, distortion or parody. Therefore, performance is a decentering of the original work. Performance is an endless migrating, returning and wandering among pieces of work. The improvization of performance calls for special attention. Performance is a whole set of portable strategies adaptable to changing conditions. Performance is a series of 'mini-carnivals' dispersed in daily life. Naturally, there are good and successful performances, just as there are bad and unsuccessful ones. The criteria to assess good or bad performances are by no means vague or illusory, there are no pre-established rules, but a series of 'living' or 'historical' affirmations and negations.

In talking concretely about 'the modernist or post-modernist repertoire' of the Chinese literary 'concert' of the 1980s, instead of haggling over whether it 'is' or 'isn't' modernist literature, or whether it 'resembles' or 'does not resemble' modernist literature, it would be better to inquire how and why and for whom it performs, plus the circumstances and the effectiveness of the performance. In other words, the focus of criticism should shift from squabbling over 'what it is like', 'how to name it', 'what it is about' to a study of 'what its function is'. The units for analysis should include not only a comparison between genres, styles, and conceptions, but also the relationship between discourses and their various functions.[6]

---

[6] You Yi, p. 174. You's paper analyses splendidly the ordinary people's absence from 'popular discourse' (the proletarian discourse which is also the State discourse) in the past few decades. It examines how the State, posing as the 'broad masses' or 'people's general spokesman', has assigned the mute discursive role to the individual and the ordinary people. Besides showing the emergence of different new discursive relations in the 1980s, the paper demonstrates that the discursive function of 'unrealistic literature' is to reconstruct the imaginary relationship between history and man, to reconstruct the

In exploring Chinese literary history, one would need to go deep into the actual historical scenes before those UWOs (Unknown Writing Objects), which seem to be composed by 'the other's shadows', could be described, named and positioned. The historical content of the so-called 'ahistorical', 'forward-looking' writings, could then be explored; the Chinese message within 'Westernized' literary genres, the seriousness within the cynical 'language games' could be delineated; and the linkage of Chinese discourse with various other global discourses (say Latin American literature and Eastern European literature) could be clarified, and the whole struggle of Chinese literature fighting against historic amnesia and aphasia, striving to tell 'its own story', could then be grasped.

The performance still continues. Only if we dance with 'the other' will we be able to survive, to have and to tell our own story.

---

historical richness. If the discursive functions and not styles were taken as the analytical units, the problem of 'Westernization or not' would seem to be a 'pseudo-formulation'.

ABANDONED WINE

O

FICTION — II

GOING HOME

Duo Duo

translated by Harriet Evans

Seventy miles north of Scarborough in the north of England there is a small coastal town called Wearmouth. Nine hundred years ago all the people who died in this town were buried in the same graveyard. The place where I lived was a small house at the end of the graveyard.

I am already very old. My eyes have long been accustomed to the grey skies and the green pastures, to the wet winds and the dim light of England. Whether I am a farmer or a writer doesn't really matter much at this age, but whether I am a cemetery attendant or a gardener makes an enormous difference. Not all the people in the small town would be able to agree to someone from another religion caring for their graves, so it was natural for them to feel the same about someone buried here after his death.

I was quite content to be a grave gardener, and often strolled over the fields, which I liked to watch carefully, particularly at harvest time. It was doubtless because I used to walk with my hands behind my back that I used to be able to hear the shouts of children through the wind. "Good morning, Li." " Good evening, Li." I was never in a hurry to turn around to answer their greetings. I simply bowed affectionately in the direction of the fields, narrowing my eyes to watch the fierce wind plundering the waves of wheat and the church steeple which concealed itself deep in the wheat fields. Every time the harvest season came around I would say to myself that the Chinese people's god is not in the church but in the fields.

Many years passed, and whether or not I spoke with the people in the small town was no longer important. They and I grew old in an unchanging relationship. The children of the adults who used to call me Li still call me the same. Sometimes when they come to pay their respects to their buried parents, I stand there for a little while together with them.

My arrival and residence in this rural burial ground and church had long ago lost all reason, or rather the initial reason had long since lost its initial significance. I looked after the land for the four seasons of the year, and as long as it didn't rain I would go into the fields to look at the sky. I didn't go out if it rained, but I had to go out if there was a storm. When it rained heavily, I would sit on the long bench of the church opposite the small square, holding a red umbrella. At such times, when I looked through the window of the shop, people were usually making some comment like, "There you go, the Chinese bloke is waiting again."

They were absolutely right. I was waiting.

I was waiting for the arrival of another person from China. I thought that he would definitely be a young person, possibly with a backpack, and that after leaving the coach station and turning the corner by the second hand bookshop, he would find his way directly into the small square. There he would catch sight of me in the heavy rain, and would come over to listen to me telling him a story. If he is willing to listen, I shall be able to depart this world, or as Chinese people put it, I can go home.

All night long I seemed to be repeating my will and testament. When I woke in the morning, the sky was overcast, and the sound of thunder could be heard in the far distance. I got up as soon as I heard the first raindrops on the grave stones.

But when it came to putting on my raincoat, I put my hand through the stitching of the lining at the underarm seam three times, and when I closed the door behind me, I felt as if part of my body was caught on something, as if I had an extra tail. I hadn't gone far out of the door when another odd thing happened: there were two newly dug graves side by side. Then an old woman came up to me and greeted me. "I'm really happy to see you." How come her words contained another meaning? I couldn't help but turn towards her because her two large rubbery legs seemed to convey an invitation of some kind.

The rain stopped as I sat on the bench in the small square by the street. There was no one around, and the only sound was the church bell — was someone being buried? I realized that at least I had had one such extraordinary experience.

It was when I was still a student in London, and I wanted to get out of the city to relax a bit, and I found myself in Wearmouth. I left the coach station, and found myself in this small square. It was before they had set up a tourist shop that sold plastic penises. Small house after small house appeared, as if out of a dream; a small bundle of newspapers, still waiting to be picked up, lay on every doorstep. There was no sight of anyone — today, as every day — all that could be seen were some fat horses which, because of the rise and fall of the green slopes of the pasture, seemed half buried in the land. By the time I reached the breakwater, the beach was already full of people — probably the entire town was there. The people were evenly dispersed over the beach, facing the sea in the late afternoon light. No surprise movement altered the appearance of the water, and no strange occurrence interrupted the scene. Some of the old gentlemen nervously twitched their hands, shaking their dogs' leads, but the dogs were not there. The children uttered not a sound. These gentlemen and their wives, old and young, hair all smoothly combed, standing so solemnly and respectfully, were all looking at something that I could not see. There was something stirring in their hearts, and their silence must have had a meaning. It was as if a silent gesture was all that was needed for them to go down to the sea together. I didn't know what they were waiting for, but I knew that they had some reason to wait, while I did not.

I reached middle age in London, but still every day I followed the road to and from school carrying a bag for my books and swinging my arms, as if a young boy inside me was pointing to this and that. Near to Paddington Station there was a cluster of chimneys and all around the square at King's Cross were grey houses which reminded me of a coal yard in Beijing, near Xizhimenwai. Against the backdrop of Hyde Park at dusk, the pool for washing hands in front of the slaughter house in Ox Street distinctly appeared before my eyes; at the entrance to a bank on Piccadilly, the door of a Beijing grain shop, flashed up in an instant, or it could have been a cab rank outside Gongmenkou or a crowd of people queuing for their number in front of the hospital in Xisikou; from a small alleyway in Euston I could still see a white horse flash past Guanganmenwai.

My past in London rumbled away into the distance following an underground train. Once I was scrutinising one of those moving metal coffins when I bumped into a Chinese person and as we momentarily faced each other our eyes seemed to unmask the expressions on our faces. Then, when half-intentionally, we looked at one another again, our eyes contained a definite message: what on earth are you doing here? Yes, and what the hell are *you* doing here?

So it wasn't until later that I went to Wearmouth.

It was because of this that I always remembered that odd day when the people of Wearmouth went to look at the sea, as if they thought that the sea was about to leave them and so wanted to send it on its way.

The church bells continued to ring. So today was Sunday after all, and everyone was at church. But what was that old woman doing going to the cemetery on her own? As I was thinking about this the big doors of the church opened and old couple after old couple walked down the stone steps supporting each other, and someone took off his hat and nodded to me and said "Happy Easter."

So today was Easter Sunday.

The priest and his helpers also came out, followed by a group of children wearing choir robes, all chubby and making gestures of greeting to the crowd of people, and to me. The church doors then closed again, and after Mass the people began to disperse to eat their splendid meals of roast pork or fried duck with their families; everybody had a coloured egg and perhaps some people would dress up as Easter bunnies and parade in the street and whoever bumped into them would have good luck. Facing the closed church and the shop, and returning once more to the deserted street, I sat down alone and, unmindful of what I was doing, spat out the word: 'gruel'.

No matter how I tried I could not put this word into a sentence, but now — today — I can only think of, "Gruel is my mother." I have often cried over this — since old men are as unable to control their tears as well as young men do.

As I wiped away my tears away I went on thinking — every time the clouds in the sky float on, they take away some past events. The old woman had chosen the day of Jesus' resurrection to visit the grave, she understood the meaning of resurrection.

In fact, when she was young, she used to love coming to the cemetery, and from the distance, would watch me tending the flowers. Sometimes she would greet me, sometimes not, and when she didn't she would stay a bit longer. She loved taking her shoes off and going barefoot, and she would think her private thoughts as she wandered around. I never knew how to say her name properly — Maria, Julia or Moira. But I was young then, and liked to call her name. When I saw that her expression was a bit abandoned and distant, I called her less. Maria was a servant. Her employer was called Smith. Mr Smith liked to wear a fancy Scottish tweed jacket, and he also liked to talk with me, sometimes at length because he had long had a problem with his throat, so Maria's main task was to help him to talk, to translate his guttural sounds into, "Hello, I have lived enough and really would like to leave this world, but I should not be hasty, you Chinese people understand this." Or it was, "I haven't lived enough. Live enough? That's a Chinese way of thinking."

It was probably because Maria liked to come on her own to the cemetery for a period of time that I could sometimes hear something different in the sounds Mr Smith used to make. It was something like, "So you have had a good time then?" And he would make so many sounds that even I could recognize that this was, in fact the case. So I would say back to him, "So you have had a good time then?" And he repeatedly nodded his head.

Mr Smith has been lying in his grave for many years now. Maria opened an antique shop selling furniture, glassware, crockery, hanging clocks, lamps, mirrors — anything that was from the Victorian period or earlier. She had thousands of objects all piled up in her shop, probably left to her by Mr Smith. Sometimes, I went in with the idea of asking whether she had a coffin. But I was afraid of shocking her. She opened her doors every day, not to make money, any more than the reason I went in was to spend money. Old Maria was wearing bifocals, and as soon as she saw me, she pretended to be reading a book. She first read from left to right, and then from right to left, and finally from top to bottom. That was because when she was young, in a pub in London she once saw three people sitting down and reading, one was English, another Jewish and the third was Chinese.

There were no other Chinese people in Wearmouth apart from me, so naturally there were no Chinese bookshops. All there was was a sign opposite Maria's antique shop with the Chinese characters for 'Phoenix Restaurant'. The first time I went to the restaurant I was really happy, but when I asked whether it was Sichuanese or Cantonese food, the owner waved his hand at me, so I asked whether it was a Chinese restaurant, and again the owner simply waved his hand at me. I realized that what he meant was, "Don't ask." So I simply sat there for a while without ordering, or wanting anything to eat, but I paid a tip, simply to see a painting hanging on the wall. "Is it painted by a Chinese person?" The owner waved his hand. "It's not by a Chinese?" The owner waved his hand again. "Let's speak English then." He still waved his hand. Several decades seemed to pass by in his wave, and in my old age, when I come again to look at the picture, the owner is no longer around. The picture will still be around even when I'm not.

It was an oil painting, a Chinese palace standing in a jade-green hill, with a gateway nearby and a pavilion in the distance. That was all — I mean, there were no people. It was warm and sunny in the painting, and the landscape was rich and luxuriant. There were rays of light but no sun, and a sense of timeless, magnificent structure. It was impossible to see in it any reference to historical cycles of rise and fall.

I never tired of looking at it, it was a gift granted by heaven, with the sincerity and warmth of the mainland's terrain — it was something that a people which had spent so long looking out onto the sea had no means of fully absorbing.

So every time I left the Phoenix Restaurant it was like leaving a clinic where anxieties — whatever they were — were cured. The light in the painting was extremely soft, like music, or like the Chinese language. The last time I heard people talking Mandarin was on the underground in London.

"Or we could simply go back. Why don't we just go back?"

"Who said we shouldn't go back? Can we get back? If I were Ma Yo-Yo I would go back."

"He's called Yo-Yo Ma."

"I don't care which Ma he is, their piss is all worth three thousand pounds."

Talking of this conversation makes me think of another story.

In the small zoo at Wearmouth there were a number of lions, tigers, and there was also a whale, but they were all painted on stone, and little kids less than five would spend a lot of time pointing at them excitedly. Apart from this there were seven or eight crocodiles who spent their whole lives coiled up in a heap, sleeping all day, with lopsided teeth which made me think of the seeds spilling out of the watermelons which lie around all over London's Chinatown. My thoughts were interrupted by a child's question:

"How come they are so ugly?"

"They're just very old," the parents answered.

I like to watch them more and more, the older I get. I can watch them for a good few hours. Watching them, I don't feel tired, the radar in my brain no longer needs to turn. I particularly liked to watch one crocodile imprisoned on its own. It looked exactly the same as the others, but if that were so, why did it need to be shut up on its own? Many years ago I thought of asking the keeper, but by chance I happened to hear him talking with someone else which made me give up my idea of raising the matter.

"That Chinese guy is a bit odd."

"I agree," said the keeper. "He make a some surreptitious movements...."

"What?"

"It's nothing much. It's just that he surreptitiously ..."

I listened, surreptitiously, and, surreptitiously, they talked.

"It's nothing. It's just that he surreptitiously picked his nose a couple of times...."

The two of them laughed, surreptitiously.

Their laughter was very similar to the sound of rain. Then it really started to rain. I called out to myself, "Why, it's started to rain." But as soon as I blinked the rain stopped, and when dusk fell, I was still sitting on the bench.

I often used to doze off, and give a start when I heard the rain begin — quick, the window's still open, the clothes are still outside on the line. It was only when I had calmed down that I remembered that it was the partition window which hadn't been shut, the window from which you could see the White Pagoda Temple. And that it was a few small garments which hadn't been brought in, and that the clothes line was still hanging in number thirty-five, at old Mrs Shi's. Every time this happened I got so panic stricken that I couldn't do anything, and would have to find someone to talk with as soon as possible. Maybe it was for no other reason than that when I had nothing to do, I would talk to myself. When I had something to do, I would go to the zoo and see the old crocodile.

There was one occasion that I simply could not bear, all because of two leather shoes swaying endlessly in front of my eyes. Two shoes with worn down heels. The more I shut my eyes, the more vigorously they moved, until I finally realized that several years before I had seen a shoe tread on some phlegm on a street in Chinatown, and it had taken six steps altogether before it rubbed off. I didn't want to see that shoe any more, so I slipped out of the cemetery on to the street, and in the distance heard someone saying in Chinese — "... I love you ... I love you...." in a completely foreign tone. I looked to see who it was, and discovered that it was a fair-haired girl who was speaking to herself as she walked along, head bowed, as if she was carrying something on her back. "I love you, you fuck me, I love you, you fuck me." Who had taught her this? by the time she had disappeared I had forgotten the two shoes....

But there was still a sound which continued to ring. I hadn't been dreaming, or so I thought, because in England I never had dreams. It seemed like a dream that respected logic — not something I could have dreamed.

By the time I finally understood that what the sound came from was a hand-pushed milk cart rumbling along the cobbled road in the distance, I realized that I had slept through Easter on the bench. It was already light, and even though I hadn't had any good dreams, I heard a voice greeting me.

"Good morning, young man. How come you're lying here? Aren't you worried that I'll steal your wife?"

The milkman came up to me. Was I on this bench waiting for a young Chinese boy, or was the boy waiting for an old Chinese man? The milkman pulled at the peak of his cap with a couple of fingers, and pushed his cart on. He saw that I didn't want to share the joke with him.

I haven't liked jokes for a long time, and anyway, with English jokes, I always want to laugh when I don't understand, and never laugh when I get them. For example, a life insurance salesman. The first thing he said when he came in was "If you die we will pay you one hundred thousand." I was just on the point of waving him away when he mumbled, "Arm or limb, thirty thousand." I got up, but before I had taken a step, he was more glib, "Leg, fifty thousand." I opened the door and pointed outside, but before I could get a word out he was already saying, "We will compensate for everything, kidneys, blindness, dumbness, we guarantee to for compensate everything."

I walked through the small town towards the cemetery. The clouds made the sky brighter than on a clear day. It was impossible to open your eyes, they were so white, and it was impossible to tell whether it was morning or evening, winter or summer. I pulled myself together, and in one glance saw the keeper, eyes squinting in a smile, standing at the entrance to the zoo.

"Good morning, young man. Have you come to look at the sea?"

I stopped. "I've seen enough of the sea. I've come to look at the crocodile."

Every time I strolled up to the small zoo, the keeper was always there with his hands in his trouser pockets. "Good morning, sir," I say to him, and he begins to pull his hands out of his pockets, but he replies before he has pulled them out, and every time he brings them out it is always with a big bunch of keys, which he hangs on a bit of wood that looks like a penis or the handle for flushing the lavatory.

"To see the crocodile? Forty years ago there was an old Chinese guy who used to come every day." The keeper seemed to have reached an understanding of something.

"Forty years? Must be seventy years."

"It's really funny, Chinese people always like to look at the crocodile."

"There have been crocodiles in China for a long long time, so Chinese people have seen enough of them, but England hasn't got any so we have to go on looking at them."

The keeper shrugged his shoulders. "Well, have a nice visit."

"Thanks."

When I bent my legs to sit on the ground and face the old crocodile, it was as if I were facing a graveyard.

The cemetery was too still and quiet. Even when there were children playing around, it was still too quiet. Looking at the cemetery made me feel at ease. I always took good care of it, The grass is always exceptionally lush. A few horses used to cross over from the hills to stroll about there aimlessly. "Okay, go home now," I would call to them. "You've been playing around here enough now, so go home, this isn't the right sort of place for you to hang about in."

They were really intelligent, because even though they were big and tall, and loved galloping about and grazing, as soon as they heard me calling to them, they would unhurriedly move on. But there was one horse which used to go wild in the cemetery, galloping about all over the place, so I would have to call to it separately, "Okay, Young Four, I know that you can gallop, but you should still go home."

He was disobedient, and sometimes came rushing towards me, head down as if he wanted to butt me. I knew that he wouldn't really, that when he reached me he would turn his head and run off again. I called him 'Young Four' because he looked so very young. I reserved 'Young Seven' and 'Young Eight' for the crocodiles, for the two of them that were always squashed under the other big ones. The old one that was kept on its own I called 'Third Master'.

Every time I bent my legs to sit on the ground, the keeper would tactfully move to one side, or would simply go to the doorway to have a cigarette, but today he stuck close to me. "May I trouble you a minute? It's just my own curiosity."

"Go ahead."

"You haven't noticed any change in him?" He pointed to Third Master.

When I realized that someone who could not make a joke was making a joke, I went completely flat.

"What I mean is, you don't think he's dead, or artificial, do you?" I didn't answer. "No? Because it has occurred to me, even to me, that I haven't seen any change in him for several decades, and no one has ever paid any attention to it, but there was a girl who wanted to examine him more closely. She poked her head in through the bars, but unfortunately I wasn't around. Her scarf was too long and hung down low — but luckily she hadn't knotted it."

"And then?"

"Nothing else happened." The keeper put his hands in his pockets. "The girl still works as a typist in the BBC block which a Japanese company bought up. The scarf must still be in his stomach. She was Japanese." A bit self-important, he moved over to the side.

He was quite fat when he was young, and his bottom looked too compact, as if he deliberately held it in. Now he was old, and his bottom had spread out, but his eyes still didn't smile and his thin lips hadn't changed at all. They looked more like the rim of an unused condom.

The drab eyes of Third Master were the same size as a wasp, and his cumbersome body made me think of the wooden shoes people wore in ancient China. I shook my hand in front of his eyes.

"Five pounds." The keeper signalled that he wanted to fine me, but immediately started fumbling around in his pockets until he drew out a handful of coins which he put in Third Master's big mouth.

Third Master made no movement, there wasn't even any saliva in his mouth, but with his mouth full of money, he looked cunning and secretive.

"I'm sorry, I was only trying to learn from the old man." The keeper spoke with great assurance. "He's done this on at least one occasion. In my opinion, the old man looks at the crocodile simply to test him, as if he wanted to prove something. He also talks to him, for a long time at a stretch. There seems to be some mutual debt. To tell the truth, I wish he would die off. I really don't understand him, but he reminds me of a story...."

"I have a story, would you like to hear it?"

"The story goes like this. An English gentlemen went travelling in China, and took his dog into a restaurant. The waiter asked him what he wanted to eat, and the gentleman asked if it were possible to do something for his dog. The waiter replied, "Glad to be of service," and went off with the small dog. It was a pedigree husky, snow white all over, and with an equally beautiful name, Bianca...."

"... which was also the name of the dish," I interrupted.

"There's another story that I reckon you definitely won't have heard. Do Chinese people celebrate Christmas, or any other festival — what is China's biggest festival?"

"Spring Festival."

"That's right, Spring Festival. England has another festival called Valentines' Day, and one year it happened to be on just the same day as Spring Festival. The old Chinese fellow invented a kind of Chinese hamburger, the outside seemed to be a rice flour bun, with a sausage inside — and he walked along the street holding a basket of these things shouting, 'Today is a Chinese festival. Try a Chinese hamburger.' The people of the small town all politely declined; only one young woman exchanged words with him. "So Valentine's Day is China's biggest festival?" That instant, the old man was transformed. He was first stupefied, and then did something unthinkable. He savagely took a bite out of the Chinese hamburger, and squeezed the sausage out of the dough, laughing obscenely at the young woman as he did so. That wasn't the end of it though. He spent the whole night of Valentine's Day shouting and crying in the graveyard, frightening everyone around. Afterwards he denied it all absolutely, claiming that it was just some ghosts howling, and that squeezing the hamburger was something he had learned from British students. It was definitely not a Chinese tradition."

"That was serious," I sighed.

"There was something more serious," the zoo keeper said, moving his face closer to mine. "That old Chinese man had come to see the crocodile every day for years until both he and it had grown old. One day, just like every other day, I had a cigarette outside and returned to find the old man missing. He hadn't left by the front door. That much I knew for certain."

"You mean that it had eaten him?"

"I didn't say that. I only said that he had gone missing."

"You're lying."

"No one in this town has lied for nine hundred years."

The keeper had a youthful look to him.

"You might not believe it, but I'm not lying," he continued in a serious tone. "Anyway, the old gentleman had disappeared and the crocodile hasn't had a shit since."

At that he turned his head so as to prevent me from seeing whether or not he was smiling. I guessed that he was giggling for the few coins in his trousers pockets were rattling. "Would you excuse me?" He went out, leaving me with the story of the old Chinese man.

After many years of not saying anything to one another, this guy had eventually set me up with a story. This was unacceptable. I heard his voice over and over again. This was unacceptable. Unacceptable. I struggled to stand up and bent down to make my way into the enclosure. I had to begin the story again.

I walked back and forth over Third Master and that damned old man several times until they crumbled to a pile of powder as white as cocaine. When I say "walked back and forth", I actually meant "trampled". They were totally desiccated. But had I not walked over them, there would still be a crocodile with an old Chinese man and a Japanese scarf in its belly and a big handful of British coins in its mouth. Now they had disappeared and there was only me inside the enclosure. The old Chinese man was no more, and there was just me in a story about him. Only the story was still not finished.

When the keeper re-emerged, half of his face was paralysed and couldn't be pulled back into place. I had never liked that face. In my opinion a church-goer would not have that kind of face.

"My God."

"My God. The old China man has been resurrected."

"You knew." The keeper showed remarkable self-control. "You knew it was only a joke."

"It was good as a story but lousy as a joke." I stopped in my tracks. "Let me tell you the story again. One day you saw an old Chinese man walk into the zoo. You went for a cigarette. When you returned the crocodile was gone with only the old man standing inside the enclosure. That day is today." I raised my leg and shook my trousers. There were bits of Third Master's body clinging to them.

"Please stop there old man." The last few hairs on his head were about to drop off. "That's enough. I only want to remind you. Don't take advantage of April Fool's Day. There isn't any advantage in it."

"Well, I want to remind you that today is Easter Sunday."

"That was yesterday. Today is April first. The day after Easter Sunday happens to be April Fool's Day. Please don't pretend you don't understand. You know perfectly well that you can play any number of jokes today. But what you said was simply too much. It's unacceptable. Legally speaking it's a crime against humanity, a crime against our cultural heritage. Or do you think it's nothing but money?" The keeper's two small fists were about to strike his own lower belly. "Wait. Please don't go."

His leather shoes scuffed the ground all the way back to his office.

Of course I am waiting. I am waiting in a story as though I'm waiting in a cemetery. During my life the graveyard gave me a sense of substance. It gave me more than I could get by myself. For this I have to thank the light that can be seen in England. It's as if time could be easily pushed back three hundred years. I am like the sea, the church, the graveyard, or all those immobile things. I am only a part of it. I haven't uttered a single word to anyone for years. I don't even have a dog. My only acquaintances here are the bartender, the butcher and the baker. I recall the life I once had. Every morning I took a piece of bread fresh from the oven. Next I walked into the butcher's and the owner handed me a packet of minced meat. It was half a pound. He didn't even need to weigh it. In the evening I went to the King's Head and had a neat scotch. I had no worries. Now all I have to think of is the cool autumn, the cold air that comes in through the crimson painted door, and the leaves hanging golden on the trees. I miss them. I don't know where they've gone. The more I miss them, the sadder I become. I remember a big courtyard. Whenever the tree waved, something dropped onto the roof. I could see it clearly through the window paper. But just as I was about to run out, Mum's shout stopped me: It's a walnut from the tree in your Third Uncle's garden. You are not allowed to pick it up. It was in the afternoon, or in the middle of the night, the sound on the roof again.

It was not until the police car with its screeching siren came nearer, rattling the glass, that I realized I should not have let them see that there was only a joke trapped inside the crocodile enclosure.

That's why I have to retell the story once more.

I sneaked out of Third Master's enclosure and climbed another fence. There I saw the heap of crocodiles, the young ones with their mouths open to the sky like pairs of scissors. I sighed. The greatest mistake of all is that time is never on your side. As I moved my hips, not without great difficulty, through the fence, I heard the sound of grinding teeth.

It was my mother munching on a pomegranate shortly before her death. Her lifelong wish had been to eat fresh pomegranate. My lifelong wish was to fetch her to be buried here in this graveyard so that I could see her and wash her headstone every day. If there were passers-by I could also tell them that I was looking after my mother. I wanted to talk to the church about this matter on many occasions: she wouldn't take up much space. She was in a small urn, not a coffin.

My last glimpse was of a British police officer's cap — it was similar to the cap of an Air China pilot. They didn't stop me since they had to let me finish the story.

VACATION

Duo Duo

translated by John Crespi[*]

Of the five on the trip, Robin and his Chinese girlfriend who can't speak Chinese make up one couple, Li and Annie the other. To help spread the costs of renting the car and the cabin, they have taken along Tommy, Annie's teenage cousin. The drive out is rather unpleasant, as the driver, Robin, keeps making quick turns that pile the three in the back seat up into one another; twice at least he has swerved steeply to evade heavy trucks coming head-on. Li sits numbly in his place, until his head again jounces against the ceiling of the car, and he hears Annie, her voice stern now, say, "Hey! You're not the only one in this car you know!" Unruffled, Robin makes a pretence of getting a more honest grip on the steering wheel. The mood in the car grows heavy, as if they were on the way to a funeral. Li moves quickly to fill the silence: "Actually, it wouldn't be so bad to die this way, seems to me." For that Annie presses the sole of her Birkenstock down on top of his foot, and keeps it there until they stop.

From Toronto it is two and a half hours to Georgian Bay and its more than three-thousand little islands, each with a cabin built to let. Dusk is nearing by the time they get to the shore, where a flat-bottomed launch carries them to the islet. Along the way the launch bucks and heaves as if riding on a sea serpent's back.

Li can't work out what Robin's problem is. Aside from him being Annie's former classmate and admirer, their history is to him a blank. All he knows is that on the trip out Robin keeps talking about some sort of cave, a thirty-million year old, six-hundred foot deep cave. Li still isn't too clear on Robin's girlfriend's name (it's harder to remember than either a Western or Chinese name). Tommy sits in stubborn, stolid profile — seventeen years old, this little chunk of granite. The five of them are all staring off in at least three different directions. An image comes to Li: Robin has seized the helm from the boatman and charges straight into a rock, hurling everyone off the boat and onto the shore.

[*] And revised by John Crespi, Gregory B. Lee and Daniel Wang.

Waves brush the banks all night as the island lays silent. Several times Li is on the verge of saying something to Annie, but fears his words will transform themselves into the question: What are we doing here, with them? Annie has squeezed her knees in between Li's legs and lets one arm rest on his abdomen. No, no questions, because once it starts we'll run on all night. And that's hardly the point of taking a vacation, right?

Although he has never regretted it, Li has never had halcyon student days to think back on, and never in his life has he made progress under a teacher's guidance. At the job he holds now — Chinese instructor — he deals with his students kindly enough, so there's nothing really to reproach him with.

But for the very reason that this is a vacation, being roped in together with these relative strangers is all the more stupid. How would Annie answer his question?

"No, I totally disagree. They're not strangers at all. Which is all the more reason you should try to get to know them."

"Why?"

"Well, you have to face facts."

"I don't want to face facts!"

"Then you'll just have to accept the logic that the situation has advanced too far for simple denial to negate an accomplished fact."

Whenever Annie uses complex, declarative sentences in a debate with Li, he feels that the English language is devastated by its own logicality. He wants to strike at the heart of Annie's argument with the perfectly succinct phrase, but finds himself at a loss. Not only that, debating is practically Annie's career. Just take a look at her CV: A Bachelor of Arts in French at Montreal, then a Master's in English at Vancouver; after that, during eight years of indecision over whether to pursue linguistics or English literature, she got a degree in sociology from Kingston and another in anthropology from Waterloo; then four years in Toronto, where she has only just graduated from law school and passed the bar examination, leaving her where she stands now — wavering over the decision to study for her first Ph.D. or fourth MA. Her extended career as a student temporarily on hold, along comes this three-day trip to Georgian Bay together with Li. So what will you do with your life when you're finished studying? Every time Li asks, Annie has a ready answer: I'll never be finished. Li interrupts, How old are you now? Annie asks back: What does age have to do with anything?

Li rolls over in bed, counting the hairs around Annie's nipples and mulling over how much he hates picturing his girlfriend as the

stereotypical North American female university student — smokes a
little pot, listens to rock and jazz, eats health foods, rides a bicycle to
the library with a load of books, her broad buttocks smothering the
tiny little bicycle seat....

Li lifts Annie's arm off his body and sets it down. He feels as lonely
as ever, even with Annie, though he can't let it show because if he
does, so will she. He picks up Annie's arm and sets it back on his
abdomen.

It is nearly light before he gets to sleep.

Li pads, bleary-headed, to the toilet. Coming out of the bathroom,
he realizes that the house is totally silent, and that there are bread
crumbs all over the breakfast table. He goes into the kitchen and opens
the refrigerator. It is the old-fashioned, bulbous kind, the kind that
with its door open resembles a human body split apart, its internal
organs ready to slither out. A cracked egg leaks yolk. Tommy is sitting
alone in the living room, his hair dripping wet, facing out towards the
bay.

"Good morning. Been swimming?"

No reply from the young man. Li tries another question.

"Where's everyone gone?"

"Out."

"Did they take the boat?"

No more response from the youth. What makes this kid so stubborn
all the time?

"Could you tell me what time they'll be back?"

The youth shakes his head. Bemused, Li strides back into the
bedroom, covers his head and sleeps. The pillow still holds Annie's
scent, and her belt hangs, sword-like, straight down from a clothes-
hook. Li sees his mother gliding through the air above him.

Whenever he sleeps alone, Li sees his deceased mother in big cotton
trousers gliding through the sky. He understands that she is searching
for him, and that he is waiting, waiting for her to return to that old,
sheepskin-covered rattan chair, head sagging, drooling, asleep. "Are
you feeling better, Mother?" he asks. "Yes, yes, better than yesterday."
His father lies in bed and yawns. He naps until three in the afternoon,
and won't let his rest be interrupted by Mother before then.
Sometimes Li wonders how the three of them made a family. They all
accepted themselves as a family, that was all, and their forty years
together developed an inertia that kept them from wanting to live any
other way. A broad window lets in sunlight. From the distance come
the cries of a peanut seller. A fire burns in the stove, heating a kettle of

water. The old cat rests on Mother's big cotton trousers. Li buries his head against Mother's legs, calling: Meow, meow, kitty kitty. Mother is gone somewhere far, far away in her sleep, and all he can do is call, over and over: Meow, old kitty kitty, old kitty kitty. Li rolls over in bed and hears the rustle of his mother's gliding, like the sound of leaves rubbing against each other in an old, withered tree.

The weather is clear and bright under a wide and nearly cloudless sky. One after another Li kills three mosquitoes that had attached themselves to his back, then gets up and goes outside. The Canadian flag, the red maple leaf, flutters in the breeze. Another flies on the island opposite. There are two ways to circumnavigate the island: one by traveling inland, pushing through the trees and underbrush; the other by clambering over the boulders lining the shore and at times wading through water. Li chooses the latter because he fears withered trees, bleached and petrified like bones, as well as lichen and fungus with their stench of decay. All these are things that remind him, of something.

Back at the cabin after scrambling around the island, he smells a stink on his hands, the sort that would be left from burying many dead bodies. Tommy sits silently on a boulder in front of the cabin. Li waves at him with a pack of cigarettes. The young man shakes his head, and Li lights one for himself. In the distance across the vast lake people are visible. From time to time boats motor past, and sometimes people wave from them. It occurs to Li that until now he has only seen Tommy in profile.

Back inside the cabin, Li leafs through the books left there by the owner. Cookbooks, gardening manuals, fashion magazines, and children's readers. Li picks one at random and suddenly finds himself engrossed: A peaceful old farm village with pigs and sheep and silos and chickens. Two young hens dream of going off to a beautiful, beautiful place. So why not go? One night they slip away from the barn to discover new worlds. They rush off to the big city and stride proudly along the streets. They cut through a supermarket, where startled ladies and gentlemen stand aside for them. They go to many marvellous places until at last in a fancy hotel a policeman catches them. They are hung upside-down by their feet on meathooks in a big marketplace, and then a container truck takes them away to a chicken farm where they are stuck into little separate cages. Several times a day a worker in rubber boots pours out their feed and checks the air temperature. When the fat manager discovers they can't lay eggs, he sends them off with a batch of other 'rejects' to a dark and gloomy

274

slaughterhouse. The two hens run away and hide in an old abandoned mill, where they huddle together and dream that an angel is feeding them grain from a golden scoop. They long for the peaceful old farm village....

Li drops the book, rushes into the kitchen, and chomps down two handfuls of peanuts. The two hens have disturbed something inside him. When Annie used to come over to his place, he'd unlock the front door and then hide himself, out on the balcony, behind a curtain, in a closet, and wait there until Annie found him. It was a game he used to play often as a child, after dinner, out for a stroll with his father. He remembered the intense delight of hiding behind a pile of cabbage on the streets of Beijing. The same magic thrill ran through him when Annie, gently chiding, was searching for him. He crawled out from under the bed and hugged her legs by surprise. He loved to see the startled expression on her face. They held each other for a long time, motionless. Annie stroked his head, and he looked up, "Mama, mama, mama." Annie looked down at him, enunciating clearly, "I am not your mama."

"Mama, mama," he went on. Again, Annie said, "I am not your mama."

"Mama," he continued.

"Listen. I'm not your mama. I might become your wife, but certainly not your mother."

"I've heard a lot of old men in the West call their wives mama."

"Look," Annie went on in a no-nonsense tone, "I'm not your mother."

"Why can't you use a little imagination?"

Li felt wounded somewhere inside.

"What does this have to do with imagination? I've never called you daddy?"

"Because I don't want to be your daddy."

"It's best if nobody pretends to be anything."

"But that would let one of us off, and I don't want that."

Li squirmed back and forth through Annie's legs.

"Be a little animal, Mama."

"I can be a little animal, but I won't be your mama."

Annie really makes Li want to cry. She is such a simple girl, so delicate from frenetic studying and a plain diet, her grasp of the world so narrow, her adherence to social conventions so total. She has her bath every evening and is up and onto the computer every morning, the alarm clock set unequivocally at six-thirty a.m. This is the Annie who, with her head buried between two pillows and one hand on the alarm clock asked: What right do you have to feel sorry for me?

"Oh, mama, mama." He gazed at her, wide-eyed and helpless.

"I'm not your mama."

"Why not give just a little, just for a while? Not even just for a little while?"

"No. I told you already, I'm not your mama."

Li crawled on the floor, not wanting to believe in Annie's blandness.

Li takes a bottle of beer outside the cabin, still thinking how through the hot, muggy night he punished Annie with silence. Annie lay facing the wall. He had shifted over to the far edge of the bed and was tracing figures on the floor with his finger. When they made up after a fight, Annie could just do it, no reason needed. He needed a reason. But what was it? It wouldn't come to him. All he could do was ask, over and over, Why can't you see it, Why can't you? She just couldn't. He wanted her to see her own predicament. Your life is like a war, do you know that? She agreed to that completely, so what was the use in saying it? She's just incapable, incapable of changing anything. Annie, you're a practical-minded girl, you can take on any good, solid task that comes your way. But what does your life really amount to? Have you thought about it once, even once?! Annie has no desire at all to meddle with his understanding of her — what could it have to do with her? Annie, listen, we're each other's front lines. Sure, no question about it. Better to say nothing, hold it all back, let this stifling summer night smother me. He massages his abdomen. This suffocation has somehow made him fatter, or maybe it's just gas, because when he looks in the morning, it's gone.

Still no sign of Annie and the rest. The lake lies wide and calm as ever, but it is a lifeless calm, the calm of vacation. Tommy sits alone looking out at these other lives. Li has an urge to tousle the young man's hair, but his nerve fails him. If he were a horse or a big dog, it would be different.

The boat circles around from the back of the island. Li raises his beer bottle to the passengers.

"Sorry, Li, but I didn't want to wake you." Li is glad to see Annie in high spirits. "We went to a little market on the opposite shore.... Sorry?" Li asks her what general direction it was in. "Oh, it's complicated, you go around the island across the way ... no, around a whole lot of islands. Nothing worth seeing. Some people selling paintings and sculpture. We met a Russian girl called Lyuba, from Chernobyl. Just turned thirteen. I talked some Russian with her."

"The Glorious Fatherland, the Glorious Capital, the Glorious Land of Socialism."

Li loudly recites the Russian he learned in middle school. Robin and his Chinese girlfriend look on gleefully, but aren't interested in talking to Li. Li thinks he might ask Robin where that cave is located.

"Too bad, though. Lyuba can only stay on Georgian Bay until Saturday. She has to go back. Some very nice Canadians paid the money for her to come. We all wish that she could stay a while longer, and we're worried about her future. Hey, look at that." A small snake is lying across a rock. Annie's reaction is the same as when she feeds the pigeons in Toronto.

"Don't move. It might be poisonous."

"That's right. There are only two kinds of snakes on the island, poisonous and non-poisonous." This comment from Annie infuriates Li. Tommy darts in front of Li and deftly catches the snake by the head.

Robin comes over, his girlfriend beside him, her arm around his waist. "Having fun?" "Great fun." Annie puts her arm around Li. The four of them stand in a face-off, as if ready to begin a square dance, or burst into laughter. The teenager wraps the snake around his neck.

Annie has sunblock on now, but probably put it on too late — her skin is as red as if she'd been stung all over by hornets. Still she insists on sunning herself. Li looks again at Robin's girlfriend. She was born in Toronto, but her distant place of origin shows through in that clingingly manipulative way she has. Li lies back on a rock and finishes two bottles of beer. He feels enervated. By the time the alcohol has begun to wear off, the others have swum out to a massive rock out in the lake. Annie is there, waving to him to come over.

Looking up from its base, the rock appears quite tall. After climbing to the top and looking down, it is in fact not even fifteen meters high. Annie comes up from behind and hugs Li around the stomach.

"Cheese belly." Li wants to pat his belly, but Annie won't let him. "Cheese, beer, and gripes."

"Easy now." Annie covers Li's mouth with her hand, afraid he'll say, "I'm getting old."

Robin and his girlfriend help one another climb down the rear face of the rock. Tommy, chest out and holding his breath, stands at the rock's edge. His body is well muscled, his hair tied back in a small ponytail, and his toes grip the rock so firmly they seem nearly to sink in. Li has seen fine-looking young men like Tommy in many places, at figure skating competitions, for instance. Li cocks his head to look down at the water, a little mistrustful of the lake's depth, and noting that the leap outward will have to clear more than two meters to avoid the boulders below. The young man leaps with precise control, arms spread, chest forward, head back, legs straight and taut; in less than two seconds Li's entire youth flashes past — he too has dived like this.

The young man bursts from the water and shakes back his hair in a supremely winning way. He smiles, directly at Li, it has to be at Li, and Li understands what is required of him. But his feet won't budge an inch. He feels he has reached an age that allows him to comfortably decline a challenge, to wave it off with no sense of shame. He descends along the rear face of the rock. The wind is blowing at him face-on, and in the distance he sees trees bending and heaving from the gusts. The clouds too move drunkenly. Normally Li can see hundreds of spectacular shapes and visions in the clouds; now all he sees are drifting, cottony giants with contorted eyes and twisted mouths. Li suddenly senses Annie near him, still there with him in the world, here on this rock.

"Why don't we leave Toronto, go to a small village in Ontario and get down to making forty babies. Thinking about it, sitting here on this rock, it sounds perfect, don't you think?"

Annie isn't giving serious attention to his heartfelt words. She just leans close into him.

"That was great, champ." Annie turns, "Let me give you a kiss."

The young man climbs up onto the rock. With an emotionless sweep of the hand he brushes Annie's arm from his shoulders. Annie replaces her arm. He brushes it away again, adjusts his ponytail and the amulet over his chest, and leaps away into the air. This time when he surfaces he doesn't wave to Li.

"As you've probably already guessed, we have a little bastard on our hands. What can you do with someone Tommy's age? He never says anything, and always has that stubborn look on his face. He does know how to dive, though."

"Uh-huh. I need a cigarette."

As the sun descends a vague coolness comes into the air. They decide to take the rowboat out. Li watches as the others go about competently gathering up fishing tackle, oars, a sail, and surfboards, and put on life vests. The last to get in the boat, Li sits in the stern. They cast off and row out into the tranquil lake. The water spreads into the infinite distance and waves slap the shoreline with the sound of the sea. No one on the boat looks like they're enjoying themselves, however.

After dinner the five of them sit in a circle of cane chairs, no television, telephone, or electric lights; just a pair of candles to gather around as fatigue from the day's outdoor activities affects them to varying degrees. The hour is still too early for bed, but slapping mosquitoes while listening to the waves grows tedious quickly. Li reaches for a magazine. On the first page is a photograph of a young girl, with a caption below that goes, "Dearest Karen, It's been three weeks, but my eyes are still red and swollen. Still I keep asking myself, Why didn't I get in the car with you on that day? I'll never forget how sad that car looked. Karen, I'll never have a better friend than you. Karen, I love you." After reading this letter from a girl to her friend killed in a car accident, Li notices a word that keeps reappearing in the magazine. He asks Annie what a "teenager" is. A young person between thirteen and seventeen years old, she replies. Robin adds that Canada has approximately five million teenagers. His girlfriend corrects him: Was it five million or nine million? I remember that five thousand teenagers commit suicide a year, or was it nine thousand? The discussion turns to the teen magazine, and closes with the conclusion: God himself can't understand teenagers.

Listening to the talk, Li feels himself of an age where birth and death are both far away. Tonight he wants to be in bed face to face with Annie, again with her arm resting in that hopeless way on his abdomen, her, asleep, while he lies awake without the strength either to get up and go read in the kitchen, or to get himself to sleep right away. He is at the age where getting to sleep is harder than waking. What he used to do was shake Annie awake, but when she realized he wanted only to slip into her arms like a child, she would fall heavily and hopelessly back to sleep. It was a shameless thing for him to do, and he knew it.

"Good night." "Good night."

Robin and partner stand up. Tommy has long since disappeared.

Li goes with Annie into the bedroom. Immediately he feels that uncomfortable wetness. As always, he knows only too well that this is only urine, and that he's going to wet himself again and again. He goes into the bathroom, wipes himself dry with toilet paper, and returns to see Annie waiting for him watchfully. He wets himself again. He lies face downward on the bed, stretching one leg in between Annie's legs and resting it on the bed sheet. Annie is waiting for something, but he's not sure what. Annie lifts her buttocks to adjust her night-gown; he is still losing urine in tiny spasms. He clamps down on Annie's heel with his own to try and stem the flow, but it only comes faster. He recalls how most of the time he is so unusually dry, like the pebbles a young boy plays with for so long and then clamps between his knees. Annie shuts her eyes and presses close to him, as if readying herself for some sort of therapy. He strains to concentrate, but wets himself again so that now he absolutely has to wipe himself dry once more. He slips hastily out of bed, hearing Annie release a sigh behind him.

"I'll be right back."

In the bathroom mirror he sees cruelty in his face and shakes violently, as though death itself has its hands on him. He is afraid of wetting himself again when he gets back in bed, but fears even more that Annie might already be asleep. Staring at the face in the mirror, he can't remember when this shameful thing started. He sits resignedly down on the toilet until his legs go numb before finally getting up and lurching into the kitchen.

He opens a beer, wondering in the cruel summer night if he matters to anyone, to Annie, to those less close to him, or to those who have died. He drinks down the entire bottle in one breath and opens another; he doesn't drink for pleasure, he drinks to be drunk, drinks because he's at the age of summing up what he is. He affirms that thought, opens another bottle, and carries it outside.

Ah, the lake, it makes him want to burst into song — Four hundred years ago the Indians here dwelt. The Indians here dwelt.... He can't think of a line to follow that one. A shadow starts in the darkness — Tommy, gazing at the sky. He speaks at length, but rapidly and vaguely, apparently about something happening in the sky, something like a star leaving its path. Li looks up too, and as he does Tommy goes back indoors. The lake slaps at the shore, though there is no wind over the water. The waves arrive from far, far off, from the wake of a passing ship, coming perhaps from the United States.

"Sorry to make you wait so long. When are we going to go and find that cave?" It's nearly noon by the time Li comes out into the living room where the other four have gathered to decide what to do. Li remembers last night's plan of going to the cave Robin had spoken of. According to Robin, the cave was a wonder to behold.

"Sorry, Li." Somehow Li can't ever fix Robin's face in his memory. "We've broken our promise. Sorry about that, really. We have to go back to Toronto today."

"You mean now?"

"No. We'll have lunch first."

Li glances at Annie. First your old schoolmate here ropes us into coming to the island; now he wants to pack us all back to Toronto.

Avoiding his look, Annie turns to gaze out at the lake. Li still looks hard at her. It's because he wants to save money on the car, did you catch that? To save money on the car he wants to go back, and so we have to go back, too. Who got us into renting a car together with them anyway?

Robin and his girlfriend go to their room to pack, where they continue their spat in hushed voices. Li too begins rehearsing to himself the all-night argument he will have with Annie the coming evening in Toronto. Thinking about it upsets him: first will come a heavy barrage of questions, then a thoughtful silence, then he'll hit home with that one phrase that says it all. He wants to come up with that phrase now. When the ferry has left the small island, he recalls how on that same island an author had once had a magical night of writing: by the light of two candles, in a deep stillness disturbed only by soft breezes passing through the room, he wrote as if possessed....

Back on the mainland Robin pulls the car keys from his pocket, but is stopped from getting to the car by Annie.

"If you insist on driving, the rest of us are walking back to Toronto."

Both Annie's and Tommy's hands stretch out. Robin tosses the keys to Tommy, and Annie and Li get into the back seat. The car winds along the wooded lake shore and past tastefully designed vacation cottages half hidden in the trees. On Fridays the wealthy of Toronto drive to the lake shore, hop into private powerboats and motor off to private islands for three-day stays. After that it's back to the city through the Sunday evening traffic.

Tommy pulls over near a tall slope, gets out of the car and runs uphill, shedding clothes as he goes. The cold war going on in the car is just peaking. Robin keeps turning around to face the back, "Listen, Annie. Let me talk, Annie." "I don't want to hear it." Robin is angry, his girlfriend is too, and Li decides to stay out of it — his set partner in argument is Annie. All he wants is to get to Toronto as soon as possible. At the top of the slope Tommy is wearing just a bathing suit as he stands erect, holds his breath, spreads his arms and leaps. Robin is motioning with his arms over the seat-back for emphasis, and his girlfriend and Annie are slapping his arms back and forth between themselves. Robin gets out of the car and runs. The three remaining are breathing heavily in anger as they watch him charge up to the crest of the slope and stare down over the edge. When he begins gesticulating at them wildly, Li recovers himself: Robin has found the cave, the six-hundred foot deep cave.

At the base of the cliff a wide field studded with rocks extends for a full fifty meters before meeting lovely Georgian Bay. Li forces himself to look far away, into the sky, his mind filled with the words he wants to say to Annie. But every time he opens his mouth, Annie's fingernails bite into the palm of his hand.

THE INCIDENT (AT THE OPEN AIR CINEMA) THAT EVENING

translated by Steve Balogh

Whatever happened that evening remains a mystery. Apparently somebody hiding behind the screen yelled, "Lion!" Even before that, most of the audience had already become increasingly alert and restive, quite apart from the alacrity with which they then fled. But then, there had never been a lion in our town — in fact there were, at most, only a few halfway decent-looking cats.

There had once been a circus troupe from up north that brought along a lion to open our eyes to a strange and unfamiliar world. But the beast caught typhus and had to be hurriedly transported away.

When the news came, everyone was left somehow exhilarated, as after some triumphant victory. So I began right away to suspect that I had misheard.

The incident took place so many years ago that people are now unwilling to have the subject brought up. A couple of days ago, while at the post office to post a parcel, I ran into Zhou who said, try as he might, he could not recall a thing.

"What lion? Which evening?" He blinked at me, unable to imagine it could ever have happened.

But I remember the event in perfect detail — how one of Zhou's toes got crushed, and his subsequent explanation of how it was broken. According to him, he did it resisting a crush of desperate people trying to force open the main door.

In fact, afterwards, all that was left of each half of the door were a few splintered planks, a dozen pairs of shoes, a hundred or more buttons and the odd ragged strip of torn-off clothing in various shapes and sizes.

I didn't leave by the doorway at all, misguidedly taking what I thought a more sensible way out. This turned out to be a newly-built surrounding wall, still ten days or so from completion.

Zhang once told me he hadn't heard somebody shout, "Lion" but "Fire," so he'd assumed that a fire had broken out.

Very quickly, he was swept up in an unstoppable flow of people —
his glasses went flying. Zhang is the sort of guy whose glasses count for
more than anything else in his life. Although furious, he was unable to
avoid stumbling along, propelled by the crush of his fellows and
bellowing with rage, ready with the punch that would give anyone in
his path a nose bleed. Later, it turned out that the opponent he'd taken
on in this way was a step-ladder, jagged with old nails.

"I was really cross. As you know, I've studied kickboxing, and even
know what to do with herbal medicines," Zhang said, scooping up a
pile of books under his arm, and raking his hair with his free hand.

After that I never saw him again. Actually, if it were not for the
things I'd heard him say over the years at the soup and noodle house,
I'd never have believed he was able to develop such skills. Everyone
knew he was skinny and small, but given that he was also well-versed
in kickboxing, the situation was totally different. Add to that the
herbal medicine, with which he could hold lions at bay, never mind
rusty stepladders.

Where had I seen that ladder before? In the sports field in front of
the open air cinema. The fire brigade used it every week for their
training. In turns, and in full fire-fighters' gear, they'd rush up and
down it over and over again. They kept repeating the exercises until
even we could do them fluently, their bodies soaked in sweat.

"Be prepared!" The whole brigade would roar in unison, and then
dismiss.

One of the exercises included taking a long roll of sailcloth hosepipe
and chasing along its length as it unrolled. I came to think that one
day I would be able to perform this exercise myself. Pity a fire never
did break out. Though if one had, I didn't have the first idea about
where to look for the hosepipe.

Speaking rationally , the impressions left by that evening were not
unlike a fire. In actual fact, however, no such thing had occurred. The
following day, as I walked past the cinema, I supposed I would find
some trace of an extinguished fire, but, no matter how hard I looked, I
couldn't find the smallest sign. The sun shone peaceably down
everywhere, an extremely old man and a small child dragged a big sack
over the grass. They were collecting up the abandoned shoes.

Several sparrows were flitting about chirruping a paean of praise to a
life whose good fortune knew nothing of the sudden outbreak of fire.

I was shocked when I saw that collapsed wall; broken bricks lay
scattered as by the passage of a wave across the street. Next to it was
the half demolished toilet. Normally people had tiptoed gingerly in

carrying a torch, but it was clear that, on this occasion, no one had hung about. They had no choice but to dive in at once. When the torrent of people had surged, I had a fleeting thought: "I am going to die right here right now." It was hard to believe such a yard could have contained so many people. It was still harder still to believe that in the winking of an eye so many could have been impelled to stampede for dear life by a still uncertain cause.

Strange though it may seem, the two poles supporting the screen had not come down in the tumult. I had always thought that the slightest wind would have blown them down. Some previous evening (probably not a Saturday) they'd shown a Hungarian musical and the poles had heaved like the rigging of a sailboat beating its way through a storm. It had been cold then and our necks had been painfully stiffened by the wind. The projectionist had as many clothes on as he could wear. A large group standing by the old fort gateway sang songs the whole time. Thinking about it reminds me that it was at this low point that a number of my meal coupons and a shirt were stolen from my bedroom.

"I'm gonna kill someone!" said Wu when he couldn't find a pair of socks. I suspect the person he wanted to kill was himself. At the time his body would periodically exude a fragrance of an indefinable nature, which made those who smelt it feel like the world was beyond hope.

"Who could want his socks?" Hu said to me later through the canteen window, with a gesture as if fanning away the smell of sulphuric acid. "Socks ! Ugh !"

So I chatted with him a while on a series of subjects such as socks, such as how to achieve immortality, such as how to track satellites after launching them into orbit and such as the price of peas. It hadn't rained and the temperature had risen somewhat. There was no indication of the desperation which would appear later that evening. A pleasant wind wafted our bodies which only inspired the desire for a snooze.

Two days after the incident Hu was his usual lucid, agile self, his speech as incisive and perspicacious as ever. He shot off to the hospital to engage at length in argument, forcing a doctor to acknowledge that Zhou's broken toe was inflicted with a blunt implement, not the result of a flat sole or whatever.

But on the fourth morning when he got up things were not well with him. We gave him chillied radish for his unfocused stare, sighs of despair and generally dispirited appearance, but he wouldn't eat it, letting it grow a coat of thick white fur in his gargling cup.

We all reckoned it was concussion from the incident that night. He refused to go to hospital for a check-up.

"Just get yourself checked over, OK?" I told him: "I got struck on the head and with a brick too. It throbbed with pain. They gave me a check-up and I'm fine now."

Hu gave me a glance. From that single glance I could tell the scene he beheld was of a distant, different landscape altogether, for example, one populated with towering crags and mountainous peaks, or else perhaps the utmost extremity of the Great Wall. We began to notice the same indistinct smell as that of Wu, but it turned out, to our surprise, to emanate from Hu.

Films weren't shown for days on end, but he would seat himself in the middle of the deserted field, lost in desolation. One day he eventually left us. His cup continued to produce penicillin and erythromycin.

What had hit me on the head had been half a broken brick all right. I had just negotiated the breach with the crush of people coming through when an invisible voice yelled at us to follow. So we just ran after it. An innocent voice could be heard shouting, "What on earth's going on? What's happening?"

Everyone recognized the laughable obviousness of this and the voice fell silent pretty quickly. All you could hear were the people behind making good their escape with a further great heave. The din was enormous. I realized I was lucky to get away with just a blow to the head. All around were people puffing and panting to the very last, desperate to keep on running. Some clutched at clothes ripped by thorns in the shrubbery. Others clamped their hands over their liver.

The film had not been stopped. On the screen a few people went right on with their exits and entrances, unafraid of lions or fires. Someone had run into a ditch. Afterwards he climbed out intending to watch the film to the end from afar.

"Is it leprosy?" he grabbed me, dripping wet. I uttered an "Aaargh" noise and fled at full pelt, unsure if he were asking me about the dramatic content or something else. And anyway being grabbed by someone soaking wet is unpleasant. As for the plot — I really didn't remember it at all.

After that I never again went to see films at the open air cinema. Once, when I accompanied a friend who was going for an operation, we took a short cut and I chanced to hear a snatch of dialogue from the film playing. A woman was talking to a man:

"You're bound to regret it one day!"

HE HAD ME FLEX MY ARM

Xu Xiaohe

translated by Steve Balogh

He wanted to see me flex my arm, so I flexed it for him. Then he made as if to sniff my armpit, taking my elbow and forcing me to raise it. I wondered what could smell so good under there. He clapped. "Right, you're on our side."

I went over and stood with the rest, some of whom were tall and some short. They all looked as though they'd all had their armpits sniffed. I reckoned there'd be more introductory stuff to do. There wasn't. The team leader came over and gave each of us a severe look. A guy with short hair was laughing, obviously to ingratiate himself. A shout silenced him.

"Quickly now." The leader pointed to a pile of mats. "Same as yesterday."

The mats were swiftly set out. Shorthair went first, walking the full length of the mat and back again, probably to check everything was in order. The team leader straightened a mat with a kick and a plume of dust floated out. From his expression I guessed all was set. I wondered vaguely what time it was.

We all stood on our hands on the mats. The team leader told us to imagine we were holding up the world. I would have found it easy to imagine this, only my nose was blocked. The team leader made a few points for our general guidance. He announced that we were to follow Shorthair's example. I was about to throw him a sidelong glance when I fell over with a crash. The team leader was furious. He pointed out a huge number of my shortcomings and that my feet were ill-formed. I hurriedly lifted up the world again. He struck me on the knee-cap, uttering a phrase I was unable to hear distinctly. I reckoned that the problem was more serious than I had imagined, but many of the others had their knee-caps struck as well.

After that we had to walk. I'd never walked on my hands before, so time and again I fell over. The team leader again commended Shorthair for walking more steadily than anyone else. Shorthair insisted simperingly that he was still not steady enough on his hands. A

woman appeared and bawled at the team leader. I didn't expect her to
have a particularly short neck, but when I looked, her neck was indeed
short. The others had all sat down for a rest. Only Shorthair was
content to continue walking on his hands across the mats.

"Redmuscles or white ?" Someone with folded arms leaned and spat.

"Me ? I'm not really sure."

" I'm Redmuscles," he said.

He shrugged his shoulders and wiped the sweat off his nose, gazing
into the far distance. I thought this could be one of the advantages of
being on Redmuscles' side.

Shorthair came across on his feet. Everyone ignored him. Where
Redmuscles was looking there were some girls doing the long jump.

"Tell a joke," suggested Wideforehead. "Who'll tell a joke ?"

"He'll tell one, he'll tell one." Everyone was pointing at a skinny
guy. Just as Skinnyguy was demurring, the short necked woman came
over to put an end to us eyeing her up. So we went back to the mats
and walked about on them on our hands. The short necked woman
was scrutinizing our efforts self-importantly from the side.
Wideforehead fell to one side as he turned around.

"What on earth are you doing?"

"I need the toilet."

The short necked woman cocked her head to one side and thought
for a while before finally gesticulating, "Off you go all of you. Hurry
up."

We all sped off in a trice. When we returned, only Shorthair was left
on the mats still standing on his hands. There was no sign of the
woman. Redmuscles spat, still showing off the superiority of
musculature. In the distance the girls were doing their long jumps into
the sand.

"Sometimes pickled vegetables are really good," Redmuscles said
while sketching on the ground.

I guessed he was drawing a pickled vegetable. Drawing a pickled
vegetable was no mean feat. But before you could distinguish what
he'd drawn he rubbed it out with his foot. Over it he made a big cross.
Skinnyguy suddenly gave a low laugh.

"Here he is, he's come," said Wideforehead. We all got up,
preparing to return to the mats. Shorthair glowed with excitement,
you could tell he'd long been looking forward to this day. In the end it
was the fellow who changed the lightbulbs in the corridors who came
in carrying his ladder. Redmuscles drew another majestic pickled
vegetable. He gave it two eyes, a mouth and feet.

"A giant salamander," he explained.

"Look everyone!" said Wideforehead. "It's the same fellow as last time."

"After him!" someone yelled.

Without thinking I chased after him. Redmuscles rushed out in front, right in front of the long jump. The girls stood and stared, unable to make head or tail of what they saw. Turning the corner, nobody noticed the sparrows which had been perching there fly off in alarm.

"He's scarpered!"

"We've lost him."

We walked back dejectedly. Redmuscles, apparently foreseeing just such an outcome, made straight for the edge of the long jump and did a hand stand, his feet almost brushing the nose of one of the girls. She dodged, giggling, and the other girls began to giggle as well. Wideforehead swallowed a mouthful of phlegm. Redmuscles jumped to his feet and did the same, not even looking in Wideforehead's direction. The man changing lightbulbs carried his ladder in both hands. Shorthair was watching, upside down, walking on his hands, crossing and recrossing the mats. Sweat poured off his head. Doubtless his armpits smelt pretty strong by now. Redmuscles had a think and then rejoined him. We all followed suit.

"So what's so good about pickled vegetables?" demanded Skinnyguy, upside down. Redmuscles did the splits without a sound, his legs in the air. I was astounded. I was considering whether I could do the same, when somebody suddenly leapt up from the mat. His action was so violent and decisive that every one of us swiftly shot to our feet and ran off after him at top speed.

I realized that it was now up to me, but I still couldn't tell whether my muscles were red or white. We ran the length of the wall again and turned the corner. There were no sparrows lying in wait this time. This was crucial.

We ran for a while on the other side of the wall, then went down a tall stairway, people joining us as we went, apparently all on Redmuscles' side. Gathering forces, we crossed a grove of trees and circled a bell tower. Our footsteps led us inside and we found they echoed with a hollow metallic clangour. More and more of us milled about in a crowd until, finally, we thronged around a couple of trees and came to a tumultuous halt.

"Oh look! One's a peach tree and one's a pear tree, red and white flowers against a background of green glazed tiles. Just look everyone!"

These words were spoken by an old man of cultivated bearing — there were such people everywhere.

"My hand's grown a corn," said Wideforehead, whispering in my ear.

We floated round the trees several times. The weather was mild. Someone suggested going over the zigzag bridge. This idea was quickly agreed. Somebody's head nodded. It was the team leader's. There are too many nodding heads, somebody still joked. At least half of them fell about, creasing up with laughter. The voice didn't seem to be Skinnyguy's.

"This bridge is really not at all bad."

"Indeed it isn't. When you draw something unfamiliar, your technique matures."

Wideforehead flung something into the lake. Fish began nibbling at it until it disappeared.

A voice bellowed: "Don't chuck your litter around!"

"It wasn't litter," Wideforehead gestured with the flat of his hand. "Just a corn."

We crossed the bridge and climbed a mound where a red wall lay across our path. We thronged towards the gate, making way courteously for one another so that we could enter one by one. I noticed that the gate had not been opened fully. The weather really was good. There wasn't a familiar face to be seen. I thought it was a bit, well, you know what.

"It's better like this; what do you say?" someone asked.

Someone else opened his mouth wide. Inwardly I wondered how he dare do this, but he'd already finished yawning. I went through the gate, inside there were not as many people as I'd imagined.

"You." A muscular but thoughtful man was watching me.

"You want to have a go on our side ?"

I took a look around. Wideforehead was nowhere to be seen.

"Come and have a go on our side."

I followed him beneath an immensely tall tree, skirted a pile of cardboard boxes on a patch of grass and walked onto the sports field. Several people stood scattered about.

"Do you know them?"

I shook my head. He looked me over closely from head to foot, having a quick think about it. Finally he said, "Let's see you flex your arm."

QUASIMODO

Liu Zili

translated by Desmond Skeel

A picture was hanging on the wall in the room. A lump of white ice was bobbing up and down on the blue waves in the black frame. It seemed to be knocking against the smooth glass.

There was a large bed in the room. A man was lying motionless on the bed. He had been ill for ages. A woman was sitting as usual in the rocking chair. She was playing with a stone in her hand. It had been removed from her husband's abdomen. It was multi-coloured and glistening. A chair with a carved back stood opposite the woman's rocking chair, on the left side of the bed. No one had ever sat in that chair.

The woman watched her deaf and dumb husband. He was at death's door. She had no feelings and no illusions. It would happen sooner or later. She just sat in the dust, day after day, waiting for the dust from another place to settle slowly. If her dignified husband was really to be buried one day amid a grand ceremony, then the Quasimodo in her heart would leave the corpse, cross the hall, kick over the large crooked-necked vase by the inlaid wall panel and sit down decidedly in the chair where no one had ever sat.

She would often engage in conversation with her husband. She spoke both for her husband and for herself. Usually her first question would be:

"Hey, do you see the monster sitting on that chair?"

"No. I can see the sunlight shining on the seat and on the legs...."

"You really don't see it?"

"How annoying! I think you should move the chair away from me!"

"No! I won't. It can't be moved. I'll see it when it comes."

Why was she waiting so devoutly for a monster, for a Quasimodo? Hadn't she seen enough of her husband's face contorted by illness, his flesh stolen away as if through lack of affection, and spasms brought on by terror? Her husband's body was currently being crushed to pieces by a new power, and was forming itself into a new indignation, one without form, without structure and without a soul. This image formed a striking contrast with his posture, bearing and intelligence before the illness.

Before the illness, his mind and body were at peace, his physique strong, his bearing elegant and his manner very cautious. He belonged to that class of men who were universally considered to have breeding. He did everything without the slightest error: making love, taking meals, going out, coming home, greeting guests, seeing visitors out, reading, writing, conducting experiments, listening to speeches … there were no exceptions. In short, he conformed to the principle of ice. He melted in the season during which it was proper to melt, and froze in the season during which it was proper to freeze. This brought down upon her an unbearable, ceaseless pressure and terror.

After the operation to remove his gallstones, a colourless crystal was extracted from his body and placed in the palm of her hand. It hadn't left her hand since. This was to be a turning point for them. Afterwards his principles, regulations, customs and habits slowly became flexible and then disintegrated, until one day at dusk the violent pain in his abdomen suddenly disappeared.

However, the turning point came too late for her. His present irregular condition was the result of nothing more than his vitality being sapped and his senses being weakened. This irregular form was not the one she had envisaged in her mind's eye. The masculinity and beauty she yearned for were embodied in Quasimodo. When the bells rang out in the snow, Quasimodo made his way over, climbing, like a spring breeze. He stretched out those arms as thick as tree trunks, and the sense of a river running dry could be gleaned from his panting.

At last he sat on the chair that was neither very large nor very sturdy, blocking the contact between his heart and hers with his ape-like body. When the towering partition curtain fell, loneliness filled the room from all sides. It was as though someone had touched a spider's web that had remained undisturbed for a century. Sorrow and misery permeated the air, which began to moan. At first she was pleasantly surprised by this, then she was frightened, and finally her soul completely left her body. The crystal in her hand dropped to the pale wooden floor with a thud. An extremely weak and muffled echo sounded in the room, just as though it were an omen. She was pinned down by four arms. Her arms were slowly leaving her body.

Her statue was later placed to the right of the picture frame by her descendants. A large mah-jong table was put where the bed had been. The inlaid wooden panel had been replaced by a fake diamond ornament.

None of this could alter her husband's fate. Time passed chaotically following her departure from this world. His limbs detached themselves from his body after having decomposed. His body evaporated. But his indestructible head floated on the ice.

There was no land anywhere near the floating ice. The clear seawater made a ringing sound against it. A colony of penguins was hopping about clumsily and crying without human feeling.

THE MASK OUTSIDE THE LIBRARY

Hu Dong

translated by Jenny Putin

The following extract appears in a book entitled *Lang Huan Ji* (*Notes from the Celestial Library*):

> *Xie Xianghui had a magic table. The top was inscribed with original freehand notes and jottings in the Li and Zhuan calligraphic styles. There was something to interest every reader. For the person contemplating taking orders, there were words to guide along the winding way of self-reflection. For those searching for something, there were comforting phrases such as 'You will find it somewhere'. And for the person seeking a cure for a particular ailment, or for the person looking for magic formulae, there were references to medicines and magic charms. And there were even notes in full to remind the student of forgotten lines and words. Xianghui treasured his table.*

At this point I should mention that I found this extraordinary book on the computer database in the library. I painstakingly copied down this excerpt and saved it on a floppy disk along with the rest of my stories so that I could read through it again in idle moments. I used to amuse myself by joining a number of stories together in one long tale, then breaking it down again into individual pieces, arranging it so that each story could serve both as the beginning and the end. The permutations were endless. Through these subversive acts, I managed to squeeze a little stimulation from my dried-up academic life. I tell no lies when I say that my infatuation with study grew out of this obsessive pursuit. I roamed enchanted round this square inch of floppy disk for days and months on end, never tiring of it. Although the game was monotonous, it was a monotony of kaleidoscopic proportions.

I was still teaching at the university. The sole reason for my continued presence (my more outspoken students called me a hanger-on) was the excellent university library. Since moving recently to new, modern premises, its vast, previously chaotic collection had been rediscovered. By means of its new, comprehensive database of good, rare and unique editions, users could access its entire extensive holding of old books. All the special reader privileges for university staff had been preserved. In the middle of the night, as I tossed and turned alone in my single bed, I was driven by the considerably enhanced attractions of the library to contemplating the necessity of filling yet another floppy disk.

I had been appointed by the powers that be to teach 'Socialist Economy'. Punning on the sound of the Chinese characters, the students shortened the name of this hateful compulsory course to 'Lessons on Ejaculation'. In no time at all the place was buzzing with obscene innuendoes. I was the laughing stock of the school. I stuck it out bravely — what choice did I have? One day, I confronted the assembled second year who responded with boos of derision. As their surprised expressions turned to anger, I realized that they regarded me as a self-centred impotent, responsible for the humiliation of our race. The rabble continued to remonstrate and cry. Then, quite unexpectedly, the normally obedient class prefect called on the students to strike, which was followed by another round of anguished debate. I turned down their nauseating invitations to join them in their discussions and retired calmly to my single room. What could I say? I talked it over with my reflection in the mirror. My position in the school was completely untenable. I had been written off by a bunch of hypocritical student activists. At the end of term, as I seduced the female student who had been dispatched to wheedle information out of me about the exams, I couldn't help regretting that I hadn't put the gag on all her giggling classmates by inviting them in for a bit of bedroom tuition. As I humped away on top of her, she couldn't resist letting out a few moans of pleasure.

But I was certainly no evil spirit that had invaded the pedagogical ranks nor even a sex maniac. True, I did threaten the nubile young girl a few times when she became hysterical, but really I just wanted to exert some control over her. It was clear to all that whilst I was forever commending other people's addictions, privately I was very much against drink and sex. Suggestible souls like myself, struggling to stay on the straight and narrow, had to be conscious of limits when it came to self-abuse. Although I was bored with teaching, I still had my ambitions. I dreamed of embarking on a new bibliographical career, cataloguing and researching old books, an interest far removed from my professional life. I spent all my spare time immersed in strange books like the *Lang Huan Ji*. I wasn't only interested in dipping in to pick out the more stimulating passages: I was particularly keen to clarify the true identity of the author and to establish the exact date of the book's completion.

The *Lang Huan Ji* was attributed to Yi Shizhen of the Yuan Dynasty, but some people suspected that it was a forgery and that it was actually the work of Sang Yi of the Ming Dynasty. It was an intriguing situation: two persons from different dynasties thrown together by a bizarre, salacious book. I would dash off my teaching duties in a perfunctory manner, then bury myself in amongst the stacks of threadbound books, losing all track of time, often going without regular meals and sleep. But after a term's work, the material I had collected was still insufficient to enable me to verify which of the two dynasties or which of the two authors was correct. Rather, the textual complexities threw up hosts of other possible authors and dates either considerably later or earlier than suggested. I was completely flummoxed. I began to question whether a non-expert like myself was up to the rigours of historical study. But I refused to be beaten. Contemplating my painfully wan and sallow reflection in the gleaming library windows, I decided against soliciting the assistance of the self-confessed conservatives in the history faculty in order to avoid exposing myself unnecessarily to their derision.

The female student went home during the vacation, so I devoted even more spare time to the increasingly hopeless task of deciphering endless volumes of impenetrable texts. I collected and went through them all with a fine toothcomb, but nothing conclusive emerged. I began to suspect that I had overlooked a key volume as I was browsing through the library's collection of everything published since the Qin Emperor burned all the books in the third century BC; or that one of the library assistants had omitted to include the reference when editing the catalogue; or that this key volume was languishing in some dark recess of the old library building among the moth-eaten, mouldering tomes awaiting incineration. And there was another possibility, one I was reluctant to contemplate: that the book of all books that I yearned for day and night did not in fact exist.

These terrible riddles wound themselves around me more and more tightly, compounding my dilemma. Baffling hallucinations seeped gradually into every pore of my daily life, dominating the inner life that I kept concealed within me, making me appear gloomier than ever. With the vacation almost over, I became even more dispirited. Not wishing to prolong my agony, I summoned my courage and set off one sunny afternoon to call on someone I had met only once before

— Yuan Rui, an archaeologist who worked amidst the architectural splendour of the museum. I picked him out from my circle of acquaintances because as far as I could see, for all the methodological differences between archaeological and historical research, Yuan Rui's outstanding work was totally devoid of the smugness that attended the scholars in the history faculty. It was formidably incisive and exacting. And I had another reason for wanting to see him: the impression he had made on me at our first chance meeting at the house of a mutual friend many years earlier. Not only had he seemed completely unconstrained by convention (reminding me of a stud horse), when he spoke, his voice was reminiscent of an exotic, untamed *kylin*, stretching out its neck from beyond the skies, snapping away at the bad-tempered clouds. People could not but prick up their ears to listen.

As expected, Yuan Rui was not at all taken aback by my presumptuous visit. Whilst he remembered me, there was nothing special in his greeting. This helped me to relax. He poured a glass of water, told me to make myself at home, then moved on to discuss the matter in hand.

"The most important archaeological discoveries in recent years belong to the future," he declared seductively. My puzzlement was immediately apparent. I waited for him to continue, but instead he lapsed into silence. He gestured with his chin towards another part of the room. I saw that in addition to some fully intact portraits painted on bricks, there were some human figures bearing animal heads and some limestone sculptures, neither small nor large. Then there was a huge lump of rusting copper and hardened earth revealing the corner of an ancient implement. Finally, there was a heap of suspicious-looking pieces of wood, displayed carefully in the centre of the office. On the wall hung a large set of framed photographs of assorted gear wheels. The exquisite metal work on the gears gleamed, like the prize product of a large company.

These cultural relics, Yuan Rui began to explain, were emblematic not of an ancient way of life, but rather of the achievements of the present day. They represented forays into the future, into a period yet to arrive. Seeing me fix my gaze in astonishment on the wall, he told me quite nonchalantly that the gears had been dug out of the Mediterranean sea-bed by a fellow archaeologist from overseas and that they were usable in today's ships, although carbon dating had proved that they went back several thousand years.

"It's a slap in the face for the archaeological purists." Yuan Rui dismissed the misgivings which I voiced in an indirect manner, as if he had prepared his spiel in advance. "But the field of archaeology is dominated by the old school. They disregard all developments from overseas and are most put out by my new way of thinking. They feign bewilderment when, as scheduled, I submit my reports with the evidence there for them to see. And then, on the pretext of safeguarding the academic reputation of their journals, these wise old men of the archaeological establishment refuse to publish my findings, fearful lest they bring new ideas into the field." Yuan Rui's eyes flashed, whether with anger or excitement, I couldn't tell. He fixed his bulbous gaze on me before zooming in to examine the entire office.

Yuan Rui's authoritative and loquacious manner stunned me into an embarrassed, baffled silence. I had no choice but to abandon my original plans completely. In actual fact, Yuan Rui's verbal outpourings did address the points I had wanted to make. He pulled them apart mercilessly. Indeed, after I said goodbye to him that day, I was so agitated and preoccupied I couldn't settle or sleep. It was as if Yuan Rui's spirit had taken hold of me.

What was this invading force that seemed to have garrisoned itself permanently in my head? I set about trying to clarify what Yuan Rui had said.

"Historical contradictions are not only symbolic of the past, they embrace the future embodied in the past. Or, to put it another way, the future has already happened in the past. As far as we and our forebears, or the present and the past are concerned, it is not that the former succeeds the latter, but that they coexist at the same point in time." According to Yuan Rui, both the present and the future exert powerful influences on past lives, just as the past affects the here and now. He explained repeatedly why, in view of this, it was inappropriate to regard history as a retrospective phenomenon. On the contrary, just as the fears of people in the past were the product of premonitions of our existence, so our present day troubles and disasters are the legacy of our descendants. I asked him to give an example to illustrate. He honed in immediately on the subject of the circulatory system, asserting that whilst acupuncturists and masseurs had been practising their healing arts for thousands of years, they were still unable to offer medical explanations for their procedures. But what fascinated Yuan Rui in particular was the fact that the system of acupuncture points, more complex than an integrated circuit, was discovered in the pre-Christian era. I reminded Yuan Rui that the earliest references to acupuncture appear in *Huangdi Neijing* (*The Classic of the Yellow*

Emperor). "True," Yuan Rui acknowledged. "By the way who wrote that book?" He took a deep breath and in an emotional tone went on: "Those awesome riddles from the distant past belong to some point in the future and were originally bestowed on our ancient ancestors by our descendants. But all along, out of sheer ignorance, they have been interpreted as miracles and tidied away quite dangerously in the cupboard of tradition by eras too proud of their own achievements. It's insufferable! As we pass from one generation to another, all we can hope to do is return those baffling phenomena we are unable to fathom to their original time. But those times have yet to arrive."

"So what about things like women one has enjoyed, refreshing mouthfuls of tea, or even a set of scrolls depicting a Buddhist monk sitting cross-legged under a pine tree?"

"These are not the work of trouble-making future generations," Yuan Rui replied. "They are timely, enjoyable and aesthetically pleasing. They are completely harmless. And because one cannot attach a price to them, they are meaningless. It follows, therefore, that there is no real difference between loose women and chaste virgins and cultural relics and antiquities. The only worthwhile thing to do is to copy our descendants by burying our outstanding achievements for the benefit of times past. But in fact, we have already done that, many years ago, before we even came into being or were able to open our mouths. The facts are there for all to see in the writings of disaffected scholars and exiled officials. And ..." Yuan Rui lifted his right hand triumphantly to show a large, yellowed ring, gleaming shamelessly on his raised middle finger. Smiling openly, he went on, "This solid gold ring was discovered in a grave. It probably dates from the late Microlithic period. At that time, class divisions were just beginning to appear, and yet the ring testifies to the existence of a surprisingly comprehensive and stringent taxation system. But what I want to tell you is more important. Although smelting processes had not been discovered then, the standard of workmanship on the ring is as high as we see today. Indeed, no one will believe that the ring is as old as it is." My surprised expression evidently pleased him. "In truth, I've stolen it. Well, you can't tell the difference between this ring and the common or garden rings you find in the jewellers. Trying to make ends meet on an inadequate income is the most depressing thing known to humankind. Here we are, stuck in a dreadful city, living on what can only be described as poverty wages. So to pull myself out of this ignominious existence, not only do I mix with old farts, I also do some business with those irritating antique dealers."

Yuan Rui's candour left me speechless. It was obvious. The pictures engraved on the bricks were not depicting fine-waisted, slim-shouldered salt makers and hunters from the Eastern Han at all, but rather the lifestyles of future generations. The pile of rotting wood was not kindling, but the 'wooden bird' that Lu Ban, the sage of carpenters, and Mozi, the philosopher and carpenter, once rode — the remains of a future light aircraft. Neither was that lump of hardened earth and rusted metal the decayed remnant of a poisoned torture instrument, nor was it, as some people would have it, a weapon concealed in roadside undergrowth by a 'Robin Hood' character. It was a poorly disguised miniature radio from the fifteenth century. Yuan Rui had picked these things out of the museum stacks to substantiate his wild, arrogant hypotheses. No one had bothered with them before. And of course those wide-smiling, triangular-headed figures from the distant past were not totems, but self-portraits of people from a future age. Finally, Yuan Rui closed the slim volume that had been lying open on the desk — a copy of the *Yi Jing* (*The Book of Changes*). "You see, I'm researching this too, just like everyone else. But as far as I'm concerned, it was written by our descendants."

With the start of the new term, I flew about in a state of muddleheaded sobriety. My moral character went into decline and I paid increasingly scant attention to the school calendar and to arrangements for lectures. What is more, I no longer washed my feet before going to bed, a habit that I hitherto had been unable to control and that I equated with getting out of bed in the mornings and immediately putting on one's watch. Furthermore, I wantonly altered the pattern of my lifestyle, deliberately blurring the difference between dawn and dusk. At lunchtime, as I lay supine on the lawn next to the lotus pond, the roar of Yuan Rui's words in my ears covered the screech of the horns that hung over the treetops and the ring of the bell which signalled the end of the lunchbreak. But I did not stir. Time had laid siege to and worn down a thousand generations, was wearing away at the rows of school buildings, the playing field, the new library, the lads with their bone handled knives and the girls in their dresses, but its intense fire would never wear me down. I who was subject neither to life or death, neither new or old, would tick on with every stroke of the second hand. In my terrible, unceasing daydreams, I returned repeatedly to Yuan Rui's motto in my battle against the whinging sycophants at the university. This was the motto: it is only because we have been tricked into believing that things that were originally very close to us are a long way away, that we have come to regard the stars that we see before our eyes as unattainable.

The female student became the love of my life. We were inseparable, our desire for one another insatiable. It was an open secret. From the whispers it was evident that our behaviour had scandalized the chaste character of the university. A teacher who lectures on the 'Socialist Economy' having it away with a spotty-faced female student! How unseemly! I knew just what they were thinking. "And sometimes they do it the bushes or under the desks in the classrooms." In the past, the humiliation would have been unbearable, but I had grown impervious to such matters as my mind had become preoccupied with more awesome discoveries. Moreover, had I been unable to put myself in their shoes, how would I ever have understood the motivation of these tittle-tattling good-for-nothings?

The students were distracted, as if planning a new offensive. My lectures attracted fewer and fewer students, just as I had hoped. In order to preserve my energy for reading in my eyrie in the library, I would often feign illness to get out of teaching and increase my free time. I had become a glutton for old books, the leader of an army of starving book worms which burrowed its way unimpeded through the labyrinthine stacks of old threadbound books. (I should say, however, that following my visit to Yuan Rui, I had ceased to regard them as a labyrinth.) I wanted to sing for joy! The Celestial Library! My Celestial Library! A secret tower, an exquisite repository, God's very own pleasure-ground. Even now I could go in with my eyes closed and pull out a book to prove that our forebears sensed our every breath and cough. Each and every one of the weird and wonderful technologies that are part and parcel of contemporary society were known to and shaped by past lives. And what is so strange about that? As I explained to my audience in the lecture theatre in a tone reminiscent of Yuan Rui, "A computer, a genuine microsystem, which is nothing out of the ordinary for primary school students today, was a rare treasure, a weird and magical table to a thirteenth century collector like Xie Xianghui."

And yet I could not go as far as Yuan Rui who had no compunction about either offending or sucking up to the authorities. My upbringing had nurtured in me a cautiously independent spirit which, aroused by Yuan Rui, had found its true expression in this collection of old books. Thanks to him, my interest was no longer confined to the arcane realm of textual criticism. It lay instead in extracting intimations of the future from every smile and scowl of times past. I discovered that in living in a world laid out by future generations it was remarkably easy

301

to regard the gifts of our descendants as constructs of the present, as artificial mysteries or deliberate frauds. The fine conviction that there is no existence beyond ourselves had blinded us to the truth. It was as if our mental cogs had ceased to turn, as if we were suspended upside down, caught up in a complex world of trivia, our overloaded minds unable to assimilate the past and respond to the future. This is what I found so unbearable. I would go on and on talking to myself in this vein. Then one day, as I sat in the library in the gloom that heralds an approaching storm, I confronted with tears of shame an image of my ancestors. There beneath his brows, I saw in his eyes a glimpse of the last of my descendants engulfed in flames with no prospect of salvation.

"Before the fire, everyone will rush in to grab their favourite book which they will have chosen after a thorough appraisal of the other ten thousand volumes." There may well have been some truth in what Yuan Rui said, but the fire never happened. Instead the library was saved by someone who had the foresight to move it to a safer location. This zest for life is not only there to indulge the hereafter; it also enables the past to get its own back. But most compelling of all, it is about seizing the pleasure of the moment. I surmised that it was precisely because Yuan Rui understood this so well that he was able to take on his bewitching dreams. And it was also why I chose to bury myself in the library, just like the warriors who went into Troy hidden inside the wooden horse, who endured the long silence, the fear and the burning darkness for the sake of conquering this legendary city.

The success of my campaign grew in proportion to my astonishing collection of strange writings and anecdotes. For example, in *Notes on the Extraordinary* by Li Junsuo of the Tang Dynasty, there was a piece about a fisherman who netted a looking glass in the Qinhuai River. When he peered into the glass, he was taken aback to discover that "all his vital organs and the blood coursing through his veins were clearly visible." Scared out of his wits, he relaxed his grip and the glass fell back into the river, lost forever. My analysis of this piece found no reference to the following, "On looking in the glass, everything to the left, right and the three directions to the fore was visible ... it was as if the army were right in front of his face." So the first looking glass was not the telescope described in another work from the Tang Dynasty; in this instance it was a form of X-ray machine. I could not but feel proud that I had unconsciously accumulated so many treasured writings on my floppy disk. I kept thinking that I would gather all my discoveries together in a book. My lover was excited by the prospect.

As a result, she not only drifted away from her trouble-making colleagues, the frequency with which she did my typing rapidly came to rival that of our lovemaking. Whenever I observed her absorbed in her work at the computer and the stretch of thigh visible above her knee, I had to struggle to suppress my desire to sing out, "Oh God! Lock us up in the library together for ever more! I shall want for nothing else. A mere scholar such a I could not be more fortunate! Immersed in this vast collection of books with my lover constantly at my side." Her physique in particular was so perfect that she might have been Emperor Yan's very own test-tube creation, impeccably-formed and enduring, faultless in every respect. When I clasped her tightly in my arms, the grace with which she received my amorous advances was reminiscent of the seduction of Chang E, like a future Apsaras.

It was another six months before I once again had the urge to call on Yuan Rui. I made meticulous preparations before the visit to ensure that I would be up to him in conversation. Naturally, it was another fine day and I was in exceptional spirits as I tapped lightly on that familiar office door which, being unlatched, opened at my touch.

An elderly man cordially invited me in and asked me to sit down. Each word that he uttered gave me new insights, "Yuan Rui has been remanded in custody charged with abusing his official position to sell off our national treasures." Then, just like Yuan Rui in that first meeting, he sank into silence for a moment before going on to appraise this subordinate whom he had taken so much trouble to cultivate. "He was an outstanding lad, but unfortunately got taken in by bogus scientific thinking. He would seize hold of all manner of trumped-up discoveries, and then he became completely possessed by an iconoclastic fervour — Daoist sorcery to be precise — which he used to shoot down the reputation of the archaeological profession and to subvert humankind's greatest legends. In the end, well, not only did he give himself up completely to a life of luxury and dissipation, he stubbornly maintained that he was the descendant of the extinct Zhong people."

The old man went on in this rather stepfatherly tone. I felt as though I had walked into the wrong room. There was nothing on the walls apart from a sheet of white paper bearing the words, 'Guidelines on the preservation and management of historical relics' written in red. The ancient radios and the things that had been arranged around the floor had all disappeared. In their place, where Yuan Rui's pile of wood had previously been, was an imposing bronze mask. The mask bore an immutable enigmatic smile, as if it were laughing at the office.

After that I made a point of never going back to see it. Once was enough. The mask's face returned to haunt my dreams, accompanied by a murky little laugh. Its two animal ears and in particular its bulging, cylindrical eyes frequently startled me out of my drunken slumbers, propelling me back into a disturbing, off-screen reality. News of the mask's excavation seemed to flow from everywhere, from the newspapers, the television and even people's conversations in the street. But ever since its discovery, after Yuan Rui's arrest, it had become my recurring daydream. As far as I was concerned, the exact location of that elusive place where it had been unearthed was none other than Yuan Rui's office. When I assembled my misgivings about the location, the uncertain origin of the mask which had been lying dormant for a thousand years, and its huge, proudly protruding, beak-like nose and put them together with the image of Yuan Rui's shameless, greedy face, I found myself looking at an old-fashioned picture puzzle, steeped in an atmosphere which the old man had so perceptively described as 'iconoclastic fervour'.

An imaginary flood (even more autocratically) had destroyed the library and the archaeological digs. As the waters receded, fake books and earthenware pots, and even real-life pigs and horses, which gave off a putrid odour in the burning summer heat, were left floating on the surface. One day as I was wandering aimlessly and hungrily along the street, I was verbally accosted by an old acquaintance of mine. After exchanging pleasantries, he asked me whether I had heard that Yuan Rui had committed suicide. I just shook my head.

To this day I have never been to check whether the report was genuine. I keep myself to myself, far removed from all those books and the equally vast and varied world of street gossip. Privately, I am of the opinion that the criminal who looks down other criminals is more criminal than the rest. Compared with Yuan Rui we are all patriots. When criminals quite rightly humiliate a smug little wastrel who has sold off the family silver to foreigners, they care not one jot nor tittle that he gave a priceless ring to a prostitute in payment for services rendered, neither are they bothered that he is a crazy heretic.

Before this, I had gone to visit him on the labour camp farm. His head had been shaved but he was still recognisable. It occurred to me then that the torment of time, regardless of whether it is time spent in prison, is of no consequence to a man who turns his defeats into victories. Yuan Rui appeared more free and easy than ever. In a

304

departure from his former reserve, he raised his middle finger in an exquisite, strident gesture of defiance and called out to me to show his unabashed contempt for the place. Before he was marched away by a guard, he suddenly remembered to ask whether I had read the *Lang Huan Ji*. Without waiting for a reply, he proceeded to tell me that the book was kept in the university library next to a private edition of the official *Yuan Histories*. Whilst he correctly identified the *Lang Huan Ji*'s location, he could not recall any details of the edition or the name of the author. He had not lost his ability to talk and he went on to dismiss all the grandiose official histories as garbage, with the exception of the *Lang Huan Ji* and the tens of thousands of similar works. "Only these books," he said, "can make you long for a woman, squander your wealth and drink yourself senseless. Only these would dare to pick your pockets and pawn your things to untrustworthy persons, as they have done in the past and in the future. And only these books would entice you to come to the labour camp farm on the pretext of enjoying the fresh air that is unavailable in the city. And only ... You're smiling. We understand each other you see, because we're both descendants of the Zhong. Go off and read it! The human testimonies are all there. We cannot ignore them. If the book is still in the library, and you should happen to browse through it...."

In the end, I didn't tell him what had happened. Thereafter, the female student's belly began to grow larger by the day. Her reward for this would be severe punishment and repatriation to her home town. I was dismissed from my post. Apart from my occasional forays into the high street, I rarely came across groups of students from the university. My wonderful dream of being incarcerated permanently in the library was over, and the stories I had so painstakingly recorded on my floppy disk I deleted in a fit of pique. The historical misinterpretations enshrined in the epics were restored to their true form — the deception of the wooden horse was discovered, Troy remained intact, the bookworm army was routed. By some fluke, I managed to escape. I wandered back and forth along the edge of the dried-up moat beyond the university's imposing walls thinking of the dissolute Helen and of Yuan Rui. As time goes on, I fear the *Lang Huan Ji* will be tucked away on the top shelf in the library, and I shall never be able to read it.

NOTES ON AUTHORS AND TRANSLATORS

CORRECTION: In the previous volume of *Chinese Writing Today*, entitled *Under-Sky Underground*, the translation of Li Tuo's '1985' was mistakenly attributed to Anne Wedell-Wedellsborg of the University of Aarhus. The draft translation was in fact done by DENG Wei. Our apologies to all involved for the misattribution.

Jacqui ADU-POKU is a graduate in Chinese from the University of Westminster, School of Languages.

BAI Guang studied mathematics as an undergraduate and computer science after graduating, both at Beijing University. In 1989 he moved to the United States where he studied at Stanford. In 1992 he went into business in California.

BAI Hua was born in Chongqing in 1956 and graduated in English from the Guangzhou Foreign Languages Institute in 1982. He studied Comparative Literature at Sichuan University and is currently working as a journalist in that province. He has published two collections of poetry.

Steve BALOGH is a graduate of the School of Oriental and African Studies, University of London, and a freelance translator who lives and works in Cumbria.

BEI DAO (pen-name of Zhao Zhenkai), born 1949, is one of the finest and best-known of contemporary Chinese poets. He was a founder editor, with Mang Ke, of the original *Today* magazine and was crucial to its revival in 1990, continuing to act as its chief editor. His collection of short stories, *Waves*, was published in English in 1987, and he has three selections of poetry in English translation currently available, *The August Sleepwalker* (1989) and *Old Snow* (1992) and *Forms of Distance* (1994). Bei Dao now teaches at the University of California, Davis.

John CAYLEY is a poet and literary translator as well as the founder editor of the Wellsweep Press. A collection of his translations and original poetry has recently been published as *Ink Bamboo* (Agenda & Bellew: London, 1996).

M S CHANG DE HUANG is an Argentinian-Chinese scholar of literature. She studied at Beijing University and the University of Illinois (Champaign-Urbana). She is currently working in Hong Kong.

CHEN Jianhua received his first Ph.D. from Fudan University, Shanghai, and is currently preparing a second thesis for presentation at Harvard University. His most recent publication is a literary and social history of the Jiangsu and Zhejiang regions from the fourteenth to the seventeenth centuries.

CHEN Yanbing holds an MA in Creative Writing from the University of Notre Dame and was recently appointed a University of Iowa Arts Fellow. His translations of contemporary Chinese poetry (collaborating with John Rosenwald) have appeared in *Talus, Chicago Review, Manoa* and *Another Chicago Magazine*.

CHU Chiyu studied English at the Tianjin Foreign Languages Institute and received his M.Phil. in Comparative Literature from the Chinese University of Hong Kong. He currently works for the Hong Kong-based Chinese-English translation magazine, *Renditions*.

John CRESPI worked for five years in Taiwan as a translator before pursuing graduate studies at the University of Chicago where he is now a doctoral candidate. He specializes in both contemporary and modern Chinese literature.

DUO DUO (pen-name of Li Shizheng), born 1951, is a prominent young poet and prose writer associated with Bei Dao and other members of the so-called 'Misty' (*menglong*) group of poets. Before leaving China he worked as a journalist. A collection of his poetry, *Looking Out From Death*, was published by Bloomsbury, London, 1989. He has also been widely published in Holland where he lives and works.

Harriet EVANS lectures in modern Chinese studies at the University of Westminster, London. Her major study, *Women and Sexuality in China* (1996) is published by Polity Press in the UK and Continuum in the US.

GE FEI was born in 1964 in Jiangsu province. He began to write as a student at Shanghai National University, where he now teaches. He is considered one of the most important writers of the younger generation in China.

GE Mai, born 1967, graduated from Beijing University, when he became a poet in the 'Modernist' school. In October 1991 he committed suicide by throwing himself into the lake on the campus of Qinghua University, Beijing.

Sean GOLDEN lived and worked in Tianjin from 1981–83, and spent three stints at the Research Centre for Translation at the Chinese University of Hong Kong, as well as offering a seminar on translation at Beijing Waiguo Yuyan Xueyuan in 1992 and visiting Taiwan and Beijing regularly. He collaborated on *100 Modern Chinese Poems* (with Pang Bingjun and John Minford), and contributed to *Seeds of Fire* (Minford and Barmé), *Trees on the Mountain* (Minford and Stephen Soong), *Women Poets of Taiwan* (Renditions Book, Chinese University of Hong Kong Press). He is currently head of the Chinese Studies Centre of the Universitat Autònoma de Barcelona, and has produced or helped to produce translations of important Chinese texts into Catalan.

GU Cheng was born in Beijing, 1956. In 1969 he went with his family to Shandong where they raised pigs. In 1979 he started to publish poetry, taking part in the literary movement associated with *Today* magazine. One of the major figures of the 'Misty' (*menglong*) group of poets, he was highly productive and influential. In 1987 he went to New Zealand, and an English version of his *Selected Poems* was published in Hong Kong, 1991. After murdering his wife, the writer and artist Xie Ye, he committed suicide on Waheki Island in October 1993.

HAN Dong was born in Nanjing, 1961, and graduated with a degree in philosophy from Shandong University (Ji'nan). He now teaches in Nanjing and has published two collections of poetry and a number of short stories in magazines.

Angela HENDERSON (who translated a piece for the last issue as Angela Geddes) is a graduate of the School of Languages, University of Westminster.

Duncan HEWITT has worked for the Research Centre for Translation, Chinese University of Hong Kong and the World Service of the BBC. He is currently freelancing as a journalist and continuing a degree in South-East Asian Area Studies in London.

Katie HILL is currently completing a thesis at the University of Sussex on contemporary Chinese art in Europe.

David HINTON has produced some of the best recent literary translations of Chinese poetry into English, including his *Selected Poems of Tu Fu*. He is the translator of Bei Dao's most recent collection, *Forms of Distance*.

Brian HOLTON teaches at the Universities of Durham and Newcastle. His translation of Yang Lian's collection of shorter poems, *Non-Person Singular*, and a poetic sequence, *Where the Sea Stands Still*, are both published by Wellsweep.

HONG YING (pen-name of Chen Hongying) was born in Chongqing in 1962. She started to write poetry in 1981, and fiction in 1988. She has published four collections of poetry, three collections of short stories and a novel. She came to England in 1991 and lives in London.

HU Dong was born in Chengdu, Sichuan province and graduated from the Department of History at the university there. In 1982 he joined the modernist poetry movement. He later moved to London, where he continues his writing of both poetry and fiction.

The critic, HUANG Ziping, was born in Guangdong province, and worked on a farm in the 1970s. His university career was spent at various universities in Beijing. He went to the United States in 1988 and in 1992 settled in Hong Kong where he teaches at the Baptist University.

Wendy LARSON is professor of Chinese at the University of Oregon. Her publications include *Literary Authority and the Modern Chinese Writer* (Duke University Press, 1992). She is currently working on women and literature, and Chinese modernism.

Gregory B LEE currently teaches comparative literature and cultural studies at the University of Hong Kong. His most recent book, *Troubadours, Trumpeters, Troubled Makers: Lyricism, Nationalism and Hybridity in China and Its Others*, was published by Duke University Press in the USA, and C. Hurst *&* Co. in Europe.

LEE Yu (Stella Lee) is a writer and teacher of Chinese origin, now living in New York.

Diana LIAO (Liao Tuanli) was born in Hong Kong and read comparative literature at the University of Hong Kong. She was doing graduate work in journalism in Paris when she was recruited by the United Nations where she now works as an interpreter.

D J LIU (Liu Dajen) was born in China but grew up in Taiwan. He read philosophy at the University of Taiwan and attended graduate schools in Hawaii and UC Berkeley. Author of several novels and pieces of prose, he now works as a translator at the United Nations.

LIU Zaifu, the well-known Chinese critic, was born in 1941 in Fujian province. He joined the Chinese Academy of Social Sciences in 1963 and became the head of its Institute of Literature in 1985. He went to the United States in the summer of 1989 and is currently teaching at the University of Colorado.

LIU Zili is a poet and writer of fiction. He was a contributing member of the *Today* group of writers from its beginnings in the late 1970s. He is now working as a journalist in Beijing.

Dean LÜ (Lü De'an) was born in 1960. He has published two poetry collections and now makes a living from portraiture in New York State.

Deborah MILLS recently completed a Ph.D. thesis on the works of Lu Xun. She lives and works in Durham.

NAN FANG (pen-name of Zhang Liang) was born in Shanghai in 1962 and studied architecture at Tongji University. He went to France in 1992 and is currently studying for an architectural degree in Paris. He began writing poetry in 1981 but later turned to fiction and has since published one collection of short stories.

OUYANG Jianghe was born in 1956. He was 'sent down to the countryside' in 1975. In 1986 he was demobilized from the Chinese army and joined the Institute of Literature in the Sichuan Academy of Social Sciences. In 1992 he went to the United States, and now lives in Washington, DC.

Simon PATTON is a freelance literary translator, living and working in Australia. He has recently completed a Ph.D. thesis on the work of Gu Cheng.

Jenny PUTIN completed a doctorate in Chinese literature at the University of Oxford. She now works in northern England for a small company doing business with China.

Laureano RAMIREZ teaches Chinese-Spanish translation at our Faculty. He studied Chinese at Beijing Yuyan Xueyuan in the 1970s and lived in Beijing on and off for some 18 years, during part of that time working as the foreign correspondent for the Spanish news agency EFE. He has published translations of the *Liaozhai* and *Rulin waishi* into Spanish, receiving the National Translation award in 1992 for the latter.

Foster ROBERTSON is an American poet and the publisher of *Hyperion,* a poetry magazine. He is also an art historian and curator of Asian Art who lives in Austin, Texas.

John ROSENWALD is a poet, translator and Professor of English at Beloit College. He is also on the editorial board of *The Beloit Poetry Journal.*

Desmond SKEEL received his Ph.D. in Contemporary Chinese Literature from SOAS, University of London in November 1995. He is currently researching into various aspects of 1980s avant-garde Chinese fiction and is assisting in the writing of the autobiography of an elderly Chinese woman residing in London.

Gary SNYDER was born in San Francisco in 1930. He grew up in Washington, Oregon and California. He studied several years in Japan and travelled in India and throughout the Pacific. In the 1950s he became a part of the remarkable flowering of west coast poetry which is also associated with Kenneth Rexroth, Robert Duncan, Philip Whalen, Allen Ginsberg, Jack Kerouac and others. Since 1986 he has been teaching at the University of California at Davis in the Creative Writing and Nature and Culture programs. Snyder has fifteen books of poetry and prose in print. *Turtle Island* won the Pulitzer prize for poetry in 1975, and his selected poems *No Nature* was a finalist for the National Book Award in 1992. He has been a Guggenheim Fellow, and is a member of the American Academy of Arts and Letters and the American Academy of Arts and Sciences.

SONG Lin was born in 1959 in Xiamen (Amoy) but spent his childhood in the countryside. He was a graduate of Shanghai Normal University where he stayed on to teach Chinese Literature for eight years. He has published both poetry and prose. He was imprisoned for nine months in 1989 and left China for France in 1991. He now lives in Paris.

TANG Jie (penname of Huang Danxuan) was born in Xinhui county, Guangdong province. She graduated from the Department of Fine Arts at Nanjing Normal College. Her fiction has won several prizes in Taiwan.

WANG Yin was born 1962 in Shanghai, where he also studied literature at the East China Normal University. He started writing poetry while at university and continues now while teaching in his home city.

XI Chuan (penname of Liu Jun) is a poet who graduated from the Department of English, Beijing University. Later, he worked for the Xinhua News Agency and now teaches at Beijing School of Fine Arts.

XU Xiaohe, born 1956, studied physics at university. He started to publish poetry in 1977 and fiction in 1983. He went to the United States in 1991 and is now a freelance writer living on Long Island.

YAN Li, poet and writer, was born in Beijing in 1954. In 1985 he left to study in the USA, and in May 1987 founded *Yihang* (One Line), a journal of poetry, in New York. He has published collections in both English and Chinese.

YANG Lian is another prominent name associated with the 'Misty' (*menglong*) group of poets. He has been widely published and translated and two collections of his work have appeared in Australia, *The Dead in Exile* (1990) and *Masks and Crocodile* (1989). More recently, a collection of his shorter poems, *Non-Person Singular* (1994) and a poetic sequence, *Where the Sea Stands Still* (1995) were published by Wellsweep.

The editors have no current biographical information concerning YANG Yunqin.

YI PING (penname of Li Jianhua) was one of the earliest members of the Today group in the late 1970s and contributed poems and criticism to the first Today publication. He is now teaching at the University of Poznan, Poland.

ZHANG Zao was born in 1962 in Changsha. He studied English at the Hunan Normal University and the Sichuan Foreign Languages Institute. In 1986 he went to (what was then) West Germany to study for a Ph.D. in literature at the University of Trier. He started writing poetry in 1977, and has published two collections.

ZHANG Zhen was born in Shanghai in 1962 and studied Journalism at Fudan University. She went on to study in Sweden, Japan and the USA. She is currently a doctoral candidate at the University of Chicago.

Henry Y H ZHAO (Zhao Yiheng) is a critic, writer and poet. He studied for his MA at the Chinese Academy of Social Sciences and completed a Ph.D. at the University of California at Berkeley. He is currently teaching at the School of Oriental and African Studies, University of London. He is the editor of *The Lost Boat: Avant-garde Fiction from China* (Wellsweep, 1993) and the co-editor of *Under-Sky Underground: Chinese Writing Today, 1* (Wellsweep, 1994). In 1995 Oxford published his, *The Uneasy Narrator: Chinese Fiction from Traditional to Modern*.

J J ZHAO is Professor of English at the Suzhou Medical College. He served two years as a Chinese editor for the International Atomic Energy Agency. His many publications include articles in *Applied Linguistics and Translations Studies*.

ZHENG Haiyao works as a specialist librarian at the University of Westminster, School of Languages. Jos GAMBLE is her partner.

ZHONG Ming was born in Chengdu, 1953 and graduated from the South-Western Normal College in 1982. After teaching for two years he began to work as a journalist. While at university he co-founded South China's first unofficial poetry magazine, *Ci Senlin*. He has published several collections of poetry in Chinese.

ZHU Wen, born 1967 in Fujian province, spent his childhood in northern Jiangsu province. He studied engineering at the South-East University, where he began to write poetry, turning to fiction in 1991.

The editors have no current biographical information concerning the poet ZHU Zhu.

SKOOB *Pacifica*

Contemporary writings of the Pacific Rim and South Asia

AS I PLEASE
Selected writings 1975-1994
Salleh Ben Joned

'Anybody who wants to understand cultural politics today should read this book... anybody who wants an insight into the confrontations of East and West, of Islam and the secular or Christian world, should read this book!'

Margaret Drabble

'Here is a book to relish.'

Asiaweek

ISBN 1 871438 29 2 £6.99

IN A FAR COUNTRY
K. S. Maniam

Themes of ancient community, material progress and a sense of belonging in a new novel from the author of *The Return*.

'Numerous images and instances will strike those familiar with Malaysia as utterly accurate. Maniam has an eye for the cultural friction that lies just below the surface...'

Far Eastern Economic Review

ISBN 1 871438 14 4 £5.99

SKOOB PACIFICA ANTHOLOGY NO.2
THE PEN IS MIGHTIER THAN THE SWORD

An anthology of poetry, prose and literary criticism. Special features; Malaysian / Singaporean writing of the 1990's.
ISBN 1 871438 54 3 £6.99

UNDER-*SKY* UNDER*GROUND*

Chinese Writing • *Today* • Number 1

selected & edited by
Henry Y H Zhao & John Cayley
foreword by JONATHAN D SPENCE

Conceived in 1978 and suppressed in 1980, *TODAY* became the best-known unofficial literary magazine in China, with BEI DAO and MANG KE as its founding editors. After ten years of silence, in 1990, it was relaunched from Sweden. It is now published as a quarterly and opens its pages to Chinese writers throughout the world. Its reputation continues to grow, that of a literary magazine dedicated to the enrichment of Chinese and world culture, *TODAY* and in the future.

UNDER-*SKY* UNDER*GROUND* is the first in a series of book-length biennial anthologies which will select the best writing which TODAY has published since its relaunch. The series, CHINESE WRITING *TODAY*, offers a unique opportunity to read, in English translation, a selection of fiction, poetry, prose and criticism by some of the best contemporary Chinese writers, bringing some of these authors to international attention for the first time.

£7.95 / US$14.95 PBK ISBN 0 948454 16 4
247 pp, 20x13

NON-PERSON SINGULAR

Selected Poems

YANG LIAN

Wellsweep Chinese Poets 6
translated by
Brian Holton

Yang Lian is one of the best-known of the young poets who came to prominence in China during the 1980s and attempted to re-establish a truly contemporary Chinese literature open to the world. His work, which has found rich sources at the margins of Chinese culture — the south, the far west and Tibet — and in ancient Chinese cultural forms — such as his reading of *The Book of Changes* — is wide-ranging, exploratory, linguistically rich and deeply rewarding.

Brian Holton teaches Chinese at the Universities of Newcastle and Durham. Amongst other projects, for some years he has been engaged in producing a splendid, fast-moving translation of one of China's best-known early folk novels, *The Water Margin*, into Lallans Scots.

£7.95 / US$14.95 PBK ISBN 0 948454 15 6
128 pp, 20x13, parallel text

WHERE THE SEA STANDS STILL
A Poetic Sequence
YANG LIAN

Wellsweep Chinese Poets 6+
translated by
Brian Holton

Yang Lian (born 1955) has published six collections of poetry and two anthologies of prose in Chinese. *Where the Sea Stands Still* is the first complete publication of Yang Lian's most recent work. He considers it to be the most important piece he has written since leaving China.

Yang Lian's ever-moving 'sea' stands still in the midst of its restlessness; it is here in the midst of nowhere; and in the space of the poem, time is swept away. Because of Odysseus, the sea began its endless ebb and flow; when this sequence was written, the sea stood still, and became an illusion.

The book reproduces paintings inside and on the cover by Gao Xingjian, a pioneer of avant-garde literature in China who is best-known internationally as a dramatist.

£2.95 / US$5.95 PBK ISBN 0 948454 25 3
32 pp, 21 x 13 cm, parallel text. 4 b/w illustrations
Limited edition of 200 copies

桔
槔
出
版
社